GONE AT MIDNIGHT

GONE AT MIDNIGHT

The Mysterious Death of ELISA LAM

Jake Anderson

CITADEL PRESS
Kensington Publishing Corp.
www.kensingtonbooks.com

CITADEL PRESS BOOKS are published by

Kensington Publishing Corp.
119 West 40th Street
New York, NY 10018

All Kensington titles, imprints, and distributed lines are available at special quantity discounts for bulk purchases for sales promotions, premiums, fund-raising, educational, or institutional use.

Special book excerpts or customized printings can also be created to fit specific needs. For details, write or phone the office of the Kensington sales manager: Kensington Publishing Corp., 119 West 40th Street, New York, NY 10018, attn: Sales Department; phone 1-800-221-2647.

CITADEL PRESS and the Citadel logo are Reg. U.S. Pat. & TM Off.

ISBN-13: 978-0-8065-4005-4
ISBN-10: 0-8065-4005-2

First Citadel hardcover printing: March 2020

10 9 8 7 6 5 4 3 2 1

Printed in the United States of America

Library of Congress Control Number: 2019944529

Electronic edition:

ISBN-13: 978-0-8065-4007-8 (e-book)
ISBN-10: 0-8065-4007-9 (e-book)

For Elisa and Jill, who will always belong in our hearts

CONTENTS

AUTHOR'S NOTE

I wrote this book after several years of research into the Elisa Lam case. On a journalistic level, I faced significant hurdles, namely that after the investigation was officially closed, the three ostensible sources for information on the case—the LAPD, the Cecil Hotel, and the family—remained completely silent.

I had one critical asset, though, a primary source that changed the trajectory of my investigation: the departed left behind a wealth of online posts. Initially, I viewed these as potential sources for clues to what happened in Elisa's final days. To my surprise, what I discovered after reading and studying hundreds of pages of her writing is that Elisa and I had a great deal in common. The full extent of this affinity didn't become apparent until about midway through the project, and it truly shocked me.

Though I have been unable to interview her family (no one has), Elisa's public-facing, first-person monologues, in addition to stories and analysis provided to me by her friends, allowed me to reconstruct aspects of her life. While I did, in a couple sections, take creative license to reconstruct scenes, characterizations, and pastiches, the majority of material featuring Elisa is based strictly on her own autobiographical descriptions.

It took time (years, in fact), but I slowly began to discover new evidence in the criminal investigation. Since the vast majority of LAPD personnel and Cecil Hotel employees refuse to discuss the case, I had to cast a wide and unconventional fact-finding net. In addition to Elisa's writing and the police and court records, my sources eventually included a police informant, an investigative journalist, a private investigator, a retired deputy coroner, a forensics expert, an LAPD psychologist, several hotel tenants, a bouncer, a family member of a Cecil Hotel employee, and many others. The information they disclosed to me casts considerable shade on the official explanation of Elisa's death.

Normally, the lack of involvement by the family—who, tragically, I imagine was doubly traumatized from the sensational media coverage after Elisa's death—would have prevented me from pursuing a commercial project on the subject. However, I strongly believe that since there are already tens of thousands of blog posts and videos (many of them monetized) depicting Elisa in an antagonistic, stigmatizing, and often inaccurate light, there is room for one more entry that takes a hard dive into previously unknown facts of the case and, just as important, provides a larger context for the reality of her psychological struggles. In this sense, the book is a cross-pollination of true-crime and psychological memoir as well as a call for justice that requires equal parts criminal and sociological reckoning.

I believe Elisa's story can help others by humanizing and de-stigmatizing mental illness so that more people speak openly about their problems with friends and family and seek help. The case—and Elisa herself—became part of the zeitgeist, veritable obsessions for some (at one point garnering 70,000 organic Google searches a month on top of the feverishly viral social media activity). My analysis of this response suggests a sociological component to the case that involves analysis of pathology, conspiracy theories, identity, and the desire for meaning in the Internet age.

Elisa's story also has ramifications for criminal justice and the burgeoning websleuth movement.

My methodology throughout this journey has been simple but painstaking. I only formed conclusions based on facts or the debunking of falsehoods; I avoided confirmation bias in support of my hypotheses and continually revised these hypotheses after faithfully following the trail of facts and evidence; I let analysis of the facts lead the narrative and not the other way around; I aimed for transparency where possible (though several of my sources requested to remain anonymous out of fear of retribution); and I used primary materials as much as possible.

On a logistical note, the Cecil Hotel is referenced hundreds of times in the book. Though the hotel was renamed Stay On Main earlier this decade, I decided to stick with its original name to avoid confusion.

I plan to use a portion of the proceeds earned from this book for donations to the Lam family as well as to several cutting-edge mental health research and advocacy groups.

PART 1
DISCOVERY

That's the thing about potential; it was so close, what could have been but didn't happen and will never happen. The events did not line up perfectly. And it breaks your heart.

Fear of death is very silly to me. I am reassured that death is something that all things before me and all things after me will go through. When it comes, I will know what it is. I just hope for a chance to say my goodbyes.

I am more scared of going before my time, without having lived a full and meaningful life.
—ELISA LAM

CHAPTER 1
Missing

ON A SUNNY, WARM WINTER DAY in Los Angeles, during one of the most historic and tumultuous weeks in LAPD history, detectives ushered a grieving family before a hungry press corps that had assembled at the downtown precinct. Six days earlier, a Chinese-Canadian student, Elisa Lam, vanished from the Cecil Hotel while vacationing alone. The police had since searched the building twice and canvassed the neighborhood; now they beseeched anyone who might have pertinent information to come forward.

Shortly after this press conference, though, the LAPD cut off the flow of all incoming and outgoing information regarding the case. Looking back years later, their plea for a synergistic relationship between law enforcement and the citizenry carries an ironic, disingenuous tone.

Detective Walter Teague of the Robbery and Homicides Division, looking appropriately grave, led the press conference, the ostensible purpose of which was to enlist the public's help in finding the twenty-one-year-old Elisa. A posterized photograph erected next to the podium featured her in autumn colors flashing an ebullient smile, cascading, obsidian hair swept over one shoulder, her eyes gazing out from behind thick-rimmed glasses.

With an anxious and unsettled air, Teague outlined what the police knew so far. Elisa was last seen on January 31, 2013. She had verbally checked in with her parents every day while on her solo "West Coast Tour" of California, but on February 1 she didn't call.

And they hadn't heard from her since. Nor had anyone. No texts. No calls. All communication—including Elisa's prolific social media posts and blog entries—had abruptly ceased. Her parents reported her missing and flew with their eldest daughter from Vancouver, Canada, to Los Angeles to assist with the search.

Flanking Teague, the family looked ashen and devastated, their body language melting downward in the panicked countenance of loved ones who know something has gone horribly wrong.

The day before the press conference, on the sixth of February, the LAPD had posted flyers around the neighborhood.

"Lam is described as an Asian woman of Chinese descent," the flyer stated. "She has black hair, brown eyes and stands five feet four inches tall. She weighs about 115 pounds. Lam is fluent in English and also speaks Cantonese."

It concluded with a directive telling people to contact the LAPD with information.

Teague told reporters that Cecil Hotel management had confirmed Elisa was booked for four nights and scheduled to check out on February 1, the morning she disappeared. They also confirmed that Elisa was last seen by hotel employees in the lobby, shortly after returning from The Last Bookstore with gifts she bought for her family.

Police believed Elisa intended to travel to Santa Cruz next, but they were still piecing together the timeline of her travels.

Lead Detective Wallace Tennelle noted that particular attention was being paid to the case because it involved a foreign national.

"We've had some tips come in, not many, but nothing that has proven to be her," Tennelle stated. "Some sightings, but they proved not to be her."

When later asked about the nature of the investigation, he said, "We're just investigating whatever personal habits she may have. And trying to follow up on where she was headed to or what she wanted to see. Like the murders that I investigate, they may grow cold but we don't close them. I'm pretty sure that's the same with missings, we don't close them out."

Tennelle, whose own son was murdered in cold blood only a few years earlier, mentioned that he was keeping Lam's family updated with their progress. "We can't give them everything we have but we do try to keep them in the loop as to what's going on."

In the preceding days, the LAPD had set up a command post in the lobby of the Cecil Hotel, where they deployed numerous search teams who were paired with a hotel employee with access to a master key. This effort produced an "extensive and exhaustive search of the entire hotel, including the roof." The search lasted several days, but did not turn up any substantial evidentiary clues as to Elisa's location.

A second search was conducted, this time with a K9 unit attached. Again, the entire hotel was searched, "every nook and cranny," including the roof. Again, police obtained zero clues.

Finally, after a full week had elapsed since Elisa was last seen, the LAPD turned in desperation to the public. In an age when milk carton photos have been replaced by social media hashtags and online web-sleuth forums, word spread quickly that the notorious Cecil Hotel—known by locals as the "Suicide Hotel"—was at the heart of another potentially dark mystery.

Not even Aleister Crowley himself could have predicted how much darker it was about to become.

Missing Persons

Teague looked worried. YouTube users commenting on an uploaded video of the press conference remarked that he sounded like he wanted to cry. Indeed, with a grief-stricken family behind him, the emotional burden must have been heavy.

I've always wondered what detectives say to families when a loved one is missing. What can be said? I doubt it plays out like in the movies, where a steely-eyed detective tells the parents, "I'll find her, I promise."

Los Angeles has had its fair share of missing persons. For a city that prides itself on visibility, hubris, and conspicuous consumption, the rate of disappearance is staggering. According to the Missing Persons Unit (MPU), approximately 3,900 adult Missing Person (M/P) reports are filed annually. "Approximately 80 percent of all reported missing persons are found or voluntarily return within 48 to 72 hours." That still leaves hundreds of people who disappear from Los Angeles each year, never to be found again.

There are around 750,000 cases reported annually in the U.S. and in the majority of them, the person is found. However, many are not. Over the last few decades, hundreds of thousands of people have vanished from the face of the earth.

On its website, the Los Angeles Police Department lists the following most common reasons for a Missing Person report: mental illness, depression, substance abuse, credit problems, abusive relationships, or marital discord.

The site goes on to state the following: "The difficulty with a missing persons report is that the person missing has a right to be 'missing.' In other words, this person may have a legitimate or personal reason that he or she wants to be left alone and the police do not have the right to violate that right. This can be frustrating for family members or loved ones who may be (perhaps justifiably) convinced that foul play is involved. Once foul play is reasonably established—or the police have a reason to suspect the person's life is endangered (for example, if they require timely medication and are without it)—an investigation can be launched."

Law enforcement agencies urge family members or friends to report a missing person as early as possible. However, in the case of adults, it is virtually impossible for police to rapidly determine if they are missing or if they have simply left their old life and started a new one. And in the case of children or young women, investigators simply can't respond to every missing persons case assuming it's a sexually motivated non-family abduction. Most of the time people go missing, they either return safely or the case was a misunderstanding of some kind.

"If you just spent two extra hours and went to the hairdresser, would you want the chief of police pulling up?" said Todd Matthews, communications director for the National Missing and Unidentified Persons System (NamUs). "You don't want to be controlled or watched."

In those first crucial forty-eight hours, there is a slippery slope investigators must navigate in respecting the privacy rights of the missing while doing right by the family.

While an individual has the right to disappear, their families have the right to file a Missing Person report. They can do this at any time; there is not a requisite number of days one must wait before contacting the police. In California, a missing person is simply "someone whose whereabouts is unknown to the reporting party." In fact, in the case of children or other dependents, each hour counts and family members should report as soon as possible.

However, prematurely reporting someone missing can lead to wasted police resources. In 2017, the mother of twenty-two-year-old Rebekah Martinez reported her daughter missing, igniting a statewide manhunt only to find out that Rebekah had absconded to Los Angeles and was an aspiring reality TV star on *The Bachelor*.

Other cases don't have such warm endings. In early 2018, the parents of nineteen-year-old University of Pennsylvania student Blaze Bernstein reported their son missing. The Orange County Sheriff's Department used Blaze's Snapchat posts to pinpoint his last sighting to around midnight on January 2, when a friend dropped him off at a park. He hadn't been seen since.

In the ensuing search of Borrego Park in Foothill Ranch, police deployed drone technology. But Blaze was only found when rain runoff exposed his body, which had been buried in a shallow grave. The friend, Samuel Woodward, who dropped Blaze off was charged not only with stabbing Blaze twenty times but with a hate crime, as it was later determined Woodward was associated with a white supremacist group and may have targeted Blaze because he was Jewish and gay.

Drones are increasingly utilized in missing persons cases because they allow detectives to explore large swathes of land and then judiciously narrow in on the areas that should be searched on foot by people and dogs. In another case, the search for three-year-old Sherrin Matthews, police hired the North Texas Unmanned Aerial Systems (UAS) Response Team to scour Richardson County, Texas.

Like the Bernstein case, the search for Matthews ended with a tragic discovery. Her father was later charged with capital murder, her mother with child endangerment and abandonment.

Drones are part of a growing suite of new technological tools used in the search for missing persons. This arsenal includes predictive analytics, closed-circuit television, GPS darts, blockchain, and even experimental facial recognition. In 2008, Seattle police found a missing suicidal man by tracking his cellular phone data, in a case that would portend a controversial debate over privacy rights that persists today.

Cell phones and smartphones have assisted greatly in missing-persons cases. If police actually physically have the phone, they may be able to piece together what happened based on the most recent text messages or calls. But even if they do not have the missing person's phone, investigators can usually learn a great deal about a person's location based on "tower dumps" from network providers, which let them track a phone's serial number. They can use network towers pinged by the phone to "triangulate" a specific location.

Unfortunately, increasingly stalkers also use this technology for nefarious purposes.

However, if there is no evidence of a crime, investigators can find themselves legally restricted from accessing cell-phone information. Which is to say, there is another slippery slope for investigators, who must wield technology to help identify missing persons without trampling on the civil liberties of someone who simply wanted to disappear for a few days.

When he opened the conference up for questions, Teague was immediately asked by a reporter if they had checked Elisa Lam's cell phone for information.

"I don't want to talk about the cell phone," Teague replied, adding, "We have . . . some of her property."

The next reporter asked what, in retrospect, was an astonishingly prescient question.

"Is there any surveillance footage of Elisa from inside the hotel?"

THE SURVEILLANCE VIDEO

One week later, on Valentine's Day, a friend emailed me a link. The email had no subject or text, just a hyperlinked YouTube url. Thoughtlessly opening it (could have been a virus), I found myself watching a grainy video recorded by a hotel's elevator surveillance camera. I had no idea what the video was going to show, but I had a sneaking suspicion it would be disturbing.

One of my hobbies is curating and creating content for the website *The Ghost Diaries*, which I launched earlier that year to satiate my fascination with morbid mysteries. I was posting about everything from the paintings of serial killers to parallel universes, watching thousands of bizarre videos—some of them fascinating, some of them moronic, others outright emotionally scarring.

The Internet has democratized information and, in doing so, freed the pixels of a trillion nightmares to flow into our heads.

I didn't know it at the time, but in opening the link in the email I had opted into an obsessive quest that would change the way I think about the world and myself. I spent the next five years of my life trying to solve a puzzle that is missing most of its pieces.

The footage was allegedly surveillance from inside the Cecil Hotel. It must have originally come from the hotel manager's office, then migrated to the files of the investigating LAPD detectives and had somehow ended up posted on the YouTube account of journalist Dennis Romero of *LA Weekly*. Romero has since steadfastly refused to explain how he came into possession of this clip.

At this time the view count was several hundred thousand, but it has since ballooned to over 23 million for that upload alone.

The blurry, pixelated video showed a young woman with shoulder-length black hair in a red hoodie and black cargo shorts entering an elevator and leaning over to inspect the button panel. She proceeded to push several of the buttons and then stand waiting. The doors remained open. As she waited, so too did I, wondering why my friend had emailed the video to me. I half expected it to be a "screamer"—a once popular online ploy to trick someone into engaging with a video just long enough that they jump out of their skin in horror when an *Exorcist*-style face suddenly screams at an eardrum-shattering volume.

"What the hell is this?" I asked out loud.

The video description read: "Elisa Lam, the Vancouver woman who disappeared in Los Angeles on January 31, is seen acting strangely in new video released by police on Thursday."

"What?" my colleague said, beside me.

"Oh, uh, nothing," I said, discreetly covering the browser window with a work tab. "Where you getting lunch?"

Lunch—and food, in general—was always a popular subject in our company's ranks. Creature comforts distracted from the monotonous toil of search engine optimization (SEO) and Internet publishing.

I turned back to the video.

Presently, the young woman became interested in something outside the elevator, as though she'd heard a noise or voice in the hallway. Her body language became nervous, hesitant, like some-one who suspects there is something waiting for her but is afraid to look. Then she lurched out through the doors in the pose of a runner stretching her legs, peering down the hallway to the right of the el-evator. Except for the small patch of carpet and wall directly in front of the doors, the camera could not observe this hallway, but whatever Elisa saw (or heard) caused her to retreat back into the elevator and back herself into the corner.

Several moments passed. Hands tucked in the pockets of her hoodie, Elisa ventured from her corner and stood at the threshold, peeking out the still-open doors as though checking to see if who-ever had been there was still there. She hopped back out into the hallway and took a few playful steps to the left, back, and then to the front, where she waited, barely visible on the left side of the screen.

She returned to the inside of the elevator and leaned over the but-ton panel again, proceeding to press nearly all the buttons again in rapid succession. The elevator doors remained open.

Elisa wandered back out into the hotel hallway. She lingered there for a moment and then began gesticulating, as if conversing with an unseen figure. She waved her hands around in strange, dreamy movements, fingers splayed.

Is she sleep walking? Possessed? Her behavior actually reminded me of how I've seen others (and presumably myself) behave on psychedelic drugs.

Finally, Elisa shoved off out of frame of the surveillance camera. After four or five long seconds, the elevator doors slowly closed. And that was the end.

Using some of our search engine tools, I checked the Alexa ranking, SEOmoz score and other metrics. The case was extremely popular. Viral, in fact. Elisa Lam's disappearance was already being debated on several forums, including Reddit and Websleuths.

I perused the comment thread underneath the video and found a veritable hornet's nest of frenzied civilian analysts proposing their explanations. There were quite a few people speculating that Elisa was on drugs. LSD, mushrooms, PCP, bath salts, and virtually every other illicit substance was invoked to explain her behavior. Someone even mentioned certain kinds of vitamins as being capable of making you dizzy and nauseated, and hence susceptible to confusion or paranoia.

Others developed detailed narratives as to what was happening in the hallway. Elisa had been drugged by someone who was stalking her through the hotel. Some sadistic psychopath was toying with her and triggering a different button panel down the hallway so that Elisa's elevator couldn't depart to another floor. This person followed her and probably killed her, according to one YouTube account.

"She is hiding from someone," a commenter wrote, describing the inverse of the previous scenario, "and is trying to prevent them from using the elevator. If you look up a map of the layout of the hotel, there is a staircase to the left and I'm wondering if she tried going that way and they caught her."

I wondered if that person had actually studied a schematic of the hotel.

Another user wrote: "She was obviously trying to get the doors to close . . . The murderer was probably trying to get her to go to the stairwell, so he could grab her."

One commenter wrote that she was having a psychotic episode and that her murderer knew this. "I think her killer came across her during this episode, in the halls just outside the elevator. Possibly an employee and probably offered to help her but then felt bc of her mental state, he could take advantage of her and ended up killing her . . ."

The views and comments kept pouring in. I watched the video again, hoping to catch a detail, a nuance, an eerie face in the corner, a glitch in the matrix, a barely perceptible timeslip from one dimension to another—to give me something I can work with. Why were people instantly obsessed with this video?

The footage was blurry, almost smoky looking, and the timecode in the lower-left corner of the screen was inexplicably scrambled into what looked like alien Sanskrit. But other than that, and Elisa's admittedly peculiar behavior, the video was pretty uneventful. A woman enters an elevator, a woman exits an elevator. Yet somehow the video had accumulated almost a million views in less than a week.

I looked it up. Exactly one week earlier the LAPD had held its press conference. Elisa was still missing without a trace.

I recalled a piece of advice sometimes given to people, particularly young women, who are trying to evade someone in a building. They are told to press multiple buttons of an elevator so that the pursuer doesn't know what floor they will end up on. Is that what was happening here? I got chills imagining a stalker leaping into the stairwell and trying to intercept Elisa on the ground floor.

Other commenters delved into more fringe explanations. She was playing the Elevator Game, one user suggested; she had pressed a specific sequence of buttons in order to travel to different dimensions inside the elevator.

Another YouTuber discussed the creepy history of the Cecil Hotel. Dozens of people have committed suicide there, she claimed. Hotel guests have been murdered in cold blood. Sex offenders and serial killers rented rooms there. And the place is obviously haunted, she concluded.

I didn't know about the sex offenders, but it was most certainly true that at least two serial killers had taken up residence inside the Cecil Hotel walls. Both Richard Ramirez, aka "The Night Stalker," and Jack Unterweger, "the Austrian Ghoul," called the place home during their respective killing sprees in the 1980s and 1990s. And there certainly had been decades of grisly deaths. Did that mean there was some nefarious disembodied consciousness possessing the hotel tenants?

I had been a bit unclear on why the video was pushing buttons inside so many people's heads. But it was starting to make sense to me. I was beginning to feel the terror frozen in those pixels. It's pretty simple.

She was hiding from someone. And now she's missing . . .

Who was after her? I wondered, lost in thought. *A stalker? A serial killer? An abusive boyfriend? A deranged hotel resident or employee?*

"What about you?"

"Huh?" I looked up, startled.

My coworker was staring at me. "What are you getting for lunch, McFly?"

GOING VIRAL

My toolbar widget didn't lie. Although it was only two weeks old, merely an embryo in the life cycle of a popular true-crime enigma, the Elisa Lam case was already red-hot. In time these numbers swelled to astronomical proportions. At one point, Google Analytics clocked 70,000 organic monthly searches for "Elisa Lam," a stunning metric dwarfed only by the feverish social media activity surrounding articles, videos, and podcasts about the case, which Internet users shared by the millions on Facebook, Twitter, YouTube, Reddit, and other networks.

I left work that day in a haze of unorganized thoughts.

I recalled a recent story in which police officers had deputized a psychic to help them find a missing woman. A couple years later, the CIA declassified hundreds of thousands of files about government experiments on ESP, which, among other things, showed that police agencies regularly use psychics to help with cold cases.

"All of the police officers said they had used a psychic in a case as described in the newspaper articles," one report noted. "Eight of the officers said that the psychic had provided them with otherwise un-known information which was helpful to the case. In three of these cases, missing bodies were discovered in areas described by the psy-chic."

I wondered if the LAPD detectives had hired a psychic to find Elisa. Did they have a medium squared away in some windowless precinct room conducting remote viewing sessions, wading through the quantum ether in search of Elisa's red hoodie?

Even though I didn't know Elisa, I found myself anxious about her case.

The Christopher Dorner case—the intensive manhunt for a disgrun-tled former officer turned rogue assassin—was surely using up most of the oxygen of the LAPD. It was watershed enough for a former of-ficer to blow the whistle on the entire department and accuse them of systemic corruption. That this officer had actually taken up weapons and manufactured a one-man war against the third-largest municipal police department in the United States was sufficient cause to worry about the tenacity of the Elisa Lam investigation.

THE ASSASSIN

The Elisa Lam case made local news, but it was a second Los Angeles–based missing-person case that at this time dominated the national headlines. On February 3, three days before detectives launched an official investigation into Elisa's disappearance, former police officer Christopher Dorner released a manifesto declaring "unconventional and asymmetric war" on the LAPD. In the coming days, he would initiate targeted killings of police officers and their families before leading his former colleagues on a week-long man-hunt that ended as violently as it began.

A widely circulated photo of Dorner showed him in his Navy uniform with a beaming smile across his face. A former police of-ficer, Dorner had also been a naval reservist who was deployed to the Persian Gulf for six months to provide security on an offshore oil platform in Bahrain. In over a decade of service to the United States Naval Reserve, Dorner received multiple honors, including the Iraq

Campaign Medal, the Global War on Terrorism Service Medal, a Rifle Marksman Ribbon, and a Pistol Expert Medal.

A laudatory 2002 story profiling Dorner recounted how while on duty at the Vance Air Force Base he found a bag containing $8,000 that belonged to the Enid Korean Church of Grace. Chris reported the money to local police and made sure it was returned. He called it a matter of "integrity."

Dorner's troubles started in 2008 when he accused a fellow officer, Teresa Evans, of kicking a handcuffed detainee in the face. An internal review board concluded that Dorner fabricated the claim; he was dismissed shortly thereafter. Dorner filed a lawsuit challenging his firing, but the California Court of Appeal dismissed it.

This challenge to his integrity seems to have triggered something inside him, flipped a switch in his mind that left him consumed with vengeance and wrath.

Two years later, Anderson Cooper's office at CNN received a package from Dorner addressed to La Palma Police Chief Eric Nunez. The package contained a Post-it note to the former police chief that had dismissed Dorner, a video supposedly corroborating Dorner's claim against Evans, of excessive force and a gold "challenge coin" riddled with bullet holes.

Then the killings started. Monica Quan, the daughter of the LAPD's first Asian-American captain (who Dorner believed was involved in his firing), and her fiancé Keith Lawrence were murdered in Irvine. Only four days earlier Monica had joyously surprised her basketball team at Cal State Fullerton, holding up her hand to brandish the engagement ring. Keith, who had proposed to Monica next to a heart-shaped pattern of rose petals he'd carefully designed, was himself a prospective law-enforcement officer with a bright future. They were shot to death while sitting together in their car. Monica was shot three times in the back of the head; Keith took five bullets to the head and face, and two in the neck.

In an 11,000 word Facebook manifesto released soon after, Dorner outlined at least forty other officers and targets he planned to assassinate in retaliation for conniving against him. The manifesto excoriated the Los Angeles law-enforcement agencies, accusing them of rampant corruption, racism, and brutality. Dorner, an African-American, said the department had actually grown worse since the Rodney King beatings and that excessive force was an everyday occurrence. Dorner wasn't just crossing the "thin blue line" that supposedly unites all police officers together in a brotherly fraternity—he was destroying the very concept of allegiance to Los Angeles law enforcement.

"The blue line will forever be severed and a cultural change will be implanted," Dorner wrote. "You have awoken a sleeping giant . . . I am here to change and make policy. The culture of LAPD versus the community and honest/good officers needs to and will change.

"From 2/05 to 1/09," Dorner continued, "I saw some of the most vile things humans can inflict on others as a police officer in Los Angeles. Unfortunately, it wasn't in the streets of LA. It was in the confounds [*sic*] of LAPD police stations and shops [cruisers]."

Dorner's claims included officers falsely incriminating people they knew to be innocent. He claimed officers let shooting victims bleed out just to accrue overtime hours from the resulting court subpoenas. They shared and joked about cell phone images of the grisly deaths encountered while on the job. They regularly brutalized civilians and lied about it.

The rambling document oscillated between eloquent pleas for social justice and descriptions of his favorite TV shows and actors. He professed his admiration for President Obama and Senator John McCain and his continued respect for the nation's military veterans and the federal rule of law. Dorner advocated for gun-control measures while threatening wholesale death with a military-grade arsenal of assault weapons. Using the language of terrorist insurgents, he promised to engage in "unconventional and asymmetrical warfare" and warned his former colleagues, his brothers in blue, that they would "live the life of the prey." He knew all of their contingency plans and protocols, he said, and would systematically dismantle and thwart all attempts at containment.

By the end of the ensuing manhunt and standoff, an effort that conscripted thousands of LAPD officers, five people were dead and six people sustained non-fatal injuries.

The week Elisa Lam disappeared, the Dorner manhunt went into full swing. This same police department—charged with the unprecedented task of neutralizing a former officer turned rogue assassin and executioner—was now carving out time to investigate another missing-person case.

As one case fizzled out in dramatic violence and the other became mired in mystery, I would find other disturbing parallels.

For now, I could only consider that Elisa had vanished only blocks from Skid Row, one of the most dangerous neighborhoods in Los Angeles. Were the detectives interrogating hotel employees and residents? Were they canvassing neighbors? Maybe Elisa had simply made a new friend, with whom she was staying; she had lost her phone and didn't have Internet access. It was unlike Elisa, according to her family. But missing persons have been found alive under much stranger circumstances.

One thing was for certain: Elisa would not be part of the 65 percent of missing persons who return or are found alive within the first forty-eight hours. After seventy-two hours, your survival rate plummets. Elisa had been missing for a full seven days.

But the surprises and anomalies in this investigation were just getting started. Five days later, an unlikely discovery cemented the case as one of the most bizarre death investigations of all time.

CHAPTER 2
Found

THE TAP WATER OOZED out of the faucet as a thick brownish red sludge and almost looked like it was saturated with red blood cells. However, you can't waterlog blood cells enough to expand them to be visible to the naked eye. *Whatever these grotesque globules are,* Natalie Davis thought, standing over the faucet in her new, temporary bathroom, *I'm better off not knowing.*

Steven and Gloria Cott saw the same thing. They had not checked into the Cecil Hotel expecting their room to be adorned with silk curtains and crystal cutlery. Nor had they more faith in the purity of the hotel's tap than any other municipal source of water. However, they had most certainly not planned on brushing their teeth with water that looked like it had been dredged from a corpse-infested swamp and pumped through the crotchety pipelines of an eighty-year old, 600-room building in the decrepit heart of downtown Los Angeles.

And for this reason, Steven Cott lodged a formal complaint with the hotel management. Upon his approach to the concierge's desk and his subsequent verbal grievance, the hotel manager, Amy Price, managed to suppress a groan. It was the third complaint over the hotel's tap water that night, and the tenth that week. Some residents complained about the water pressure, reporting that the water only dribbled out of the faucets; others said it smelled, and that it had a "funny, sweet, disgusting taste."

Amy Price knew the protocol on dealing with the complaints of hotel guests. In many cases, especially at the seedy Cecil (which boasted the patronage of two serial killers, multiple sex offenders, several horrifying murders and over a dozen suicides) guests weren't so much protesting a specific grievance as they were expressing a general uneasiness with the hotel itself. There was little Amy or any of the other managers could do about this without a solid re-investment into infrastructure by the hotel owners.

The fact of the matter was, the Cecil Hotel was an old establish-ment in a very run-down neighborhood and its primary clientele consisted of travelers, transients, and low-income locals looking for the cheapest possible lodging—ranging from $65 to $95 a night. Spend much time on the downtown Los Angeles Main Street, mere blocks from Skid Row, you find yourself looking for commercial refuge with a quickness.

On this particular day, the consistency and frequency of the com-plaints over the water had Amy a bit on edge. Maybe there really was something wrong with the hotel's water. Perhaps a pipe had burst; maybe the supply had been contaminated. She had started to think it was time to actually check the situation out. That's when Steven Cott came to the desk describing what looked like red-brown sludge with blood cells.

In the morning, Amy dispatched a maintenance worker to the roof to make sure the hotel's water cisterns were properly func-tioning.

A GRIM DISCOVERY

On February 19, 2013, Santiago Lopez clocked in at the Cecil Hotel just like any other day. Of course, it wasn't like any other day. A young woman who was a tenant of the Cecil was missing, and police had been trundling around the building for two consecutive days. One detective even questioned him briefly.

But besides that, it was a normal day. He couldn't possibly have known that within only a few hours, he would have one of the most haunting visuals imaginable permanently sewn into the fabric of his memory.

Santiago had been a maintenance worker at the Cecil for three years. Most people didn't know that in addition to being a hotel, the Cecil also offered permanent occupancy on some of its floors. Some of the residents had lived there for decades. While the rest of Los Angeles remained fragmented into harsh class divisions, the Cecil still stood proudly in the heart of a gentrified downtown neighborhood as a home for low-income tenants.

It made the job of maintenance somewhat more complicated, as the staff had to balance the demands of overnight transients and vacationers with the needs of people spending their lives there.

In contrast to some of Los Angeles' other famous hotels—the Roosevelt, the Biltmore, etc.—the Cecil had long since relinquished the limelight and glamour and had devoted its resources to housing disenfranchised people.

But the Cecil shared something in common with the other hotels and many other spots in the City of Angels: a grimy reputation filled with strange, unsettling stories. Santiago had never been one for ghost stories and murder conspiracies, but there was something undeniably peculiar about his employer's history. How could so many awful things happen in one place?

Within ten minutes of starting his workday, he already had a lengthy to-do list. A litany of small repairs, unremarkable duties, and, frankly, annoying follow-ups. It turns out some people don't know how to properly operate a faucet. He didn't know that was possible. It was kind of one of those tasks one internalized into muscle memory after years and years of habit, starting in early childhood, like flipping on a light switch or flushing the toilet.

Yet in the last few days, there had been a multitude of hotel tenants reporting impairments in their showers and sinks. The reports were both consistent and varied. Consistent in that they were coming from all over the hotel at a steady clip, and varied in that the complaints concerned everything from pressure and delayed flow to strange-smelling water, funny-tasting water, and even "dark water."

He received two complaints from the guest in Room 320, who said the water pressure was too weak to get the soap out of his hair while showering. It wasn't a first-world problem, of course. And while shower quality is a sanitary condition, it's hard not to want to make a baby-crying sound when someone complains that they can't get the soap out of their hair.

The Cecil Hotel is configured in an E-shaped pattern, with a main building flanked by three interconnected wings that, in all, contain 600 rooms. On a usual day, Santiago found himself taking care of business on one wing, then moving on to the next wing, and so on to the next. He consolidated tasks to prevent himself from having to run back and forth to different wings.

Unfortunately, it was mid-morning and he had already visited each wing twice, running around like a chicken with its head cut off. Nothing pisses guests off more than water problems.

In Room 320, he noted impaired water pressure. The tenant glared at him when he was unable to fix it. Santiago said he would return within the hour. He didn't like leaving tasks unfinished but he'd run through the initial diagnostic list; he couldn't do anything more until he ruled out larger issues.

Next he took the elevator up four floors and to Room 720, which is serviced by the same water line as 320; in this room, too, the water pressure was impaired.

Walking back down the hall, he felt a prickly sensation in his hands. It was just in his head, he knew, but it always seemed to happen on the 7th and 8th floors. He tried to minimize the amount of time spent on these floors.

Throughout its history, there had been "jumpers." Guests who committed suicide by leaping out the windows of the hotel. And people were brutally murdered, their killers never brought to justice.

Santiago's next stop, fortunately, was on the 4th floor. Unfortunately, it was room 451, located in the middle wing. Upon arriving, he realized it was the same room that had been involved in another very strange story from a couple years earlier. A man staying there reported waking up in the middle of the night with the sensation of being violently choked. He came to the front desk trembling and drenched in sweat and said it felt as though an invisible person had gripped his throat. He demanded another room; when he learned one was unavailable, he packed up his belongings and left.

Same room. No choking report, though. Just low water pressure.

Incredibly, this same room had yet another bizarre annotation. The previous year, a young boy by the name of Koston Alderete took a photograph of the outside of the hotel. Upon close inspection, the photo seemed to feature a wispy gray apparition coming out of the window of a 4th-floor room. After studying the configuration of the hotel, Santiago determined that it was the window of room 451, directly three floors below where yet another jumper had committed suicide decades earlier.

There was another water complaint coming from the 9th floor—in an entirely different wing of the building, of course.

The note referencing the complaint just said, "Room 943 – water pressure."

The guest who answered the door was a young woman named Natalie. She seemed unnerved. Santiago ran the tub water. It wasn't red at the moment but he could see the residual stains left over from earlier.

Usually discolored water is the result of deposits in the pipes. Red would most likely be the result of rust. It can also be sediment stirred up by the water heater. Obviously, that's not what you want to see, but it's usually completely harmless.

Santiago told Natalie this and added that he was running tests and that her problem was a top priority. He said he would check back in with her shortly.

"Thank you," she said, and then as Santiago opened the door to leave, Natalie asked him, "Do you know if anyone has died in this room?"

Santiago stopped in dead silence, staring down at the floor. Then he met her gaze.

"Someone has died in every room here," he replied.

It was clear now that he would need to inspect the rooftop tanks to ascertain the cause of the problem.

Using his maintenance key, Santiago bypassed the alarm to the rooftop access door on the 15th floor. This alarm, if triggered, would issue a highly unpleasant noise that can be heard across the 14th and 15th floors of the hotel, as well as at the front desk on the first floor. Of course, the noise was only theoretical; the alarm had never been triggered in the time Santiago worked at the Cecil, so he didn't know what it actually sounded like or if it worked at all.

Besides the emergency fire escapes, the access door was the only path to the hotel's roof.

In his sworn testimony later given to the Superior Court of the State of California, Lopez confirmed that on the date of his inspection, the rooftop alarm was in working condition before he deactivated it in order to proceed to a flat, gray nondescript slab of concrete. There he observed four 1,000 gallon water cisterns clustered together at the edge of the hotel like cylindrical gargoyles overlooking downtown Los Angeles. A gravity-based system pumped water from a main water line below street level upward into the cisterns, supplying all of the hotel's drinkable and potable water.

Each tower was ten feet tall and six feet in diameter. Situated on a four-foot platform, accessing, much less servicing them, was not easy. He ascended a narrow ladder to the first platform; to reach it he had to slither between the tanks and plumbing equipment. That brought him to a second ladder that he scaled alongside the tank itself and that delivered him to the top.

The first thing he noticed, he would later testify, was that the lid to one of the tanks was open. Each cistern lid was 18" by 18" and quite heavy. What the hell was it doing open? The police had been on the roof looking for the missing woman—could they have left it open?

Rising to his feet, Santiago dusted off the grime that accumulated on his pants during the climb and took in an eagle-eye view of downtown Los Angeles and beyond—a decollage of shadowy structures under a salmon-colored late afternoon sky crossed and dotted with contrails, drones, and helicopters.

He looked down into the open lid. Recessed in the dark cistern, something caught his eye—a color where there should be none. The color red.

As he later reported to the hotel manager, detectives and court

officials, when Santiago looked inside he saw the body of a woman
floating face-up in the water, approximately twelve inches from the
top. After nearly two weeks submerged, her left eye was bulging
and skin slippage had warped her face into something ghoulish. The
woman's clothes, including a red hoodie, floated beside her.

CHAPTER 3
The Investigation Begins

AUTHORITIES RECEIVED A CALL from Cecil Hotel management shortly after 10 A.M. on February 19. The Los Angeles Police Department, according to Officer Diana Figueroa, dispatched officers to 640 South Main Street shortly thereafter. Captain Jaime Moore of the L.A. Fire Department said his department received a separate call from the hotel management reporting that their maintenance staff had discovered a body.

Upon arriving at and inspecting the scene, Moore stated: "There are three of these tanks, inside a portal, with sealed water cisterns on the roof. The body is inside one of these tanks."

He had mistaken the number of tanks (there were four) and it isn't known which tank he was referring to when he called it "sealed." Virtually every later report would state that the water tank lids were not sealed. Were these reports wrong? Had Elisa been sealed in?

Moore said that the size of the hatch granting entrance was too narrow to accommodate the equipment necessary for removing the body. Subsequently, the tank was drained and cut open from the side with lasers.

At approximately 1:45 P.M., LAPD Officer Bruce Borihanh confirmed that a body had been found inside one of four rooftop water tanks of the Cecil Hotel.

"Our urban search and rescue team is working on the best method to recover the body and maintain as much . . . evidence as they possibly can to support the investigation that's being done by the LAPD and robbery/homicide investigators," said LAPD spokesman Sgt. Rudy Lopez.

That the tank had to be cut open from the side with lasers underscores the exceedingly awkward physical dimensions of the rooftop platform where the tanks stood. It was partially an effort on behalf of law enforcement to preserve the state of the body from any nicks and cuts that may arise from dredging it upward through an 18" by 18" opening. Pictures from the scene show a phalanx of firefighters and law enforcement officials spilling off the sides of the water cistern platform and huddled on the control room roof above the tanks.

The grim tableau served as a reminder as to why it was so strange that a body was discovered there. That Elisa, or indeed anyone, had somehow accessed the cistern struck many as borderline incomprehensible, a mystery worthy of Sherlock Holmes. The coming debate over whether the task was even physically possible for Elisa, who in the videotape was manifestly disconcerted and missing her glasses, was just getting started online, as well as the equally important adjoining question of why she would have sought access in the first place.

Later that day, Elisa's parents confirmed the body was hers.

At 4:36 P.M. Coroner Supervising Investigator Fred Corral notified Senior Criminalist Mark Schuchardt that a criminalist would be needed once the decedent's body arrived at the Forensic Science Center.

Under an hour later, Mr. Schuchardt was staring at Elisa's body, which lay supine on a service table in an advanced state of decomposition, with bloating, marbling and discoloration to the face, abdomen, and upper legs. The hands and feet were waterlogged, which did not surprise him once he learned the body had been submerged in a water tank for days or weeks. The woman's soaking wet clothes lay next to her along with a wristwatch and a hotel key card, which had also been submerged.

Mark collected forensic evidence until 6:50 P.M., at which point the clothing and other personal effects were bagged and placed into evidence.

This information, as well as the additional fibers and debris found on the clothes, would not be publicly disclosed for another six months, when the full autopsy and toxicology reports were released. Other details, some of them critically important, would not be revealed until the next year. Some of them were not ever revealed.

CONTAMINATED WATER

Of the many simultaneous investigations that began that day, the one most devoured by local news concerned the LA County Department of Public Health, which sought to determine if the Cecil Hotel drinking water was safe for consumption. While they awaited the results of this investigation, public health officials with LA County's Environmental Health department temporarily condemned the Cecil Hotel's water supply and issued a "Do Not Drink" order.

Suddenly there were news reports about infected water. Eighty-nine-year-old Cecil Hotel resident Bernard Diaz, who had lived in the hotel for thirty-two years, said management did not tell him about the water situation. He and others only found out that the health department was quarantining the water supply while watching the news. An hour later, Diaz said, a news anchor on KTLA announced that a body had been found in one of the water cisterns on the roof of the building where he lived. Imagine finding out on the 6 o'clock news that your drinking water has been contaminated by a dead body.

Tenants and short-term residents who had stayed at the hotel recalled instances of water coming out of the faucets and showerheads dark, discolored and, in some cases, containing sediment; they realized in horror that for nearly two weeks they had drunk, brushed their teeth with, and bathed in corpse water.

"The moment we found out, we felt a bit sick to the stomach, quite literally, especially having drank the water, we're not well mentally," said Mr. Baugh, a British tourist.

Another tenant described the taste of the water to news reporters as almost "sweet."

"The water did have a funny taste," said Sabrina Baugh, who had been drinking the water for eight days. "We never thought anything of it. We thought it was just the way it was here."

Terrance Powell, a director at LA's Department of Public Health, said the size of the water cistern and the presence of chlorine in most Los Angeles public water made the likelihood of contamination pretty small, but he could not rule it out.

"Our biggest concern is going to be fecal contamination because of the body in the water," Powell told reporters.

When an initial test for coliform bacteria—indicative of human waste—came back negative, officials tried to assuage residents' fears of contaminated water. But no amount of mental gymnastics could absolve the odious truth: a cadaver had been marinating in their drinking water.

In the days following the rooftop discovery, fifty-five of the hotel's guests chose to leave the premises and were relocated. Approximately fifteen guests, many of them lower-income full-time residents signed waivers and remained. They received bottled water in replacement of the possibly contaminated hotel water. Two guests, Steven and Gloria Cott, filed a class-action lawsuit against the hotel within the next month.

The cistern in which Elisa was found was taken "offline" and additional samples were taken from different parts of the building to be retested. The hotel's entire water system was flushed and refilled with chlorine-rich water. Until the new tests came back, the hotel restaurant was shut down and water at the Cecil was only to be used for "flushing."

"So many things have happened in this place that nothing surprises me," Diaz told a reporter.

CAUSE OF DEATH

The preliminary autopsy was unable to determine the cause of death. Ed Winter, L.A. County assistant chief coroner stated that it was "deferred, pending additional tests." Winter further stated that the coroner's office wouldn't be releasing any partial or preliminary information until it had the results of blood, urine, and toxicology tests. That information could take anywhere from six to eight weeks to be released. At least, it was *supposed* to take that long.

Though he didn't divulge much information, Winter did shed a little light on his thought process when he stated a few of the questions for which he would seek answers. "What was in [Elisa Lam's] system? Were all the organs functioning right? . . . Any prescriptions, was she on meds within a therapeutic level or did she take too many or was there none?"

In other words, it's reasonable to assume based on this statement that there was at least some consideration going into the theory that Elisa was under the influence of drugs during the surveillance video. Had Elisa willingly taken an illicit substance—a psychedelic or narcotic that rendered her in a dissociated, confused state? Or had she been drugged?

INITIAL QUESTIONS

With Elisa no longer missing and her body found in suspicious circumstances, police now found themselves with a potential murder investigation on their hands. As they waited for an autopsy and toxicology report to shed light on the empirical facts of her cause of death, detectives began working the case.

The primary detectives assigned to the Elisa Lam case were veterans Wallace Tennelle and Greg Stearns.

Elisa's body was found naked; her clothes (if, in fact, they were her clothes; one item listed as Lam's was a pair of men's shorts) were found floating in the water coated with "a sand-like particulate." Pending the results of the autopsy, we didn't yet know whether she had been assaulted in any way. A rape and fingernail kit would hopefully answer the critical but disturbing questions that must invariably be asked when a missing person's clothes have been removed.

No crime scene photos or photos of her body were released; nor did the LAPD release any information regarding DNA collected from the roof where her body was found. This is, of course, standard. In a homicide investigation, detectives are methodically careful about what information they release because there are certain details of the crime scene that only the perpetrator could know. When they question suspects, they look to glean these details from them.

The age-old tactic is surprisingly effective. During the investigation of serial killer Jack Unterweger, who had lived in the Cecil

Hotel during one of his murder sprees, detectives from both Vienna and Los Angeles carefully safeguarded information pertaining to the condition of the prostitutes Unterweger had murdered. Details, such as the meticulous and particularly vicious and fatal nooses he fashioned with his victims' bras, were known only to the detectives and the killer.

In the case of Richard Ramirez, who had also lived at the Cecil Hotel, the LAPD did not publicly disclose details of the killer's Avia sneakers and .25 automatic ballistics during the manhunt so that Ramirez would not see it in newspapers and eliminate the evidence. Then-Mayor of San Francisco Dianne Feinstein blurted out the information at a news conference and it was subsequently plastered all over the city newspapers.

The disclosure infuriated the LAPD and could have compromised the manhunt, as Ramirez saw the article and only then learned what evidence they had on him. He subsequently discarded the .25 and the sneakers when he read Feinstein's leak. Fortunately, he was apprehended anyway.

In the Elisa Lam case, there was not yet a shred of physical evidence to prove foul play—and the question deck was stacked. Was Elisa interacting with someone in the hallway as seen on the surveillance tape? Why was her body in the water tank? Why was she naked? Why was she on the roof at all? How had she accessed it (or been brought there) without the alarm being triggered?

One thing we know about the initial police investigation is that they searched the hotel, floor by floor, with a canine unit. Manager Amy Price stated in the civil-case depositions that this search included the roof but did not yield any information.

Detective Tennelle testified that when the LAPD set up a command post in the Cecil, they searched "every nook and cranny of that building where we thought was a room, locked or unlocked, it was to be opened. It was to be searched."

This was a somewhat misleading statement, since they did not initially discover Elisa's body on the roof when they supposedly searched "every nook and cranny." If they had searched every nook and cranny, they would have found the body in one of the only structures visible on the roof of the hotel they supposedly searched twice.

How had police investigators overlooked the water tanks during their two searches of the hotel? There's nothing else on the roof—if the lid to the tank in which Elisa was found was up, how had the police investigators not seen it? If the lid was down—and presumably set back into place after Elisa's entry—who was responsible for this? Who closed the lid?

Search Dogs

Police have confirmed that a K-9 unit was used in the building but have not been specific about where. For example, we don't know if the dogs were used to search rooms and pick up a live scent—which one would presume police were looking for when Elisa was still missing—and we don't know to what extent, if any, dogs were deployed on the roof. This is crucial in assessing how Elisa was not found earlier in the water tank, which is itself crucial in understanding that critical evidence may have been lost early in the case. Determining if and why evidence was lost is an issue we will return to later.

Since the LAPD, by their own admission, claims to have searched the entire building, "every nook and cranny," let's assume that the K-9 unit was taken to the roof. How did the dogs miss her scent during what was then a second search of the roof?

To answer this we must first know what kind of search dog was being used, an air-scent dog or a tracking dog. Tracking dogs are often used when time is of the essence in a missing-persons case. They are called onto the scene in order to follow the scent of the person missing before the area becomes contaminated by the smell of other people. To do this, canines are bred and trained to detect heavy skin particles, which living humans shed at the rate of 40,000 per minute. They are essentially following the forensic trail all humans leave in their wake.

There is ample reason to think that tracking dogs were used as detectives may have believed Elisa was still alive. But if she was still alive at the hotel, the only place they could have reasonably suspected her to be breathing is in one of the rooms. If they believed that, this may suggest the existence of other evidence, such as suspicious tenants or employees, that led them to think using a tracking dog in the hotel would have been fruitful.

However, unless Elisa was alive in one of the rooms of the hotel, the only logical K-9 choice would have been air-scent dogs, who do not follow a specific scent but rather look for the origin of a corpse scent that they pick up on through air currents. Tracking dogs and air-scent dogs overlap in their training but only air-scent dogs look for cadavers.

If the LAPD used tracking dogs, how had they missed all of Elisa's forensic trail? It is almost certain that Elisa's DNA—and possibly her killer's DNA—festooned the staircase leading to the roof or, alternately, the fire escape on the side of the building. One would also suspect DNA to have been on the roof, on the ladder to the water tank, and on the lid to the water tank.

But if the police used cadaver dogs and the lid was indeed open, how had the dogs missed the scent? Does that suggest that her body was moved into the tank at a later date? Who would have the access and clearance to be carrying a body up the stairs? Who would have the strength to carry the body up the precarious ladder on the side of the cistern? And how would some of this activity not been picked up on hotel surveillance?

And where was the body before it was moved and why was that scent not picked up? Later, detectives admitted they didn't search rooms at the Cecil because they couldn't prove there was a crime, a statement that raises its own set of concerns.

But the biggest question remains: how did the K-9 unit miss the scent? Air-scent dogs' work retinue include the categories of Cadaver, Water, Avalanche, Urban Disaster, Wilderness, and Evidence. It has been said that most cadaver dogs have about a 95 percent accuracy rate and can detect bodies buried as far as 30 feet below ground.

The use of dogs by law enforcement dates back all the way to the Middle Ages, but it was not until 1889 that the modern era saw dogs integrated into police work. Sir Charles Warren, Commissioner of the Metropolitan Police of London, trained two bloodhounds to help him search for Jack the Ripper.

Subsequently, K-9 units became a regular asset of police investigations. Decomposition in the human body begins when enzymes and microbiome start breaking down organs and skin. When the body's amino acids dissolve, they release the compound chemicals cadaverine and putrescine. Cadaver dogs are trained to detect these with a unique skill set that utilizes the incredible olfactory powers of canine nostrils. Man's best friend can smell death—human death. The hounds become scholars at identifying the odor of our expiration.

They are trained to detect hundreds of different scents dispensed by corpses, to differentiate between humans and animals, between bodies that are submerged in water and bodies buried in rubble. However, the process of decomposition is impacted by external factors like environment, weather, and insects. Each modulation slightly changes the exact "scent of death" that will be present.

Some analysts suggested that rainfall may have thrown off the cadaver dogs. Weather reports show that there was slight precipitation on February 8 and February 19 in Los Angeles during the time Elisa was missing. However, the K-9 search conducted by the LAPD occurred somewhere between February 1 and February 6. Therefore, rain was not a factor that would have affected the scene. Forensic evidence, such as DNA from skin cells, should have been available either in the staircase and doorway of the rooftop emergency exit or on the fire escapes, which are the only ways Elisa could have accessed the roof. Forensic evidence should have also been available on the ladder to the water tank and on the lid to the water tank.

If the LAPD only used tracking dogs, it is possible that they missed the decomposition scent due to water immersion. But they should have picked up on the other DNA left behind by Elisa that would have led them to the roof. If, alternatively, the LAPD used cadaver dogs, it's especially difficult to imagine how they missed both the DNA scent leading to the roof and the decomposition scent.

On that day, did the 5 percent rear its ugly head and account for a group of trained, diligent hounds missing the scent? Or could it be that there was no scent because Elisa's body wasn't yet there?

What Happened on the Roof?

One of the biggest early questions pertained to roof access: how Elisa got up there and how she accessed the tank? How did she access the roof without triggering the rooftop alarm? Pedro Tovar, the Cecil's chief engineer, confirmed that there are four ways to get onto the roof: three fire escapes that are connected to interior doors of the hotel; and a staircase attached to the 14th floor, which according to one tenant was designed to trigger an alarm when accessed by someone without clearance.

If we assume that Elisa accessed the roof via a fire escape, we have to take into consideration that she was missing her glasses. Think back to the surveillance tape and recall that Elisa had to bend over and bring her face to within a few inches of the button panel to read the floor numbers—and she still got it badly wrong two different times. Is it realistic to think that someone with impaired vision, or who was discombobulated enough to press the wrong buttons multiple times, subsequently climbed out the side of a building—with nothing to stop her fall, the distant windy call of traffic humming fourteen floors below—and climbed a tiny ladder onto the roof?

And once she was up there, Elisa would have had to ascend a separate platform on which the water tanks sit and then slither through the narrow space between the tanks and the plumbing equipment. Then she would have had to scale the cistern itself, lift its heavy metal lid, and climb inside. But not before taking off her clothes and bringing them, as well as her watch and room keycard, into the tank with her.

If the lid was open when the police twice searched the roof, it's hard to believe they didn't see it and inquire. If the lid was closed, how did Elisa close it herself while descending into the tank?

Of course, the biggest question would pertain to Elisa's motive for doing any of this. Why would a young woman—who, we would learn, liked to stay in her room and keep to herself—scale the side of a dangerous building and then scale the ladder of a ten-foot water tank, remove her clothes and climb inside?

Almost immediately, many case analysts began to conclude this was the wrong question. With the evidence at hand, a young woman displaying behavior that suggests she is frightened and being followed, her body coming to rest shortly thereafter in an enclosed metal tank with her clothes removed on a difficult-to-access roof, perhaps the better question is: who brought Elisa to the roof and/or who arranged for Elisa's body to be concealed in the water tank?

It was a question that would be debated on countless websites, in a million plus comment threads, in thousands of videos and podcasts.

But first: would the LAPD find evidence of criminality to support these theories?

The primary detectives assigned to the case, Greg Stearns and Wallace "Wally" Tennelle, were veterans of the LAPD police force.

STEARNS AND THE "MYSTERY OF THE HOLLYWOOD HEAD"

Greg Stearns is widely viewed as a particularly skilled interrogator who uses cutting-edge techniques. He is probably best known for cracking a cold case that ended with a fellow LAPD detective, Stephanie Lazarus, being convicted of a murder she committed twenty-three years earlier.

In 2012–13 (directly overlapping with the timeframe of the Lam investigation) the department cherry-picked Stearns and Tim Marcia, who also worked the Lam case, to participate in a top-secret non-coercive interrogation training program called HIG (High-Value Detainee Interrogation Group), headed by a consortium of FBI, CIA, and Pentagon officials.

The goal was to use new interrogation tactics to reduce the number of false confessions. Stearns and Marcia led the way and applied what they learned at HIG to the "Mystery of the Hollywood Head."

This investigation-turned-cold-case began in early 2012 when a dog jumped into a ravine and found a head-sized object in a plastic bag.

The object was indeed a head and it belonged to a man, Hervey Medellin, who had been missing for weeks. The prime suspect was

Medellin's housemate, Gabriel Campos-Martinez, for whom police had a mountain of circumstantial evidence (for example, his Google search for how to dismember a body, which he conducted the day Medellin disappeared) but nothing substantial enough to hand over to prosecutors.

Stearns and Marcia took a run at Campos with their new HIG interrogation method. Though he didn't confess, by the time they were done chatting, Campos had admitted he went for walks in the Hollywood hills with the victim, in close proximity to where his head was found; additionally, he discussed a plant called Datura, which could incapacitate someone.

In 2015, Campos received a sentence of twenty-five years to life.

The LAPD has since used the HIG method—the true nature of which is classified—on another sixty interrogations with a 75 to 80 percent success rate.

Another case I found interesting involved both Stearns and Lieutenant Walt Teague. Teague and Stearns had been trying for nearly a decade to nab Tai Zhi Cui, the prime suspect in a grisly triple murder, who fled to China to escape extradition and prosecution. Police say that in October 2006, Cui entered a Koreatown restaurant and killed his ex-girlfriend, her new boyfriend, and the restaurant's owner with execution-style gunshots.

China refused to extradite Cui but instead prosecuted him in their own courts, which include a three-judge panel. Cui was convicted and Stearns and Teague celebrated justice, although they would have rather tried him in the United States.

Teague, who appeared with the Lam family during the press conference, has strong connections to China. He earned a degree and met his wife there. I wondered how much of a role he played dealing with the family.

"WALLY" TENNELLE

In the book *Ghettoside*, a polemic on black-on-black homicide in Los Angeles, journalist Jill Leovy describes Wallace Tennelle as being atypical of LAPD officers because of a specific and tragically fated conviction that officers should live in the community that they police. For Tennelle this was South Central, where he and his wife, Yadira, high school sweethearts, raised three children who all attended private school.

After serving as a Marine, Tennelle devoted his life to the police force. He initially rejected the Robbery and Homicide Department (RHD) out of principle but the homicide surge of the early 1980s ushered him in. Tennelle would go to work for the CRASH division, which was an elite, aggressive, almost renegade force within the department that would later become a controversial liability.

In the late 1980s, Tennelle transitioned to a divisional detective job but his intense work ethic, described as pathological, persisted. In 1992, he and his partner worked twenty-eight cases, which Leovy notes, was three times more than most detectives took on.

Wallace, a veteran LAPD homicide detective, knew what it was like to lose a kid. He had bought a home for his family in the same community in which he worked, the dangerous South Los Angeles area. It was in this neighborhood, the western edge of the Los Angeles Police Department's 77th Street precinct area, that in 2007 his eighteen-year-old son Bryant Tennelle was shot in the head and killed by a gang member. Bryant was wearing a Houston Astros baseball cap, unaware that its colors and shapes affiliated him with rival gang activity.

Anomalies

As Stearns and Tennelle got their investigation underway, Bernard Diaz, the eighty-nine-year-old long-time resident, told reporters that he'd heard loud strange noises coming from the 4th floor the night before Elisa's body was found.

"They said there was some obstruction to the drain between the 3rd and 4th floor," Diaz said, speculating as to the source of the noise.

Another claim, corroborated by photographs from the roof, stated that there was suspicious graffiti found near the water tanks. One reporter speculated that the messages, written in Latin, may have been a calling card left behind by someone ostensibly involved in Lam's death.

Still other reports concerned several registered sex offenders living at the hotel. In fact, nearly a dozen sex offenders were known to live on Main Street within only a few blocks of the Cecil.

There was also the matter of additional young women found dead in the area and, at this point in the investigation, the detectives considered foul play a possible explanation.

But who was responsible for transporting Elisa's body past surveillance cameras, security alarms, up several steep ladders and into the water tank?

Another question that would follow: was Elisa reported missing by the hotel staff when she failed to check out at her scheduled time? Or did they wait until notified by the police that the family had filed a missing-persons report?

Or was something else entirely going on with Elisa in the Cecil Hotel? In the coming weeks, websleuths would stumble upon new information about Elisa that further complicated their attempts to discern her behavior in the elevator. Other researchers, myself included, mined the history of the hotel itself and discovered tragic, terrifying truths about the tenants and employees who lived and worked there.

CHAPTER 4

Rise of the Websleuths

WHEN I FIRST GOT INVOLVED in the case, I didn't have the faintest clue what a websleuth was or even what constituted a true-crime investigation. The Elisa Lam case slowly sucked me in from a variety of different angles. By the end of my investigation, the experience would take a severe psychological toll and redirect the course of my life in unexpected ways.

And I wasn't the only one for whom the case had a special effect. What I would discover is that there are people all over the world who have become attached to, connected with, and emotionally invested in the case for an enormous variety of reasons. Websleuths and friends of Elisa's who want to see justice served; people suffering from depression and mental illness who have forged an online community; former Cecil Hotel residents who want the truth to come out about the criminal history of the hotel; paranormal researchers who see a darker reality cutting through and want to awaken the world; conspiracy theorists who believe a larger, more sinister narrative is playing out behind the scenes.

The case became a kind of Rorschach test; everyone who looked at it saw something different, something uniquely meaningful and uniquely petrifying.

MISSING PERSONS AND UNIDENTIFIED BODIES

It is estimated that one third of murders in the United States go unsolved. That's approximately 200,000 homicides since 1960. Since the days of Jack the Ripper and, much later, the Black Dahlia, people have always been fascinated with unsolved murders. Cold cases and true-crime sagas are a cultural obsession, an entertainment staple, but more important, they are a major conundrum for law-enforcement agencies who often simply do not have the resources to vigorously pursue the truth behind every unsolved death in which foul play is suspected.

Even the above estimates do not paint the full picture of the burden of justice, particularly in America, where one must also factor in *unidentified remains* and *missing persons*. In *The Skeleton Crew,* Deborah Halber breaks the situation down. A 2007 census conducted by the National Institute of Justice (NIJ) suggests there may be 40,000 unidentified individuals in morgues and graves around the country. Some coroners and medical examiners think the number may be closer to 60,000. Unfortunately, many agencies in the medico-legal establishment habitually overlook unidentifieds. One study suggests only 30 percent of small-town coroners even have policies for how to handle unidentified remains.

Meanwhile, at any given time there are about 100,000 active missing-persons cases. As we discussed earlier, the majority of these people are found alive. But over the years, the number of those who remain missing—a nightmare without end for the families involved—continues to rise. Many of them do not even constitute being a "cold case" because they lack evidence or an advocate.

The ability and capacity for our nation's police and law enforcement is outpaced by the rate of people disappearing, the staggering number of unidentified remains, and unsolved deaths. This is the troubling locus from which websleuths arose and became an indispensable and permanent tool in criminal justice.

There is no official origin to the concept of websleuths. They were forged out of the slowly evolving symbiotic relationship between humans, who seem to have an innate desire to solve puzzles, and the Internet, which is both the greatest research tool and the greatest interconnectivity tool yet devised by our species.

Since the earliest days of the Internet, civilians with an interest in cold cases have gathered information about them. The location of the body, the time it was discovered, salient physical details like scars or tattoos and other distinguishing features. They entered these details in rudimentary databases. The first newsgroups, email lists, and Yahoo! Groups like Troy More's ColdCases united researchers and allowed them to share facts. These embryonic forums grew quickly in the early days of Google and Wikipedia. Social media was just getting started but hadn't yet produced communities like Reddit, and improved Internet access and functionality had not yet allowed for a site like Websleuths.

Like raw cosmic matter being slowly shaped and consolidated by the force of gravity, the Internet and its ability to facilitate crowdsourcing coalesced into a sphere accessible to all. These earliest websleuths turned their sights onto classic decades-old cold cases like the Green River Killer, Tent Girl, the Lady of the Dunes, the Boy in the Box (which dates all the way back to 1957), etc. More recent and contemporary cases like those of Tupac Shakur, Notorious B.I.G, Jodie Arias, OJ Simpson, and Natalee Holloway fanned the flames of true crime as a moneymaker on cable TV shows like *Nancy Grace.*

The attacks of 9/11 had an impact on websleuths in forensic science, Halber believes. The number of victims that had to be ID'd sometimes with nothing more than microscopic shreds of DNA pushed the envelope of forensic technology and encouraged crowdsourced work.

The biggest online community used by websleuths at this time was the Doe Network, sometimes called the "Facebook of the dead," which is a crowdsourced database of missing persons and unidentified bodies. It was launched in 1999 and in time thousands of volunteers would become members and contribute information gathered from public records, media archives, and medical examiner and coroner websites like Las Vegas Unidentified and the Florida Unidentified Decedent Database. The volunteers were so tenacious and pesky that law-enforcement officials and cops called them "Doe Nuts." This set the stage for a prolonged tension over efforts to peek behind the "blue curtain" that has traditionally been drawn over police investigations.

A series of events in the middle half of the last decade acted as major accelerators for the websleuth movement. The first was in 2004 when Tricia Griffith purchased and revamped the Websleuths website, transforming the crime forum from a hostile vipers' nest into one of the most trafficked and respected platforms for crowd-sleuthing. The next year, in 2005, Reddit came online and quickly grew into a massive online community with several "subreddits" dedicated to websleuthing and cold cases.

In 2007, partly inspired by the success of the Doe Network, the National Institute of Justice (NIJ), created a massive new database, the National Missing and Unidentified Persons System (NamUs), dedicated to helping families and investigators identify remains and locate missing persons. Within only five years of its inception, NamUs users were mounting impressive numbers.

Crowdsleuthing was having a real effect, helping families find some degree of closure in cases of unimaginable loss and tragedy, delivering justice to hundreds of victims who had almost been completely snuffed out of existence.

A specific case spurred Tricia Griffith to join Websleuths and test her might at cold cases. The day after Christmas in 1996, six-year-old JonBenet Ramsey was found murdered in the basement of her home, triggering one of the most scrutinized police investigations in modern times. Replete with a potentially staged abduction, unidentified DNA, inconclusive handwriting samples, a badly compromised crime scene, fake press leaks, false confessions, and hundreds of opposing theories, the case generated a small library of books, movies, and TV specials. The JonBenet case essentially created a new niche obsession with true crime.

In 2004, Tricia took the helm of Websleuths and made immediate changes. The forums had become unbearable, Tricia told me, "a sea of jerks" threatening each other, calling each other names, and trolling the hell out of anyone and everyone. Her initial goal, she said, was not to create a popular web forum but to give a platform to disenfranchised advocates. She also wanted to help the families of missing persons or homicide victims who weren't getting media attention.

Tricia tightened the moderation on the site and made strict rules for communication etiquette and rumor regulation. She also banned a huge group of insufferable trolls. Eventually these measures had the unintended but welcome effect of attracting real websleuths . . . and lots of them. In only a couple years, Websleuths' membership grew from only 250 to thousands.

Then the Casey Anthony case hit and Websleuths truly exploded.

WEBSLEUTHS

In *The Skeleton Crew,* Halber paints a portrait of websleuths as decentralized, spread out all over the country and world, usually anonymous, and ranging from a software sales rep like Dan Brady to college students and stay-at-home moms. They are true-crime fanatics, cold-case junkies, people for whom the prospect of cracking an unsolved murder ranks higher than almost any other human accomplishment. They are cold-case lifers.

Some websleuths hunt for forensic information or file FOIA requests; others work on behalf of families who are missing a loved one or who believe their loved one was the victim of foul play. They crowdsource granules of detail based on dental records and DNA, facial reconstruction models, post-mortem photos, computer-generated color portraits, clay dummies, Google or aerial maps. They may comb through online archives collecting census, voter, and military records, marriage and death certificates, property titles, business permits, and bankruptcy and criminal files.

Halber's book chronicles the stories of several successful websleuths.

Bobby Lingoes, a Doe Network member who works as a civilian database manager for the police in Quincy, Massachusetts, helped solve a 2002 case of an unidentified body found in the Sudbury River. He crowdsleuthed the letters "PK," which were tattooed on the body's right shoulder, and found another Doe volunteer from Texas who remembered a missing man with that exact tattoo. Lingoes handed off this information to Framingham police; they subsequently identified the deceased man as forty-year-old Peter Kokinakis. He had disappeared that year from Houston.

Legendary websleuth Todd Matthews, who solved the infamous decades-old Tent Girl mystery, also solved a case using only a tattoo, a kangaroo tattoo that identified a missing woman found dead in Maryland.

Ellen Leach did what police in Missouri and Iowa had been unable to do for four years. Using a forensic reconstruction, she connected a skull found cemented into a bucket behind a dumpster in Missouri with a photograph of missing Iowa resident Greg May. It was Leach's first solve in six years of websleuthing, and she still remembers the glow.

In 2008, Tonya Finsterwald, an amateur Doe sleuth from Texas, helped solve the 1980 case of a young man, Joseph Formica Jr., who suffered from mental illness and had disappeared from near his family's home in Pennsylvania.

In another case, a websleuth's tool of choice was Ancestry.com. While searching the Doe Network, Sheree Greenwood saw the picture of a victim's bones and the garments worn prior to death, which included white tennis shoes, jeans, and a red T-shirt with a Native American graphic and the words "Wynn family reunion" with the date of the event and a list of names. Greenwood methodically hunted down the family members and the shirt designer and ultimately identified the deceased as Brenda Wright.

Halber says the websleuths and their crowdsleuthing techniques have not only solved a number of cases but are "transforming law enforcement's relationship with the public."

Indeed, it is important to remember that at the very beginning of the Elisa Lam case, LAPD law enforcement called upon the public to get involved with providing clues as to her whereabouts. They were not only open to but soliciting a co-relationship between the citizenry and the police, knowing full well that this meant deputizing websleuths to look into the case. Once they showed the surveillance footage, though, they couldn't close Pandora's Box.

Tricia Griffith says she knows for a fact that law-enforcement officials use the *Websleuths* site to gather information and keep an eye on the threads. She has tracked the IP addresses logged into the site and determined that multiple precincts have accounts they use to monitor activity on certain cases. Griffith is convinced that despite any outward posturing or criticism, a growing number of detectives consider the work of websleuths valuable.

But the relationship is not an altogether cozy one and, in fact, in the majority of cases, investigators are outright dismissive of websleuths and consider them impediments. Historically, law enforcement officials—be they police officers, detectives, or any number of deputies from local, regional, and federal task forces—do not want to talk to the public. And not just about the details of an unsolved murder. Transparency at all levels has been opaque since the inception of major urban police forces in the mid to late nineteenth century.

This is not necessarily always due to some conspiratorial hush-hush campaign. The reality is, as Halber notes in her book, criminal investigations, especially homicides, can easily become mired in communication breakdowns between jurisdictions, agencies, police departments, coroner's offices, and municipalities and divisions within municipalities.

In other words, the public-service officials have enough trouble with internal communication. Fissures within the law-enforcement community can be just as divisive as public relations problems. The fallout from this has been seen in cases such as the Black Dahlia and the Hillside Strangler, in which squabbling among agencies and failure to share information across jurisdictions arguably allowed killers to get away with murder.

When it comes to websleuths, there's a reason law-enforcement professionals took to using the moniker "Doe Nuts" when referring to them. They view websleuths as mentally unstable amateurs who do not have the training or the temperament to solve a case. More importantly, they are seen as dangerous lynch mobs who make false accusations based on petty evidence.

Unfortunately, there is some truth to this view. I would witness irresponsible websleuths firsthand in the Elisa Lam case. Unfounded accusations run rampant across the Internet and legitimate pieces of evidence often compete with debate threads over the most putrescent conspiracy theories imaginable.

However, diligent websleuths counterbalance this disturbance and an equilibrium develops.

Would websleuths live up to the challenge in the Elisa Lam case?

The "crime scene," the Cecil Hotel, has historically been a dangerous hotel—so dangerous in fact that there are rumors that in decades past police officers dreaded taking calls there and avoided entering its hallways at all costs.

What I would discover is that Cecil Hotel tenants, certain that they would be ignored, have traditionally avoided calling the police; further, even if the tenants could attract a caring, responsible officer, by filing a police report, they risked losing their home. So Cecil Hotel tenants didn't want anything to do with the police; the police didn't want anything to do with the Cecil Hotel; and the Cecil Hotel seemed to operate for decades with a kind of impunity.

Perhaps this is exactly why websleuths are needed. If disenfranchised victims or witnesses won't talk to the police out of fear, perhaps they will talk to websleuths, who are not ordained by the state to wield coercive force. The thought of this makes police detectives cringe but, as Tricia Griffith emphatically claims, it's a reality departments are going to have to face.

One reality I was going to have to face was that to learn more about the Elisa Lam case, I would have to get out of the academic definitions and studies of websleuthing and further into dark realms of the web itself. It was time to become a websleuth.

"BRAINSCRATCH"

Like many people who search for careers in Los Angeles, John Lordan tried multiple niches of the entertainment industry. But his heart was always in investigating true crime, unsolved cases, and conspiracies. It was a natural calling.

John launched a YouTube show devoted to tackling cold cases and murder investigations. His idea was to present a mysterious case and compile all the research he could, present that research and then use the comment threads to deputize his viewers as a decentralized crowdsourced investigation. By leaving behind all the breadcrumbs of his investigation, anyone could follow in John's footsteps—including police detectives who might not ever admit to culling evidence from a websleuth—and anyone could participate and annotate an ongoing project.

With a small but rapidly growing circle of passionate followers spurring him on, John urged subscribers to introduce new evidence and ideas. He didn't mind if his investigations forked into previously unforeseen directions. In that way, his new channel was like a multimedia Wikipedia, a transparent work in progress whereby you can actually witness, step-by-step, the formation of a theory and the research conducted to confirm or debunk it.

He called the show "BrainScratch" and one of his very first videos was about the mysterious case of Elisa Lam, the popularity of which launched his channel into motion with thousands of devoted subscribers. What he didn't know at the time was that the Elisa Lam case would be a subject he returned to many times over the years. No one could have predicted the near-cult devotee status it would attain in popular culture.

One of John's early goals with the Elisa Lam case was to eschew the paranormal angle, which he found distracting and stigmatizing. He vowed instead to focus only on demonstrable, empirical evidence. Of course, with a case like this one, such a goal became virtually impossible. And despite John wanting to avoid conspiracy theories, he couldn't deny that there was something off about this case.

He started calling out the anomalies.

There should be more surveillance footage.

While it is common for police to release video of a missing person—especially if that person is a foreign national—the only practical purpose for that surveillance video was to help identify Elisa. But the footage is of such low quality that it does not really identify her. Ultimately, the surveillance video only served to stigmatize the victim and spawn conspiracy theories.

And it raised more questions than it answered. What about other footage from the hallways of the hotel? Footage from the lobby?

From outside the hotel? Why have we not seen any of that footage that could actually help to retrace Elisa's steps and identify anyone she might have been with? Why was the elevator video the only available footage?

The answer: it wasn't, it's just the only footage the police allowed us to see. In time, we learned there was additional footage of Elisa. And the content of that supplemental footage will give you goosebumps— but that disclosure wasn't made until fairly late in the investigation.

Elisa's cell phone(s) was never recovered.

The police were reluctant to talk about Elisa's missing phone from the beginning. As I mentioned previously, the fact that at least one of her phones was missing prevented police from looking at who Elisa communicated with prior to her death. However, it is technically possible to track lost phones, and it seems that this could have been of assistance to the investigation.

More important, you do not need access in the phone to track the phone and to extract information—metadata, for example—from the carrier, provider, and cellular towers.

It is also not certain that the phone wasn't recovered. An early statement by the LAPD suggested that Elisa's possessions from her room had been stored in the hotel's basement. Could her phone have been among these possessions?

Since the investigation was still active, the police would say nothing about the location of Elisa's phone, adding the first of countless enigmatic wrinkles to the mystery.

Much later, an unlikely witness disclosed to me a shocking revelation regarding the location of Elisa's belongings.

Elisa's Tumblr account continued updating for several months after her disappearance.

A month after her death, Elisa's Tumblr account posted something new, a Virginia Woolf quote that read:

> *Why, she reflected, should there be this perpetual dispar-*
> *ity between the thought and the action, between the life of*
> *solitude and the life of society, this astonishing precipice*

on one side of which the soul was active and in broad day-
light, on the other side of which it was contemplative and
dark as night?

As bloggers and websleuths became more and more obsessed with
the case over the next year, the account would periodically update
with random images and messages from Elisa. A girl repeatedly saying "I like being alone . . . I like being alone." A *Scream*-like abstract drawing of a person in a car with the title "Human Identity in
the Urban Environment." A Tarot card of the Hermit.

Throughout the course of the parallel investigations that would
ensue, the blog would spit forth a new post on behalf of the deceased.
Paranormal buffs said they were messages from the grave. Murder
conspiracists said they were evidence that the killer had acquired
Elisa's lost phone and was using her Tumblr account to tease and
mock investigators.

The most logical explanation for the posts is that Elisa had set up
the auto-updater feature on her Tumblr account. This would have
allowed her feed to automatically aggregate posts from her favorite
accounts. But given that her phone was missing, it was hard not to
wonder whether maybe the new Tumblr posts were messages from
her killer.

The effect was chilling, as illustrated by a message written posthumously to Elisa by a former classmate:

> *What haunts me is that your Tumblr reblogged my posts*
> *at the end of February and beginning of March 2013, which*
> *distressed me to no ends at the time.*

There was suspicious graffiti found on the roof.

In one of John Lordan's early "BrainScratch" videos, he reported
on photographs displaying graffiti on the roof of the Cecil. The
photos were taken when the Fire Department removed Elisa from
the tank. The vulgar tags included the Latin phrase *Fecto cunt her
suma,* which is inscribed on a surface close to the water tank where
Elisa's body was found. According to some online accounts, *Fecto*

cunt her suma translates either to "in fact she was a cunt" or "it's the best pussy" in Latin.

There are a couple of reasons why the graffiti should be considered important. For one, in later statements the hotel management insisted that the rooftop wasn't accessible, a determination that became legally critical when the Lam family eventually filed a civil lawsuit against the Cecil Hotel. The fact that someone or multiple persons had tagged the roof meant that at least one or more people had breached the security there.

Furthermore, tagging usually implies that there will be an audience, meaning there may have been the expectation that others would see it. All of which leads to the conclusion that hotel residents or others may have habitually occupied the roof. One former Cecil tenant told me that she used to drink beer on the roof on a regular basis. It can only be assumed that she wasn't the only one. Could one of these occupiers have had something to do with Elisa's death or known the killer?

Another point to consider is an oddly synchronistic post from Elisa's blog. On 31 January, the day she went missing, Elisa posted the following statement on her Tumblr account:

> *Cunt again? It was odd how men . . . used that word to demean women when it was the only part of a woman they valued.*

This was several days into her stay at the Cecil. Had Elisa already been on the roof and taken offense at the message? Perhaps she objected to the graffiti and offended the artist. Or (a more extreme possibility) had someone Elisa knew or someone who had followed her blog—on which she had published her traveling itinerary—tracked her to the Cecil, and left the graffiti tag as a kind of calling card?

WEBSLEUTH TRAVELS FROM HONG KONG

One websleuth, Kay Theng, journeyed all the way from Hong Kong with the intention of infiltrating the Cecil Hotel with a camera and documenting the layout.

Kay arrived at the 14th-floor elevators—ground zero of the entire case—and proceeded to ask and answer five questions:

1. Do the doors of the elevator remain open? Yes, the doors remain open when you push the buttons to other floors; they only close when you press the "door close" button, or if someone on another floor has pressed the elevator button outside the elevator to signal the elevator to go to their floor.
2. How many buttons and panels are there outside the elevator? There are just two buttons on the outside panel—up and down.
3. Does the hold button work? The hold button does work and John Lordan later tested it to learn that the doors remain open for approximately two minutes when it's pressed.
4. What can you see from the inside? On the wall opposite the elevator is a round mirror which allows you to see if anyone is outside the elevator. The placement of this mirror also means Elisa would have been able to see a reflection of herself when she was standing in the hallway.
5. What can you see if you look outside the elevator? There are two blind spots that are impossible to see from the hallway in front of the elevator. When Elisa peeked out of the elevator and into the hallway, she was not able to see the entire corridor in either direction.

Kay's next moves are to attempt to access the roof and as he does so he asks and answers three new questions:

1. How many paths are there to access the roof?
2. How accessible are those paths?
3. How close can you get to the water tank?

Kay first approaches the 14th-floor fire escape and finds it can be accessed easily and used to reach the 15th floor (top floor). He avoids the main roof access, the stairs used by the hotel employees to reach the alarmed, locked door, and instead climbs the fire escape to reach the roof. It doesn't seem particularly difficult to reach the water tanks.

He concludes his video, "This is not a supernatural event, it is very likely to be a murder. We don't want to see people exaggerate the truth. May the killer be captured soon, and the dead rest in peace."

The paranormal interpretation is far more popular in Kay's home country of Hong Kong but he wasn't buying it. Like John Lordan, Kay didn't want the idea of ghosts and demons to distract people from what was really going on. And he certainly was not the only websleuth who suspected foul play.

MURDER THEORIES

Without the Internet and its attendant websleuth community, the Elisa Lam case would have likely disappeared from the public radar soon after its initial reports had made the rounds. Depending on your point of view, it can be argued that this was either a blessing or a curse. The voracious consumption of the case is nothing short of amazing, a sociological phenomenon that would be haunting in its own right even if it were not predicated on the discovery of a corpse in a rooftop water tank.

The Elisa Lam case was a uniquely Internet-based phenomenon. While the initial investigation and subsequent discovery made both local and international headlines on cable TV stations, the case never became a featured darling on *Nancy Grace* or other cable exploits. Maybe it lacked a certain scandalous sexiness when compared to the cases of Scott Peterson, Jodi Arias, Casey Anthony, or Amanda Knox. Or, one could easily argue, Elisa Lam did not fit the criteria of a ready-for-TV celebrity victim.

She wasn't white. TV true-crime producers often gravitate toward white victims. This phenomenon has an actual psychological designation, the "missing white woman syndrome" (MWWS).

Elisa's case also brings up un-TV-friendly issues. How often do shows on ID (Investigation Discovery) delve into mental illness? Even when the station did eventually run a three-part series, *Horror at the Cecil,* which devoted an episode to the Lam case, her struggle with depression and bipolar disorder were hardly touched upon at all.

Or perhaps it was because the case didn't have a clear antagonist. There was no cinematic murder suspect lurking in the shadows.

Enter the Internet.

A variety of homicide theories would soon follow: They included Elisa being drugged and either dying from accidental overdose or malicious poisoning (perhaps by a romantic interest who had an expectation that prolonged exposure to water would eliminate the trail); another theory posited that Elisa was killed elsewhere in the hotel, possibly in a bathtub where she was already naked, and then transported to the roof and deposited into the water tank; a frequently articulated theory held that Elisa had been killed by a hotel employee, or a friend of a hotel employee, who subsequently edited the surveillance tape so as not to appear.

As people waited for the LAPD detectives to make an announcement or release the results of the autopsy and toxicology reports, speculation was rampant, and more and more websleuths deputized themselves to investigate the mystery. There was something about the case that called to people.

Two body language analysts pored over the surveillance video, studying Elisa's movements and micro-expressions. A YouTuber analyzed the timecode of the surveillance footage and discovered some anomalies. One rogue websleuth actually believed she had found the killer and organized a trolling campaign to make the suspect know he was being hunted.

Perhaps the most important discovery came about without much fanfare. It turned out Elisa had scrupulously documented her life online through blogs and social media. This made it possible to reverse engineer Elisa's final weeks and days in her own words.

Shortly before she went missing, it turned out, Elisa had posted a message saying she had been harassed by "creepers."

CHAPTER 5

The West Coast Tour

IN ANY CRIMINAL INVESTIGATION, phone calls, text messages, or any communications from the deceased are highly prized pieces of information. Sometimes these missives and dispatches are enough in and of themselves to solve a case or to put investigators on the fast lane to identifying and interviewing key suspects.

In Elisa's case, there were no known text messages because her phone was missing. Nor were there phone calls—besides verbal recall of the conversations with her parents while traveling—available for analysis. No friends or acquaintances from the trip immediately came forward with information except for two women who shared a room with Elisa at the Cecil Hotel. These women appear to have been impromptu roommates that Elisa met upon arriving in Los Angeles. At some point during their stay, these two roommates reported to the hotel management that Elisa was acting bizarre and they requested that she be moved to a different room. They have remained unnamed by the LAPD, and no additional information about them has been released, constituting yet another missing puzzle piece.

The Elisa Lam case presented a vexing twist: there were no apparent eyewitnesses, but there was a first-person autobiographical record left behind by the deceased. In time, these records would become just as fascinating and haunting to me as the surveillance video itself. A public memoir she left behind detailing the mercurial journey of her life from the ages of nineteen to twenty-one. In certain passages she reached back even further, summoning memories from childhood and late adolescence.

ETHER FIELDS

The last tweet on her Twitter page (@lambetes) states simply "SPEAKEASY" and is dated January 27, 2013, which is approximately five days before she disappeared. The second most recent tweet is from ten days earlier.

These tweets took me back to December of 2012. I needed more recent information and was hoping her Tumblr would have it.

Her Tumblr blog was entitled *Nouvelle/Nouveau*. A wall of lively media-filled thumbnails greeted me like futuristic crenellations on a digital facade. At a cursory glance, Elisa had varied and eclectic tastes in art, and her Tumblr blog contained a vast assortment of different photographs, digital images, gifs, and quotes filling up the screen.

A representation of the personality of Elisa, a young woman who no longer existed, suddenly levitated before me. A *Great Gatsby* reference; a book reading another book; TVs talking at a dinner party; Kurt Vonnegut slowly smiling; a rainbow threading through a family of otters; shadowy figures emerging from a misty, ethereal swamp; a fork and spoon parental unit holding their baby spork; David Lynch; *Inglourious Basterds*; a witchlike skeleton in robes; a gif asking, "are you expanding your mind or just going crazy?"; *Waiting for Godot*; "Travel with Hogwarts Express."

One post, in particular, mesmerized me. It was a digital illustration of a body falling from a building. I remember an article I read about the horrifying history of the Cecil Hotel, one that included serial killers, murders, and a great number of suicides. A considerable number of the suicides were people jumping from the windows of their upper-floor rooms at the hotel. The falling man image posted to Elisa's Tumblr was posted on January 31, the day she was recorded in the elevator, the day she disappeared and, presumably, died.

Her final written post appears to have been on January 29, when she wrote:

> *have arrived in Laland . . . and there is a monstros-*
> *ity of a building next to the place I'm staying when I say*
> *monstrosity mind you I'm saying as in gaudy but then*
> *again it was built in 1928 hence the art deco theme so*
> *yes it IS classy but then since it's LA it went on crack*
> *Fairly certain this is where Baz Luhrmann needs to film the*
> *Great Gatsby.*

There was no direct text from her that was more recent, from the thirtieth or the day she disappeared.

Going backward, I read more of her writing, attempting to reverse engineer her timeline: on January 27, she gave a "shout out" to custodians and other working-class people who get "shit on"; she says "the Speakeasy was AWESOME" but that she lost a cellphone; on January 26, she posts that she's going out that night and hopes that no "creepers" harass her; on the 24th, she summarizes her activities prior to Los Angeles, in San Diego, mentioning that she's staying at a hostel and "reckless[ly]" told a guy there that she liked him.

Prior to that, she's planning for her trip, which she called her "West Coast tour." Her planned destinations include San Diego, Los Angeles, Santa Cruz, and San Francisco. On January 12, she mentions that she would appreciate "suggestions and meet-ups."

Elisa had been planning her trip for a while and was excited to see California. The information presented a solid travel itinerary from Elisa herself mixed in with more Tumblr madness: a man missing his head labeled "where's your head at"; American Psycho; a demon sitting in someone's head whispering, you suck; Carl Sagan; a tribute to weird people; David Bowie; more Fight Club; more Great Gatsby.

I began collecting Elisa's writing into a Google document so that I could read her posts without sifting through the other Tumblr posts.

Then I remembered someone mentioning a second blog. This one, called Ether Fields, was hosted on Blogspot and took a more traditional form. My eyes swept over a post dated over six months before her death. It was titled "Worries of a twenty something" and captioned: "I spent about two days in bed hating myself." I clicked on it to read more.

The post continued:

> *Why don't I simply do the things that I know will make me feel better?*
> *It isn't rocket science. It isn't that difficult. Get out of bed. Eat. See people. Talk to people. Exercise. Write. Read. If you want to do something with your life, well ok just go ahead and do something.*

The post continued on for several more paragraphs in which Elisa admonished herself for various reasons.

I was about to move on to the next post when I noticed that someone had left a comment below the blog entry. Someone named Emma wrote: "You REALLY need to speak to someone in real life about what you're going through."

She continued on with a strenuous appeal for Elisa to seek help for depression and low self-esteem. It appears this was the only comment prior to her death because the very next comment began:

> *Elisa,*
> *I don't know you and we have never met or even knew of each other's existence until your tragic fate. When I first heard of the news and saw your picture, I don't know why, but I felt torn and drawn to you . . . I became obsessed in finding more about you.*

The author of the comment said reading her blog was like looking in a mirror and seeing a version of himself, a reflection of his own despair. The next comment responded to Jeff telling him that it was *not* silly for him to write to a dead person because Elisa's thoughts live on in the minds of those who read her blog. These comments were left one month and two months after her death, respectively.

There were many more comments. I was a bit startled by the reality that months after her death, complete strangers felt an emotional connection to Elisa and were flocking to her blog to leave digital epitaphs.

I sought out Elisa's blogs with a specific purpose in mind: to determine if her posts revealed anything about her cause of death. But I soon got caught up in reading her thoughts and comments left by others. There was something mystifying about getting so much detail on a stranger's life after their passing. It felt almost as if I were resurrecting her in my mind, creating a simulation of her life in which her past memories and thoughts were on a looped reanimation tour.

Elisa had decided to take a solo trip, her "West Coast tour." But why? To discover this, I had to go back further and collate posts from both of her blogs, as well as her social media accounts. By the time I was fully locked and loaded I had before me over one hundred pages of single-spaced entries.

I proceeded to get lost in someone else's past, a past that only existed on paper and that began to intersect and cross-pollinate with my own present and future.

THE LONELY REBEL

Elisa went to a small, competitive high school, where she received exceptional grades and was devoted to academics. She began taking grade-twelve level courses in grade eight.

Elisa loved to read. *Awake and Dreaming,* Lois Lowry, and all of Kit Pearson's books had gotten her through elementary school (where, she claims, she began her adventure in being a "hermit"). Her grade seven teacher assigned *The Outsiders,* paving the way for a love of reading that persisted through her life.

Her English teacher, whom she described as excellent, introduced her to short stories by Asimov, Bradbury, and Atwood; an even better grade twelve English teacher inspired a love for analyzing literature and the classics (which, she says, could be referred to as "dead white guys"). She hungrily absorbed *Hamlet, Catcher in the Rye, The Great Gatsby* (a book that would become an obsession for her), *For Whom the Bell Tolls, The Importance of Being Earnest.* She read poets like John Donne, Wordsworth, T. S. Eliot, Dylan Thomas,

Dickinson, Yeats, and Keats. Poetry, she admitted, was not her favorite. She preferred complete sentences.

Elisa wanted her education to involve "REAL discussions about life, death, love, society, humanity" and all the stuff you didn't hear on the television.

She also participated in student council and a variety of extra-curriculars, such as volleyball and cross-country running. She was diligently laying the foundation for getting accepted into a university, though she hadn't yet decided whether she wanted to stay in Vancouver and attend the University of British Columbia or light out for a new course and attend school in a different city.

In some ways, Elisa fell into the mold of her peers. She was academic but also loved *Harry Potter* and a rich variety of popular culture and consumerism. In particular, fashion, which she blogged about with feverish delight. She found comfort in her two Mr. Potato Heads, named Darth Tatar and Spider Cloud, *Twilight* books, and orange and blue hydrangeas, the movie *Drive*, Reese's pieces, a good latte, Diptyque candles, *Emily the Strange* T-shirts, Stars & Regina Spektor, *Halo,* and, above all, Tumblr. She was thrilled beyond words to find black leather Repettos for under $200.

But Elisa had an anarchistic philosophy brewing in her, a contrarian streak that at times turned her blog into a manifesto of personal rebellion and eco-feminist empowerment. She evinced a disgust for the very trends she followed, the generation she typified, and was keenly aware of the socio-emotional toxins polluting society. At one point she even wrote of wanting to visit São Paulo, Brazil, to see what it would be like to live in a country that has outlawed outdoor commercial advertising. This passage stunned me because I've considered the same trip for the same reason.

She wrote that "her generation is only interested in self-promotion, media only caters to sensationalism—gigantic web of marketing, national sport of hipsters, everyone branding themselves, was this the result of commercialism run amuck, capitalism so entrenched into our DNA that we have an intrinsic desire to sell ourselves."

Perhaps as a partial result of this rebellious nature, Elisa began to feel the sting of isolation. Unlike many of her friends, she had no desire to party or drink. Since she didn't go out with them on weekend adventures, she was labeled a prude, uninteresting, and found herself excluded from plans. And even though her high school had a large Asian population—with many second-generation students with roots in Korea and mainland China—she noticed early on that her ethnicity at times caused her to be ostracized.

Elisa also realized something about herself from a young age. She wasn't able to pinpoint an exact event that caused it and she couldn't trace how it had grown from the tiniest embryo of a sensation into a fully grown everyday reality, but Elisa knew that she suffered from an ailment that most of the others in her peer group did not. She called it depression because she didn't know how else to classify it, though it made her feel like a walking cliche, so she didn't talk about it much.

But there was no denying it. She experienced dark moods that washed over her like a storm stripping the land of its life and identifying features, torrents of negative thinking and despair that made her want to hide in bed. She'd always had a habit of hanging out under the covers. For a time, she thought it was to evade the light. But now she realized it was an early defense mechanism for avoiding the way the everyday world made her feel. It was like hibernating during deep winter, when there's no hope for food or warmth.

Maybe this is just adolescence working its sinister magic, she had told herself. As hormones began to infect their every thoughts and actions, puberty became the dark lightning that divided her school's social groups. The "haves and the have-nots" don't just apply to wealth; it's also a form of ableism that applies to physical beauty and personality.

All people experience sadness, sure, sometimes painful sadness. But did it hit them for no reason for several days at a time and essentially incapacitate them? It didn't seem so. It seemed, rather, that most of her peers were surging into professional adulthood while she was scrambling to understand her own mind and sometimes struggling just to get out of bed.

BETRAYED

Things changed again for the worse in grade twelve. Elisa documented in her blog that she was betrayed by many of her close friends. One friend's act of betrayal upset her so much that she wrote an angry letter and left it on the windshield of the friend's parent's car.

It felt like her best friends were leaving her behind, substituting other "cooler" friends in her place. This haunted her for years.

The summer before grade twelve, Elisa participated in a five-week j-explore program in Quebec. The housing was in the middle of nowhere and it was the first time she had lived away from her family. She learned a couple of truths about herself during this time. One was that she despised small-town life. She was a city girl. The quietude of rural scenes too closely approximated her own inner isolation and this overlapped with the second realization, which was that she was not good at meeting new people. She was confounded by the prospect of representing herself to strangers—and as a result, she didn't make a single friend during the entire five weeks.

Once again, she felt rejected for not going out and partying and wearing hip, sexy clothes. Everyone around her, she mused, so easily slipped into new friendships and groups, so effortlessly navigated a labyrinthine social structure she found alien and meaningless. Everyone seemed capable of wearing masks and then discarding them based on the crowd at hand.

Another source of disappointment she cites from that time is the decision she made to drop cross-country running in favor of volleyball. She called the decision a terrible one. While she didn't consider herself particularly good at long-distance running, she felt a sense of comradery and warmth from the racing team. Later, she realized her discontinuation of running precipitated an overall dearth of exercise that probably compounded her depression.

Her volleyball coach was a "dick wad," who apparently was notorious for racist and sexist innuendo; he gave her barely any game time, deferring to the popular grade eleven girls in which he saw more athletic potential. Finally, at the end of the season, he told her straight out that he felt guilty for this, confirming that she had essentially wasted her term on volleyball.

She left the gymnasium and burst into tears. And at that exact moment, the cross-country team trundled by during their practice. Teammates she felt guilty for abandoning saw her weeping as they ran by.

DEPRESSION

This feeling, a sense of existential despair, grew more pronounced. Reading some of her early posts, you can sense Elisa first coming to terms with depression, developing an internal vocabulary for how she would think about it.

> *There is no physical manifestation of my "illness." Would I become psychotic and want to off myself? I know I wouldn't do anything rash like actually jump off a bridge. I'm too much of a coward. Instead I'll just lie in my bed and let the days pass by. That's my physical manifestation, sleeping for days in bed.*

Elisa probably didn't know this, but what she was doing is actually considered a healthy way to manage depression. Verbalizing one's depression—creating a lexicon for how it feels and what its features are and then sharing those impressions with others—is considered a crucial aspect of self-care for depressives.

In one passage, Elisa described her boyfriend trying to get her out of bed and her refusing to move.

Depression is "the most debilitating, humiliating disease I have ever been subjected to. It makes a fool of you. [It] sucks out every shard of hope or motivation that you ever had in your body, and it makes you want to destroy yourself."

This lethargy is, of course, one of the hallmarks of severe depression, along with disrupted appetite and sleep troubles (both oversleeping and undersleeping).

Scientists have been trying for years to determine why exactly major depression alters so dramatically one's sense of identity. While there is much to learn, what we know is that depressive events trigger major changes to the biochemistry of the brain, affecting the movement, levels, and functionality of neurotransmitters (including serotonin and norepinephrine), synapses, neurons, gene expression, hypothalamic and cortical functions, the thyroid releasing hormone (TRH), the amygdala and possibly the hypothalamus, melatonin, prolactin, body temperature, cortisol secretion, thalamus circuitry, and more.

It is difficult sometimes to differentiate what is a cause and what is an effect, but what is clear from brain scans is that an episode of severe depression can permanently alter the brain.

Elisa's earliest references to antidepressants are vague but it appears that she sought treatment from a doctor during her later teenage years and was prescribed antidepressants. Like many people who suffer depression, at times Elisa questioned the legitimacy of the "illness" and the need for taking medication.

Part of me is still in denial that I'm not sick and this can be solved without pills. No matter the argument against, I think taking the pills is weakness. I am not strong enough, I do not have the courage or conviction to do the right thing.

And then there's always the cynic saying depression is a made up disease so Big Pharma can make us all dependent on these pills and thus they are rich.

Betrayal 2.0

A big part of accepting depression involves your social network, she wrote on Formspring:

With my friends in particular, I think I have had depression for so long that I would have hoped they would have found a way to support me. It's just really hard to take when they have absolutely no response when I say I'm having a bad day. The whole of November so far has been the shittiest in my life and my friends are busy with school and so forth (understandable) but I don't think I ask too [much] if they

could check in on me once in a while (a text message even)
especially after I basically resorted them to tears after tell-
ing them how disappointed I am in them.

Social isolation from depression may have been a factor in her
ill-advised solo trip to the West Coast. Elisa described herself as a
"fiercely loyal friend" but felt betrayed.

Elisa describes a specific night, her nineteenth birthday, on which
she was drinking with one of her best friends from high school. Evidently, this friend had, unbeknownst to Elisa, made plans to drink
with her boyfriend that night. Elisa started to cry and because of
her inebriation was especially emotional and infuriated. She tried
to physically stop her friend from leaving, at which point the friend
called her boyfriend to alter the plans so that she could stay with
Elisa, who obviously needed her. But later in the evening, Elisa noticed that three of her friends had left and when she went to look for
them, she noticed her best friend trying to slip out unnoticed.

I will never speak to this friend again. We were the closest
friends in high school and she dumped 5 years of friendship
so she could drink with a loser guy and her douchebag of a
boyfriend who insulted my sister.

This and other stories suggest that many of Elisa's friends did not
always know how to help her. Despite her fierce loyalty as a friend,
Elisa's mercurial moods and depression may have isolated her from
the people closest to her.

BLESS THE INTERNET

The Internet, for Elisa, was a tool in the fight against depression and
loneliness. When she discovered the social blogging platform Tumblr, it was the beginning of an important relationship that she often
wrote about in anthropomorphic terms. Tumblr was her best friend,
sometimes her only friend, the "solace to her woes."

She often used the Internet for research and perusing fashion blogs, but she wasn't keen on Facebook, which felt like a facade, a social hall of mirrors where happiness would forever elude her.

She dabbled in the other platforms—Pinterest, YouTube, Instagram, and Twitter—but there was something about the architecture and community of Tumblr that soothed her. She became a frequent blogger and found a sense of catharsis in divulging her life with the anonymous invisible wall of faces.

Elisa used the Internet to communicate with others about depression.

"I am using this tumblr," she said, "as a platform to record my progress to get life in order and stop lying in bed letting the depression take over my life."

She wrote to one Tumblr user:

> Oh greyface you have unfortunately become a member of the sad club. We number in the millions and we roam the internet feeling very lonely and desperately want some sort of human connection.
>
> Bless the internet. All those who wish to find a way to express their sadness can go there and feel less alone. So many of the tumblrs I follow seem to carry the same grief as me in some way or another . . . Thanks to internet we record our lives and put it on some stage for creepers to stalk and follow so they can stop thinking about their own troubles for a moment and escape into someone else's.

Elisa knew that while the Internet allowed her freedom and solidarity, there were dangers associated with sharing personal information online. Transparency and self-expression in the age of the Internet existed alongside a dark truth: Online followers and friends can, if they choose, use your social media posts to track your movements. Later, I would find a websleuth who had done just that with Elisa's posts.

But the Internet was a necessary emotional outlet for Elisa. In what would prove to be a grim irony, the Internet became her haven, a place where she could be her true self. She spent much of her social life on the Internet, making it so poetically, eerily sad that that's where she would ultimately reside in death, as a viral horror story entombed and immortalized for all to consume.

A Brief History of Serotonin

I started taking antidepressants and mood stabilizers when I was eighteen, and have been on various cocktails and medleys of them since. I'm a valued customer of the pharmaceutical industry. They probably have a framed photograph of my face in the company boardrooms.

Despite my cynicism toward the Big Pharma industry, my desire to not be abjectly miserable consistently wins out over any sociopolitical protests.

The stigma over depression, mental illness, and pharmaceutical treatment has started to abate in recent years, but there is still a deep cultural scarlet letter embossing the foreheads of people who take psychiatric meds. Many of the prevailing viewpoints toward psychiatric illness have carried into the current era from "unenlightened" times, albeit they usually don't result in outright violence.

In the ancient eras of Greece, Rome, Egypt, China, and the Middle East people commonly attributed aberrant behavior and mental activity as spirit possession. During this and even in later epochs, people exhibiting this behavior, which today we might diagnose as being symptomatic of schizophrenia or bipolar disorder, were frequently tortured and executed.

Severe depression, mania, and delusion were marks of someone whose religious faith and will were not sufficiently strong enough to ward off evil spirits; thus they were somewhat responsible for their own affliction. This idea—that people with psychiatric illness are principally to blame for their condition—is one of the social stigmata that has carried into the modern era.

Barbaric and ill-informed treatments for mental illnesses also marked the twentieth century during the age of institutionalization. Before the discovery of neurotransmitters and drugs like chlorpromazine and lithium, doctors induced horrific seizures in patients, injecting them with animal blood, castor oil, massive doses of caffeine; they experimented with sleep therapy, early barbaric forms of electroconvulsive therapy (shock therapy, or ECT), psychosurgery (including transorbital lobotomies performed with ice picks).

Depression has never felt psychological to me. I know that sounds counterintuitive, but when it strikes it feels overwhelmingly physical, chemical. My emotions are the resulting glitched interface of flawed circuits. It doesn't matter how positive I try to be, how much yoga and meditation I do, how healthy I am—the chemicals always win. Untreated depression is like arguing with chemicals and, in the long run, I always lose.

This goes a long way toward understanding my empathy for Elisa. I understand the frustration of not being in control of your own thoughts, of wanting to be happy but instead seeing the darkest contours of your own mind on a regular, hourly basis. It's demoralizing and exhausting. It's like swimming with weights attached to your limbs and a bee in your mouth. Simply getting out of bed is a Herculean challenge; returning phone calls from friends becomes an existential crisis, a clinic in how to conceal a panic attack during small talk.

Your self-image is perpetually shattered as you struggle to put together the shards of your own identity. Simply holding it together for an hour can feel like sitting in the captain's deck of the *Titanic,* watching the pressurized cracks lengthen as you idly wait for an oceanic wall of icy water to demolish you.

Reading Elisa's passages on depression are heartbreaking for me. Parts of it feel as though she was describing my own internal landscape. But Elisa does a pretty incredible job at advocating for "those of us who don't have standard-issue brain chemistry."

"I have clinical depression and generalized anxiety disorder," she wrote. "I have a fancy piece of paper from a real doctor that says so, and I have a little bottle of pills that I have to take every day or else I want to kill myself."

The general practitioner I went to in San Diego had me on a cocktail of Prozac, Wellbutrin, and Strattera. Prozac, the most common SSRI, works to boost and regulate your brain's serotonin production.

Wellbutrin (which, I would learn, Elisa also had taken extensively) is an "atypical" antidepressant and increases the brain's production of dopamine; it is commonly prescribed to help people quit smoking, which was one of the reasons I took it. Strattera is an SNRI, a class of meds that works to regulate norepinephrine. It is one of the only non-stimulant ADD medications.

I remember what my very first doctor said to me about using meds to treat depression. At the time I was eighteen and concerned that antidepressants would make me less creative. He said that the goal in that case was to allow me to go to my edge without falling off the cliff. I always thought that was kind of a weird thing to say to a depressed teenager—but it makes sense.

Elisa wasn't on any SSRIs; however, she was on an SNRI (serotonin-norepinephrine reuptake inhibitor), called Effexor, or Venlafaxine, which she described as the only drug in years that had actually helped her. I tried this one for about six months. It had worked well but caused my blood pressure to rise.

The search for a compatible antidepressant is a maddening experience that can go on for years, even decades. There is simply no metric for understanding someone else's psychiatric disorder, no diagnostic for determining how a person's unique personality, history of trauma, genetic makeup, and neurochemistry will interact.

This is why the discovery of Elisa's blogs marked a seismic shift in my perception of the investigation. While the surveillance tape offered a portal into her final moments, the blogs offered a portal into her final years, which, some would argue, can be just as significant in determining a cause of death.

As I dug into Elisa's autobiographical prose, I identified with her struggle against depression and forged a powerful emotional connection to the case. At the same time, disturbing new questions arose.

CHAPTER 6
City of Demons

THERE ARE THREE NARRATIVES threading through this book that represent the principal explanations for what happened to Elisa Lam. The first two, which have already been introduced, are mental illness and homicide. The third is paranormal activity, the mere mention of which either just caused you to roll your eyes or sit forward in your reading chair, depending on your philosophical orientation.

It is important to understand, however, that mental illness and paranormal activity share a tragic, interconnected past. For most of human history, mental illness was considered a supernatural affliction. Those beset by depression, mania, or other debilitating psychiatric symptoms were considered to be possessed by a demon or spirit and were often imprisoned, tortured, and killed. Even relatively minor symptoms or "stigmata" signified that the victim was weak in his or her religious faith—an early example of the stigmatization of mental illness that in modern times often takes the form of accusing a depressed person of having a bad attitude or not being positive.

Linguistic relics of demonology and supernatural belief are found even in our informal conversations about mental illness. Depressives are said to be fighting their demons, or haunted by ghosts from their past.

About 75 percent of Americans believe in some kind of paranormal or supernatural activity. Around the world, this number may be even higher.

I grew up a devout atheist. In junior high and high school, I would engage in hours of combative debates with a Christian friend of mine. Strictly speaking, I was a Materialist; I believed the universe was atoms in the void. To my young mind, such things as ghosts and God were an affront to science.

In college, I loosened up a little, thanks to some experimentation with psychedelics. This didn't turn me into a spiritualist, but it dissolved some of the ego constructs preventing me from considering different viewpoints and ideas. And at the same time as I was wandering the meadows of Santa Cruz on LSD and mushrooms, I was enrolled in a physics class called "The Quantum Enigma." Due to my abysmal mathematical abilities, I failed this class. But I became fascinated by the philosophical implications of theoretical physics. Even when the term ended, I continued reading the professor's book *The Ghost in the Atom,* and when I finished that, I read other books on quantum mechanics.

What I discovered is that many of the ideas at the heart of quantum theory overlap with ideas espoused by eastern religions for thousands of years. And despite maintaining a healthy skepticism, the more I looked into it, the more I discovered that science is not necessarily incompatible with some explanations of paranormal activity. In fact, a growing body of new evidence suggests that understanding the true nature of consciousness may require unraveling the mysteries of quantum entanglement and changing the way we perceive the universe.

As interesting as some of these theories can be, however, speculation over paranormal activity became a point of friction in the Elisa Lam case. Reconciling this narrative with the reality of mental illness was one of the most challenging tasks in writing this book.

Simply said, it would be impossible to tell this story without acknowledging and exploring the legacy of the Cecil Hotel and how its tragic history has fueled urban legends and ghosts. To research this part, I interviewed psychics, guests who vacationed there, and tenants who lived there for decades. Over time, I saw the same patterns arising over and over in their stories.

It was only after I eventually stayed at the Cecil Hotel myself, however, that I took seriously the idea that a building like the

Cecil—where so many awful, horrifying things have happened—might have its own kind of memory.

THE CREEPIEST PLACES ON EARTH

The Cecil Hotel is considered by many to be one of the most haunted places on Earth. It's right up there with the Villisca Axe Murder House and Japan's "Suicide Forest." In fact, with its own moniker of "Suicide Hotel," the Cecil might be the urban equivalent of Japan's notorious Aokigahara Jukai forest, which is said to be the creepiest place on Earth. Famous YouTuber Logan Paul recently received flack for making a video there, which critics said trivialized suicide.

The Cecil Hotel has been a benefactor of the industry known as "paranormal tourism." It was always on the lengthy list of haunted spots in Los Angeles, but in the years since Elisa's tragic death, hundreds or more likely thousands of amateur and professional ghost hunters have rented rooms at the Cecil Hotel in their quest for contact with the other side.

MY FRESHMAN-YEAR ENCOUNTER

Prior to the Cecil, my only pseudo-paranormal experience was when I attended college at the University of California at Santa Cruz. I lived at the Porter College dormitory, where in the fall quarter of my sophomore year there was a demon scare on the first floor B-building.

Over the course of several weeks, nearly every student on the hall claimed to have woken up in the middle of the night screaming, convinced that something tried to choke them in their sleep. It became a big deal on campus. Students joked that a real-life Freddy Krueger, the ultimate oneiric predator, was haunting their dreams.

At the same time, my roommate Jared and I learned of a disturbing story from five years previous. One of the Porter College students, David, had some kind of mental breakdown, we discovered. One day he wrapped himself in an American flag on the balcony of his 4th-floor dorm room and shot himself in the face with a shotgun. His body toppled from the balcony and landed in the quad below.

Jared and I became obsessed with the case, but it was difficult to find news stories on the death, and few people on campus would talk about it.

One day, during the peak of my interest in the story, I sat on a bench in the courtyard terrace separating the A and B buildings. Usually there were gaggles of college kids, smoking, hollering, and reveling in their youth. That day it was uncharacteristically deserted and quiet. An autumnal wind pushed around a flurry of brightly colored leaves that whipped and ribboned. I was kind of in a trance when suddenly I realized that a figure had been circling the quad at the periphery of my vision.

During a sudden hush in the wind, that figure stopped and stared upward. From where I sat, I couldn't tell what he was staring at. But gradually it dawned on me that there was something peculiar about this figure.

I stood up and began to walk over to him. As I drew closer, the figure retreated. When I arrived at the spot where the onlooker had stood, I looked up and realized he had been staring at one of the 4th-floor balconies. Later, I checked online and confirmed that it was the same balcony where David's suicide had occurred. Obviously, this could very well have been a coincidence. But the experience felt unnatural, manufactured, as though the moment had been a performance just for me.

In a universe of chaotic randomness, isn't it natural for unlikely patterns to emerge? After all, one in a million isn't so rare in a field of billions or trillions. In fact, rarity becomes commonplace on this scale. In a large-enough sample size, the absurd becomes numerically normal, the impossible probable.

But what if this display of meaningless chaos is an illusion? As I dug further into the Elisa Lam case, I began tallying an inordinate number of experiences known as synchronicity. And as I drew nearer and nearer the Cecil Hotel itself, I began to develop a strong feeling that something sentient was aware of my interest.

THOUGHT INSERTION

Natalie Davis stayed at the Cecil Hotel during the same week that Elisa was there. She did not see Elisa in person, but her strange experiences occurred contemporaneously with Elisa's final days. Though she is formally credentialled as a psychic medium, Natalie thinks of herself more as an "indigo child."

She was in Los Angeles because her Greyhound bus to Texas was furloughed. She described being anxious as she trudged through the Skid Row area of downtown, where she met numerous shady characters. Of these, one of them was a tall frightening man in the lobby of the Cecil who wanted to know what room she was staying in, which happened to be on the 9th floor (943), the same floor where Pauline Otton leaped to her death decades earlier.

At the time of her visit, in early 2013, Natalie did not know anything about the history of the hotel, so she considers her experience a "double blind," a particularly useful type of controlled experiment.

She wrote on a blog, Documenting Reality:

> From the time I first checked in, I had a very uneasy feeling . . . When I had first entered the room, I walked over to the window and the first thought that came to my mind was, "Wow, if I wanted to kill myself, I could just open this window and jump . . ." At this point, looking back, I'm convinced that that thought was sort of "inserted" into my head.

This passage stuck with me early on. I recalled the number of hotel guests who jumped out of the windows of the Cecil. Then there is the photo taken of a ghostly visage hovering in the windowsill of one of the rooms. And I recalled the Tumblr image Elisa posted only hours before her death: an illustration of a body falling from a building.

Natalie's post documents a number of anomalies she experienced during her stay. The radio alarm clock started blaring even though she hadn't set it; and it went off at 1:43 A.M., approximately the same time, she learned later, that a woman had mysteriously died in the bathtub of that very room years earlier.

There were other events, too: cold spots in the elevator, phone calls with no voice on the other end, and, of course, the repulsive dark matter and red blood cells in the room's water.

TONES OF THE DEAD

Joni Mayhan has studied paranormal activity for most of her life. For a while she went through phases where she was a skeptic, because her rational mind told her not to believe in ghosts.

Joni was an anti-social kid even before she began to suspect that she could hear the sounds of spirits. Some people with paranormal abilities are clairvoyant—they can see the future. Others are clairsentient, or empathic—they can feel the emotions of others. There are remote viewers, those who can tap into the universal ether and describe events that are occuring thousands of miles away.

People claim to have all kinds of psychic abilities. Joni's gift was clairaudience—she could hear the dead.

She discovered her gift at around the age of four. It was her first inkling that she was different from other people. Some clairaudients hear music. Joni heard tones. As she moved her head, the tones changed, as though she were cycling through radio frequencies. These weren't just normal sound vibrations. They felt other-worldly, like hymns being sung to her by intelligences from another dimension.

Her parents told her that there was no such thing and to just go to bed. So Joni lived with the knowledge and kept it to herself. She was afraid to go to bed at night, she had extreme nightmares and sometimes sleepwalked. During these episodes, she could not be woken up, she lurched through the house screaming. It felt as though the intelligence had followed her into her dreams.

Joni believes that the dead can communicate through dreams. In one of her articles, she described how a few days after her grandmother passed away in her sleep, she had a dream in which she went to clean her house. When she entered, Nanny was sitting on the couch, waiting for her. "Nanny! I thought you died." She hugged her and said, "I did die, but I couldn't leave without saying good-bye to you."

I asked Joni to analyze the Elisa Lam case. I asked her if it was possible that something in the building was affecting her on a spiritual level. She discussed residual energy, vibrations of past traumatic events. Did these vibrations allow Elisa to tap into a new power, an empathic ability to feel the emotions of the dead? Did she have latent clairvoyant abilities that allowed her to see visions of bodies falling from the building? This would explain the image she posted the day she disappeared.

If she already had mental health issues, Joni said, she would have been more susceptible to something entering her psyche. Remember what Natalie said—when she walked into her room at the Cecil, she felt as though something had infiltrated her mind.

Joni believed Elisa was murdered by someone at the hotel who was taken over by a dark entity. Perhaps the dark history of the hotel spoke to an employee or tenant, gave them negative thoughts and impulses, turned them into puppets.

I had my doubts. It was impossible to prove that such experiences weren't just aberrant mental activity, neurotransmitters and synapses firing the wrong way and triggering a fictional perception. A great number of people with illnesses like schizophrenia and bipolar disorder experience visual and auditory hallucinations that bear a striking resemblance to descriptions of paranormal activity and demonic possession.

Was it possible that paranormal believers conjured these experiences out of some emotional need to make sense of their lives? Or could it be the experiences are actually symptoms of undiagnosed affective disorders? I couldn't help but be skeptical because I hadn't clocked a true paranormal experience myself.

Then again, I'd never been to the Cecil Hotel.

SENSING THE PAST

Los Angeles, nicknamed, the City of Angels, is teeming with ghost stories. Visions of Marilyn Monroe at the Roosevelt; the voices of suicides from under the Colorado Street Bridge; the dark activity reported at 10050 Cielo Drive, where the Manson murders took place. These legends are subsumed into the architecture and mythos of the city itself.

The Cecil Hotel isn't home to any celebrity ghosts, but it's nonetheless considered one of the most cursed, haunted buildings in the city. In many ways, the Cecil can be thought of as a real-life Overlook Hotel, a building with a horrific past dating to early in the century—a place capable of broadcasting and transmitting images and feelings from that horrific past into the minds of its temporary caretakers.

Was Elisa capable of sensing this past? When I played the video of Elisa in the elevator for Joni, she saw a young woman who was absorbing something traumatic from the environment around her. There is something about Elisa's movements in the video that make people very uncomfortable. Why does a non-graphic video that would be rated PG-13 in the theater disturb them so much?

It is the staggered steps and glances, almost a tortured buoyancy, the seemingly preternatural sense that something is following her; the coiled, serpentine movements of her arms, wrists and fingers, which progress into a kind of narcotized conductor's gait, as though she is adjudicating the meaning of something that only she could see, marking the downbeats of a melody that only she can hear.

In time, as I learned more about Elisa and some of her psychiatric struggles, the term "psychomotor agitation" surfaced. Soon we would have a philosophical showdown centuries in the making, an almost throwback Cartesian debate between materialists and mystics, abridged for a century in which psychopharmacology is the new talk therapy and arcane YouTube videos are the new religious ecstasy.

The ultimate question is what drew Elisa to the roof that night? The demon, the killer, or the mind—which of them stalked and manipulated her, which of them called to her from the roof, from the dark waters of the cistern, and whispered to her such an unimaginable fate.

Dark Synchronicity

Radio host Clyde Lewis had studied the history of the Cecil Hotel for decades, particularly the legacy of the Night Stalker. When a new tragic enigma arose there, one accompanied by one of the most mysterious pieces of surveillance videos ever released, he was one of the first to offer a unique interpretation.

His radio show *Ground Zero*—considered one of the first paranormal radio shows, alongside *Coast to Coast AM*—used to dovetail the legendary late Art Bell's program in one of the hottest time slots in radio. Over the years, Clyde's popularity has grown into the radio equivalent of a cult classic.

Clyde had once spoken about a concept he described as "the synchronicity of evil." The original theory of synchronicity, of course, came from C. G. Jung, one of the few preeminent scientists who went down a rabbit hole of parapsychological research. Though it created a personal and professional schism with his longtime friend, Sigmund Freud, his work also created a theory of "acausal parallelism." Jung believed that seemingly random coincidences can be connected across time and space and endowed with cosmic meaning.

On his show, entitled *Lam to the Slaughter: Dark History, Dark Water,* Clyde devoted several hours to the Elisa Lam case. In this episode Clyde's guests were a married websleuth couple, Frank Argueta and Genevieve Federline, who run the website/podcast *West of the Rockies* and had been investigating the case.

"Sometimes the 'Devil' is in the details," Clyde intoned with his brassy voice. "When we look through the glass darkly, we can see that the ordinary can be twisted into something that is dark and foreboding."

The backdrop of synchronicity in the Lam case is the incredible history of gory awful deaths of a similar nature continually happening over and over again. Dozens of unnatural deaths, suicides, and murders—violent, fatal despair sustained for over eight decades.

Then you get the *Dark Water* movies, which seemed to have predicted in a fictional setting exactly what was to transpire in the hotel years later. Clyde's guests, Frank and Genevieve, explained that in 2002 a Japanese horror movie named *Dark Water* came out. The name of the daughter in the movie is Cecilia, which phonetically is close to Cecil. In 2005, an American remake, starring Jennifer Connelly, featured a little girl named Ceci, which is also extremely similar. Additionally, in the 2005 version, Connelly's character is named Dahlia, which evokes the Black Dahlia, who is historically associated with the Cecil Hotel.

The little girl's red jacket in the 2005 version looks remarkably like Elisa's red hoodie, and the 2002 film has Ceci wearing a red coat as well as holding a red bag.

But the kicker, the creepy coincidence that played a role in the Lam case going so viral online, is that in both films the main character, the little girl, falls into a rooftop water tank and drowns. The water from the tank creeps down into the rooms and water supply. Sound familiar?

It doesn't end there. The films both feature scenes in which characters are pressing buttons in an elevator while being watched on surveillance screens. The framing of these surveillance videos looks like exact set-ups of Elisa's real-life footage on YouTube. The behavior of the characters in the elevators is also similar to Elisa's behavior in the Cecil Hotel.

It's as though the creators of the *Dark Water* movies unconsciously tapped into a premonition of the future; or, inversely, as though reality shaped itself based on human creations and did so independently of linear time.

Fittingly, the tagline on the original promotional poster for the 2005 *Dark Water* reads, "Some mysteries are not meant to be solved."

As bizarre as the *Dark Water* parallels looked, another synchronicity in the case emerged that was even more disturbing. In fact, it was almost unbelievable.

Evidently, there was an outbreak of tuberculosis in downtown LA—the largest in a decade—at the time Elisa died. The outbreak was particularly bad in Skid Row, a poverty-stricken area that cradles the Cecil Hotel. The Center for Disease Control (CDC) estimated that around 4,500 people were exposed and, accordingly, they dispatched a team of federal scientists to conduct tests.

There is a specific test that is designated for the diagnosis of this particular strain of TB. The name of this test—incredibly, impossibly—is the LAM-ELISA test.

A medical article from 2005 described the test:

"A direct antigen-capture ELISA based on the detection of mycobacterial lipoarabinomannan (LAM) in unprocessed urine was evaluated for its usefulness in clinical practice. In Tanzania, 231 patients with suspected pulmonary tuberculosis (TB) and 103 healthy volunteers were screened with standard TB tests and with the new LAM-ELISA."

In a final touch, the test was developed by a team of scientists at the University of British Columbia, which happens to be where Elisa attended undergraduate courses.

When I first heard the name of the test, I was almost angry. It's as though someone was tweaking reality to mess with our heads.

The concept of synchronicity has its critics, of course. Finding meaning in coincidences is fraught with intellectual peril. After all, in a universe that besieges human consciousness with so much information, isn't it mathematically inevitable that certain patterns, some of them freakishly improbable, will emerge? Is this just another example of humans finding meaning in the chaos?

Or is there something significant to be found underneath the chaos?

CHAPTER 7
Further Down the Rabbit Hole

I SPOKE WITH TWO BODY LANGUAGE EXPERTS about the tape, both of whom I met in person to discuss the case. The first, Dr. Jack Brown, provides a second-by-second breakdown of Elisa's body language, as seen on the surveillance tape. He published the analysis on his website *BodyLanguageSuccess.com* and it quickly became his most popular post.

Sandirella Hu, a legal consultant/body language analyst, explained that body language analysis is based in social science and has a wide range of uses: Poker players use it to study other players' microexpressions, to read bluffs and tells; lawyers use it to select jurors who will be sympathetic to their cases; some people have even used it to try and determine whether their spouses are marrying them for love or money.

While there isn't unanimous support for the science of body language, it has earned its place as kind of "populist truth telling" because it is often applied to otherwise inscrutable media recordings. Some armchair detectives on YouTube, for example, applied body language analysis to a clip of Jimmy Kimmel asking Barack Obama about UFOs.

BODY LANGUAGE ANALYSIS

According to Dr. Jack Brown, when Elisa first enters the elevator, she is relaxed and not fearful. He surmises this from her nonchalant gait and wide berth of arm movement.

After pressing the buttons, she flattens herself against the wall in a gesture that many interpret as apprehension. But Brown says this behavior does not necessarily indicate fear—her body language is neutral, which he deduces from the spacing of her feet and the relaxed position of her arms.

Then she lurches out of the elevator to look down the hallway. And here's where things change. Upon retreating back into the elevator, she backs into the left front corner. Her hands form a "Fig Leaf" configuration and her feet are close together. According to Brown, this is consistent with anxiety and low confidence but, again, does not necessarily indicate fear.

Body language analyst Sandirella Hu also concluded that Elisa's body language changes when she peeks out into the hallway. She goes from being relaxed at 0:33 to looking up and becoming nervous only moments later. Hu offers two explanations for this change: she saw someone who triggered a fear response; or, she was thinking about someone, which caused some emotional dissonance. Hu believes that Elisa then returned back into the elevator for security.

At this point, Elisa jumps out of the elevator, with a two-step jump that has a "playful quality to it." Elisa keeps her hands in the "Fig Leaf" position but widens her stance, a movement which indicates greater confidence. Brown believes the contradiction of the fig leaf anxiety and wide-step confidence is evidence of an emotional dissonance in Elisa.

Hu agrees that Elisa's hop out of the elevator at 0:54 seems playful. She also agrees that there is some kind of emotional dissonance taking place and that Elisa is experiencing an unusually frenetic cycle of emotions in under a minute. This could be due to any medications she was taking, any medications she should have been taking but wasn't, or the effects of rapid cycling, which can occur in medicated or unmedicated people with bipolar disorder.

Then comes the most important sequence in the video, at least in terms of body language analysis. Brown describes it like this:

For about 16 seconds Ms. Lam displays an "*Elbows Out Laterally with Armpit Exposed & Behind the Head Hair*

Preening Display." This was, at least for some time, performed bilaterally [see below]. The movement, as she
reaches up to begin this extended preen—was fluid, slow
and deliberate—which is very important. *This display clus-
ter context is a strong and highly reliable indicator of sexual
interest.* The person of her interest is either present outside
the elevator—or she is actively thinking about this person.

Hu also describes Elisa's "hair preening" as a definite sign of
attraction or sexual arousal and says it could have been triggered
by someone she saw in the hallway or the thought of someone she
knows or recently met. Was this person someone she met in LA? Hu
thinks the person is current, someone she's either expecting to see
that night or actually seeing in the hallway.

When Elisa next returns to the elevator, she does so while using
two arms to steady herself. This is indicative of either lightheaded-
ness, vertigo, or emotional distress. John Lordan notes that in his
visit to the hotel he observed that there is a mirror on the wall opposite the elevator and suggests that Elisa was anxious because she
saw her reflection.

A bilateral hair adjustment leads to what Brown calls a MAP
(Manipulator, Adaptor, Pacifier), an action he says means she is trying to "dial up her alpha" and be more assertive.

In the next image, Brown believes that Elisa Lam smiles. It may
be an insincere smile, a "social smile," which may be illustrative of
her emotional dissonance, given that she is supposedly alone in an
elevator. She gestures with her hand and her fingertip touches her
chest, which indicates an increase in anxiety.

Back outside the elevator, Elisa exhibits a series of dramatic nonverbal actions.

"This may be part of the body language of a conversation taking
place with someone who is out of our view or it may be a sort of a
rehearsal for an anticipated upcoming conversation/interaction—or,
as many have speculated, is possibly due to narcotics. Although our
view and resolution is limited this does *not* have the nonverbal signature of fear."

Her next few actions are described as if Elisa is playing charades with the air, and then becoming excited, joyous, and optimistic.

These actions at 1:56 are one of the most discussed segments, as it looks like she is talking to someone while making strange finger movements. In her analysis, Hu questions whether her stretched fingers is a sign that she is in the middle of a hypomanic episode. It's as though energy is shooting out of her fingertips. Is she counting something with her fingers? Elisa does make a lot of lists. Or is she rehearsing her conversation with the new guy she is going to meet?

Brown's conclusion raises even more questions:

"Ms. Elisa Lam is playing a game of hide and seek (or something similar) in this video. And although at times she displays some anxiety, there is no indication of fear. There is definitely an element of play present here . . . While what is seen here may have no connection with her demise—if the events in this video occurred just before her disappearance, it strongly suggests that the person to whom she is attracted may have knowledge of, contributed to, or be responsible for her death."

So, was somebody else in the hallway or nearby? Or was Elisa imagining someone? Some analysts have suggested that Elisa's bipolar condition may have been so severe that she was playing a kind of hide and go seek game with herself. Or with an imagined friend, or romantic crush.

The body language analysis by Dr. Jack Brown and Sandirella Hu suggests that it is completely within the realm of possibility that Elisa was in the midst of a nerve-wracking romantic courtship of some kind. The person may have only been someone she met earlier or someone she was just thinking about.

Or it could have been someone in the hotel, on the 14th-floor hallway, just outside the elevator.

TIMECODE

Three months after the discovery of Elisa's body, there was still no postmortem or toxicology report. The Internet forums were beehives of flustered, hysterical websleuths entertaining every conspiracy theory this side of JFK. And the surveillance video continued to provide ample fodder.

The elevator tape was already disturbing and mysterious enough. You have a young woman who is either hiding from someone, mentally ill, high on drugs, possessed, or any combination of those four, displayed in her final hours before somehow ending up naked in a rooftop water cistern.

The release of the tape itself was mysterious. As John Lordan of BrainScratch noted, it does not help identify Elisa or any potential suspects. Then, when you start digging into the timecode of the footage, things get even weirder.

The purpose of a timestamp is accuracy. They are often used in court and many cases have been thrown out because of an inconclusive or flawed timecode.

The timecode on the Cecil elevator footage is beyond flawed. It is a jumbled, chaotic mess that looks less like numbers than the symbols and characters of some alien programming code.

Several websleuths did take the time to study the timecode intensely and have concluded that it represents the minutes leading right up until midnight or around that time. This is widely believed to be the approximate time that Elisa went to the roof. However, the time of death is officially and unofficially unknown.

In March 2013, barely over a month into the police investigation, a YouTuber by the name of Cody Fry uploaded a different version of the video side by side with the original. His new version was the same footage but slightly sped up to about 135 percent. His claim was an odd one: he believed that the original footage posted on YouTube had been slowed down.

Why? It's possible, he claimed, that almost a minute of footage was removed from the tape and that by slowing it down they stretched the timecode back out to the original length so that it didn't look like anything was missing.

Interestingly, if you watch the sped-up version, many of Elisa's movements don't seem as creepy as before. It's almost as if by slowing the footage down, someone made Elisa's behavior appear more bizarre. Seen side by side, the new version certainly looks more natural.

But why would someone have slowed the footage down? Was it

really to cover missing footage? How could it be proven that footage was missing?

Cody Fry ended his video with the text: "Who did the editing? Why is the time stamp blurred out? What happened to this poor girl deserves answers. Someone is covering up something."

Cody believed that footage was removed, the tape was slowed down and presented to the public with the expectation that no one would notice any anomalies.

There appear to be several additional timecode anomalies, including slowed-down footage, glitches, misfiring seconds, and, most shocking of all, fifty-three seconds of missing footage.

I was at work when I watched the video and I distinctly remember, once again, spitting out a bite of food (falafel, I believe). Cody Fry's video made a compelling case that the surveillance video had been tampered with and edited.

But who would do such a thing? Who would have the motive to mess with the videotape showing what a young woman was doing right before she died? Some websleuths, including the admin of the webpage Tribwatch, have speculated that a Cecil Hotel employee may have been involved, whether as the sole perpetrator or to cover for a friend.

The next logical question is: If the hotel presented this video to the police, how did detectives not notice such a glitch? Why haven't they addressed such a glaring anomaly? Is it the same reason they didn't find Elisa's body on the roof during their initial searches? Shall we blame incompetence or criminal conspiracy? And finally, was this a case of the hotel misleading the police or the police manipulating the public?

Or maybe both.

ELISA AND THE BLACK DAHLIA

I lived in Southern California for ten years (five in Los Angeles, five in San Diego) and generally view it as a kind of dystopian nightmare with palm trees. I was at the tail end of those years, in late 2013, when I decided to journey to the Cecil Hotel and retrace Elisa's steps.

I started by taking the same mini-trip (her last) that Elisa took from San Diego to Los Angeles. Since I lived in San Diego at the time and had friends and family in Los Angeles, it was a pretty common trip for me.

It's not clear what form of transportation she used. Amtrak and Greyhound were rumored to be her preferred travel methods, but there's at least one report of a social-media friend of hers saying that she was headed to the airport from the Gaslamp speakeasy the night she went to LA.

This brings us to another bizarre parallel in this case, which is the similarity of Elisa's final days to Elizabeth Short's. Elizabeth Short, or Betty, is commonly known as the Black Dahlia, the aspiring starlet who became a haunting, ethereal myth in the 1940s when her mutilated, dismembered corpse was found in downtown LA only blocks from the Cecil Hotel.

At first, frankly, I thought the Elisa Lam/Black Dahlia connection was more sensationalism than fact. Multiple websleuths made a big deal out of Elizabeth Short having a drink at the Cecil Hotel the night she was killed, when in reality there is no direct evidence that she entered the building that night. And even if she did have a drink at the Cecil, so what?

However, the more I looked into it, the more I found some interesting parallels between the two women and their tragic deaths.

According to John Gilmore, who wrote the book *Severed: The True Story of the Black Dahlia,* Elizabeth Short had absconded to San Diego after running up several large debts in LA. She then returned to LA for unknown reasons. While Gilmore and other historians have turned up multiple people who knew Short, lived with her, and even dated her while she was in San Diego, no one really knows what she was doing there.

She had an almost mystical effect on people. Even random strangers found themselves unaccountably smitten with her from merely a passing smile.

The website Esotouric, which debunks myths surrounding true-crime cases in LA, also runs the downtown tour Hotel Horrors & Main Street Vice. One of its writers took an interest in the overlaps in these two cases and posted a list of the eerie similarities between Lam and Short:

- Both have names derived from Elizabeth.
- Both were women in their early twenties, traveling alone, frequenting public transportation.
- Both of them had loose travel plans that were known only to themselves.
- They were both petite, attractive brunettes, with personalities described as charismatic and outgoing. Both also suffered from depression.
- Each one traveled from San Diego to downtown Los Angeles in January.
- Each was last seen in a downtown hotel.
- Neither woman's disappearance was immediately reported. Both were missing for a number of days before being discovered, dead, in a shocking location.
- And the deaths of both of these unfortunate young women has inspired enormous media attention and speculation.

I'll add one more to this list. Both Elisa and Elizabeth suffered heartbreak in the year leading up to their deaths. Elisa had written in vivid detail online how her ex-boyfriend and more recent guys had shattered her perceptions of love.

Elizabeth, in her time, had expected to marry a man whom she professed to love. This man decided while fighting overseas that he could not marry her. She'd planned to have a family with him, and news of his decision crushed her. After her death, when investigators looked through her trunk, they found dozens of letters written by Elizabeth describing her "disappointments in love."

The media attention similarity listed above is no exaggeration in either case. The obsessive online coverage of the Lam case became a hallmark of the case itself, but what many don't realize is that this kind of coverage is not new and is certainly not unique to the Internet.

During the 1940s, the news media was far less powerful and prolific, but those early newspapers still published their fair share of sensational stories. And the Black Dahlia case may in fact have changed the course of true-crime news reporting. It was, arguably, the first morbid death to receive international attention and daily news coverage and turn the victim into a posthumous celebrity.

The Black Dahlia case, which was never solved, consumed Los Angeles. At one point there were 750 investigators working on the case. The Hollywood-based *Citizens-News* and *Herald-Express* started the trend of sensational reporting, using bold headlines about the BLACK DAHLIA. At one point, policemen searched storm drains for underground torture chambers to try and find the killer. At its most absurd, one paper published an article on the case with the headline "Strange Life of Girl Victim of Werewolf Murder."

Some argue the most mysterious case in LA history was compromised by rumors and speculation. But while the police blamed the press for sensationalism, the press blamed police for secrecy. Combined, this lack of information from the police and the over-abundance of unvetted information by the media muddied the case (a scenario with close parallels to the Lam case).

The LAPD also blamed the sensationalist press for inspiring nine copycat murder cases in which the killers actually admitted to imitating the grisly death of Short based on horrid sexually violent details they read printed in the news. Of course, one might argue these killers were also inspired to kill by the thought that they could get away with it, since the police seemed unable to catch the Black Dahlia killer.

CHAPTER 8
The "Suicide Hotel"

THERE ARE FEW THINGS I DESPISE MORE than LA traffic. Even before you get into the city, the traffic on the freeways, especially the 5 and the 101, congests into junk yards the size of city districts. It's nearly always awful, but if you need to use the bathroom, it's nightmarish.

Even before arriving in downtown LA, I could feel a cloud of discomfort passing over me. The only way I can describe it is that, as absurd as it sounds, it felt like the Cecil Hotel knew I was coming. Like it was drawing me there. The feeling grew more pronounced the closer I got.

I chalked it up to having spent too many late-night hours researching the hotel's history. In preparation for my stay on Main Street, I had finally delved headlong into the sordid details. I was aware of the major parts, of course—the two serial killers, Richard Ramirez "The Nightstalker" and Jack Unterweger "The Austrian Ghoul," several suicides, and the Pigeon Lady's brutal murder—but I had been unprepared for the full scope of its tragedies.

The full, unredacted history of the Cecil Hotel is certainly not for the faint of heart.

BIRTH OF A CURSE

The Cecil Hotel was built in 1924 by hotelier W. B. Hanner, who modeled his new building off the world-famous Hotel Cecil in London. Hanner chose as the destination for his hotel the fashionable

600 block of Main Street, which, in the booming downtown Los Angeles of the 1920s, was sure to draw an eclectic mix of middle-class transients and young, working-class entrepreneurs. Multiple other hotels, including the Biltmore and the Alexandria, had found success there, so hopes were high that downtown Los Angeles would be a world center of industry, class, and culture, an engine of progress and wealth in the still-young twentieth century.

Already, the city's growth from a veritable backwater to a major metropolis—despite considerable geographical curses, including earthquakes and a complete dearth of natural water sources—was nothing short of amazing.

The distinctive design of the hotel, steeped in the Beaux Arts style (an amalgam of French neoclassicism, Gothic, and Renaissance elements), featured a marble lobby with stained-glass skylight windows, potted palms, alabaster statuary, brass, gold-tone and marble "particulate." It was the work of Loy Lester Smith, who had been allocated a $1 million budget by Hanner. This budget also covered the cost of the hotel's furnishings, replete with red Spanish leather, walnut Windsor furniture, specially made carpets, specially made iron lamps, period chandeliers, hand decorated parchment shades, mattresses made of specially felted cotton and pillows stuffed with goose and duck feathers.

Buoyed by the success of the nearby Biltmore and Alexandria, as well as the multitude of buzzing department stores, banks, and early skyscrapers, Hanner was confident his investment would pay off. After all, downtown LA was, at this point, considered the Wall Street of the West, particularly the Spring Street Financial District that so closely bordered the Cecil's Main Street environs. His hotel would be an opulent Art Deco beacon of entertainment for traveling businessmen.

Neither he, nor any of the cigar-chomping financial elites, had any way of knowing that within five years, the United States would swan dive into a decade-long Great Depression that snuffed out the population's financial and psychological well-being. Nor could they have possibly gazed half a century into the future and foreseen the downtown's descent into permanent postwar poverty.

Conceived as both a short-term and a long-stay hotel, the Cecil wasn't just tailored to traveling businessmen; it also drew hardworking Angelinos looking for permanent homes. This unique blend of identities persisted throughout its entire history. Early on, the transient nature of many of the guests caused the Cecil to be the nexus of several criminal pursuits.

For example, in 1927, John Croneur, a Slavonian, was arrested in his room for running from police at the Hayward Hotel and stealing a diamond hairpin at the Rosslyn Hotel.

There was the tale of Cecil resident George Ford, a successful morphine and opium dealer with a stash of $10,000 worth of opium, who was arrested in a sting at the nearby Astor Hotel. An elderly man was picked up at the Cecil, "in peril of death," after drinking poisoned liquor that had killed three other men.

Even before things went sour from the economic downturn, the Cecil seemed like a magnet for troubled minds scraping against an indifferent universe. In April 1929, a thirty-three-year-old woman from San Francisco named Dorothy Roberson was taken to the hospital after wandering around the hotel for three days. According to reports, she was distraught over the sudden death of her husband and had tried to poison herself with prescribed barbiturates.

In the early 1930s, the darkness of the Great Depression descended upon the city like a total eclipse. Unprecedented economic destitution left a trail of devastation across the entire country. And in the shadow of this strife, a fatal curse, propelled by a string of grisly suicides, took root at the Cecil Hotel.

The earliest known suicide at the Cecil took place On November 19, 1931, when a Manhattan Beach resident, forty-six-year-old W. K. Norton, checked in under an alias and then poisoned himself to death. The next came under a year later, on September 1932, when a maid found twenty-five-year-old Benjamin Dodich dead from a self-inflicted gunshot wound to the head.

A year later, the building clocked a non-suicide fatality when a young man was hit by a truck and smashed against the hotel.

The suicides resumed in 1934, when a former sergeant in the Army Medical Corps, Louis D. Borden, who was fifty-three years of age and depressed over his failing health, slashed his own throat and bled to death. He left a note naming a Mrs. Edna Hasoner as "the sole beneficiary of the little I leave."

The next documented suicide occurred about three years later, on March 15, 1937. Twenty-five-year-old Grace E. Maguro checked into the Cecil and spent the night with a sailor from the U.S.S. *Virginia*. In the middle of the night, while her companion slept, Grace got out of bed, climbed up into the moonlit window frame and jumped from the 9th floor. Her body was found early the next morning entangled in the telephone wires, framed like some ghoulish abstract art exhibit for shocked passersby to interpret.

The next year marked another suicide attempt as well as an elderly Cecil resident drowned in the ocean. Meanwhile, criminal activity continued: A teenage stickup bandit was arrested at the Cecil with a note found in his pocket that read "You are covered. Open that cash register and shell out. No tricks or else"; a woman advertising a child-care position was choked and robbed by a man who had come to her room at the Cecil to answer her ad.

The curse resumed promptly in 1938, when a marine fireman named Roy Thompson jumped from the window of his 14th floor room and landed in the skylight of the building next door. He left no note.

In 1939, a naval officer Erwin C. Neblett, thirty-nine, of the U.S.S. *Wright* was found dead in his room after ingesting poison. The next year, there was another fatal poisoning.

A café manager, who lived at the Cecil, died in a nearby bar called the Waldorf Cellar after a gun battle with a bartender, who had been his childhood best friend.

The backdrop of these suicides was, of course the Great Depression, which took a wrecking ball to the global economy and mired millions in hopeless poverty. In the first three years, between 1929 and 1932, which are often considered the peak, worldwide gross domestic product (GDP) dropped by approximately 27 percent, causing 15 million people to lose their jobs. By comparison, during the peak of the 2007–2009 Great Recession, the global GDP fell by about 4.3 percent.

The Cecil Hotel continued to offer upscale accommodations but much of the high-end clientele, those who could still afford to dwell in deluxe establishments, defected to other downtown hotels like the Alexandria and the Biltmore. Over time, this lost business drained the hotel of its financial resources and resulted in the Cecil becoming one of the seedier hotel destinations in the city. The transformation was slow but steady, like geological erosion applied to a city. And when the United States entered World War 2 and eventually emerged from the Depression, it did not turn back the clock on the Cecil Hotel. Its golden days were over . . . while the curse lived on.

In September 1944, nineteen-year-old Dorothy Jean Purcell, who was staying in the Cecil with her husband, went into labor and delivered a baby in the bathroom down the hall. She didn't know she was pregnant, thought the baby was dead, and without waking up her husband, Ben Levine, a thirty-eight-year-old shoe salesman, she threw the baby out of the window; it was found on the roof of an adjacent building. One juror described the act as "almost beyond belief." An autopsy surgeon confirmed the baby's lungs had filled with air and hence had been alive during the fall. In November 1947, another man jumped from one of the Cecil's 7th-floor windows, killing himself. This is the same year the Black Dahlia was brutally killed only blocks from the Cecil.

In 1954, Helen Gurnee jumped from her 7th-floor window and landed on top of the hotel's marquee. In 1962, twenty-seven-year-old Pauline Otton had an argument with her husband and jumped from the 9th floor, landing on a pedestrian on the street below and killing them both. The man's hands were still in his pockets. In 1962, Julia Moore leaped from her 8th-floor window at the Cecil and landed in a second story interior light well.

In 1964, "Pigeon Goldie" Osgood, who was known locally for feeding the birds in Pershing Square (friends said she was the "benefactor of the square's bird population," fed birds too small to forage for themselves and scared away bigger birds), was stabbed, strangled, raped, and killed in her room at the Cecil. A local laborer

Jacques Ehlinger, who was found with blood on his clothes, was at one point suspected of killing her and another woman in the area who died a similar death, but police ultimately cleared and released Jacques. Goldie's murderer was never found. Friends pooled a fund for flowers, which they laid in Pershing Square. "We just wanted her to know we remembered."

In 1975, an unidentified female Cecil tenant jumped from her twelfth-floor window, landing on the Cecil's second-floor roof.

At some point, residents of the Cecil and locals of the downtown area began to call the building the "Suicide Hotel." It's easy to see why. From its inception all the way through the 1970s, there were dozens of suicides there.

Over the next decade, a new gruesome phase of the hotel's history played out: Two of the most grisly serial killers in recorded history took up residence at the Cecil and stayed there during their murder sprees.

THE NIGHT STALKER

In the early morning hours of July 5, 1985, twenty-year-old Whitney Bennett changed into her nightgown and lay down in her bed. Down the hall, her parents had already retired for the evening after hosting a get-together earlier in the night. Whitney had gone to her own party that night and didn't return home until 1:00 A.M.

She fell asleep unaware that the killer was already in the house, in the hallway just outside her room, acclimating to the dark like a chameleon. The Night Stalker decided he was going to kill her with a knife for maximum pleasure. He later said that "you can feel your victim dying through the knife" in a way that is close to sex, better than sex.

When she woke up—a miracle in and of itself—the room was dark, and she was dizzy with pain. She was lucky to be feeling anything, for someone had ruthlessly beaten her with a tire iron. Her head and face were so badly swollen and bruised that she was barely recognizable. The weapon now lay on the floor next to bloody footprints leading to the open bedroom window.

She was one of the luckier victims of Richard Ramirez, the Night

Stalker, who terrorized Los Angeles in the mid-1980s with a string of brutal murders and rapes.

The tall, gaunt man had scruffy black hair and haunting eyes and carried a distinctive smell that victims described as "wet leather." That night he couldn't find the right kind of knife so he used a tire iron instead, planning to beat the entire family to death, rape Whitney, and then take anything in the house worth money.

He entered Whitney's bedroom through an unlocked window and struck her numerous times with the tire iron. He then wrapped a cord tightly around her neck, intending to rape her as he choked her to death.

Ramirez unzipped his pants and tightened the cord. He was about to rip her underwear off when suddenly a series of sparks appeared on the wire cord around Whitney's neck. A blue haze materialized in front of him. It was unlike anything he had ever seen before and it took his breath away. He assumed it was the power of Christ intervening in his murder, a thought that shook him to his core.

As he let go of the cord, Whitney gasped and gulped oxygen. Ramirez left through the window, leaving behind a badly injured but live victim whose court testimony would later help send him to prison.

He later told biographer Philip Carlo that he believed the blue haze departing Whitney's body was her soul.

Like most killers, Richard Ramirez wasn't born a homicidal satanist. As a boy, Richie was quiet and courteous; he protected his sister and other girls from bullies. But as he grew older, Richie developed an obsession with violence. As an early adolescent, one of his heroes was Jack the Ripper. This is where he got the idea of wearing all black. He fantasized about being more famous than the unknown Jack, of emerging from the fog to snuff lives like a living incarnation of death.

There are many explanations offered over the years regarding the origin of Richie's violence: birth defects from nuclear testing in Los Alamos and/or industrial chemicals from his mother's workplace; his dad's horrific temper and domestic abuse; temporal lobe epilepsy; petit mal seizures; sexual abuse from a school teacher; and even emotional trauma from getting kicked off his high school football team

There was a near perfect storm of biological, genetic, and psychosocial factors contributing toward a pathology that would eventually turn Richard into one of the most feared serial killers of all time, a man who terrorized the city of Los Angeles in the broiling hot summer of 1985.

To escape the terror of his father's temper tantrums, Richie took to running away and sleeping in the nearby Cordova Cemetery, where eventually he would lose his virginity to a nice girl who later reported nothing negative about him. Richard also camped out in the desert and learned to navigate in darkness by reading the stars. When he was older, he took psychedelics under the desert moon, and in his hallucinations, he saw demons raping people.

As outlined in meticulous detail by Carlo in the biography *The Night Stalker*: *The Life and Crimes of Richard Ramirez,* Richie was practically groomed in his teenage years to be a criminal. His brothers taught him the art of stealth burglaries. His cousin Mike was Richie's most substantial and darkest influence. Before Richie was even a teenager, Mike returned from Vietnam and regaled his wide-eyed cousin with stories of battling the Viet Cong in the jungles. But these weren't Hollywood war stories: these were real war stories, the real legacy of America's military intervention abroad; horrifying accounts of torture, cold-blooded murder, and rape.

It started when Mike told Richie that early in the war, U.S. soldiers learned that Viet Cong fighters believed they wouldn't go to heaven if they were missing a body part. Mike and others took to cutting off the ears (and other body parts) of their enemies, which is the origin of notorious ear necklaces. Mike also showed Richie his photo collection, which contained images of distraught Vietnamese women being forced at gunpoint to perform oral sex. In one pic, Mike is actually seen holding the severed head of one of the women.

Not only did Mike teach Richie to shoot a .22, he added to Richie's skill set as a criminal, coaching him on how to avoid gravel, clotheslines, garbage cans, and dogs. Mike taught Richard tricks of guerilla warfare: how to become invisible while on the hunt and how to kill with efficiency. And he instilled in Richie an ideological rebellious-ness, a sense of social justice, us versus them, "the poor and down-trodden, against them, the rich and influential." Kill or be killed.

Eventually, Mike's lust for violence led to him shooting his wife in the head at point-blank range, a crime for which he was found not guilty by reason of insanity. Richie observed this murder; he was standing only a few feet away when Mike pulled the trigger.

When Ramirez started his killings, he was fueled by cocaine, Satan, and rock music, the American Dream—the God, mom, and apple pie—of 80s counterculture. Ever since he was a teenager, Richard had fantasized about violent sex and brutal acts of torture and murder. It was as if extreme sadism was hard-wired into him. For years he was able to control these impulses but ultimately he had to find a release. He started with an attempted rape, for which he was caught, arrested, and released without any repercussions—certainly not therapy.

His first successful rape victim was a woman with whom he had smoked PCP. He left, then snuck back in through the fire escape. During the act, he relished the woman's fear more than anything else. It was ultimate power, as though with Satan's help he'd wrested control of the universe from God himself. He enjoyed the act so much he decided he had to have more.

His foray into physical violence was supported by his belief in Satan, whom he imagined was personally pleased by barbaric acts. As a young man, Richard read the Satanic Bible by LaVey and stole a car just to drive to San Francisco to meet him. Richard became a servant to the Dark Lord, but was a "lone practitioner" because he did not trust collectives and considered many in the Church of Satan to be cult-like. He also suspected that they may have been infiltrated by police.

Much later, the Church made Ramirez an honorary member.

Around this time, Richard started shooting up cocaine and before long he was so addicted, he spent upward of $1,500 a week, a habit he supported with burglaries. When injected directly into the blood-stream, cocaine unleashes a euphoric flood of dopamine that fueled his fantasies about sadistic killing.

Meanwhile, his ultimate dark fantasy, of owning his own mansion in which he could build a basement specifically for the purposes of torturing and murdering women, smoldered inside him. Richard saved up his burglary money for this future torture chamber.

Ramirez loved rock music and imagined his favorite bands wrote songs that channeled the spirit of Satan. And like Charles Manson before him, he was convinced some songs were written just for him. Although instead of classic Beatles tunes like "Sexy Sadie," Ramirez was enraptured by AC/DC's "Night Prowler" and Billy Idol's "Eyes Without a Face." "Night Prowler" had to be for him—it was about sneaking into someone's home and killing them.

He also felt a strong connection to violent horror movies, especially ones that had occult undertones. *The Exorcist, Nightmare on Elm Street, The Texas Chainsaw Massacre.* These films captured for Richard the true terror and thrill of murder. Even as a kid, when Richard went to triple-feature horror movies, he smiled at the parts others screamed at. He imagined he was the monster from which the characters in the movie were running. The bad guys were the protagonists in his mind. The nightmarish killers were the real heroes of the story; they were being true to their inner nature, the inherently violent, chaotic nature of the universe itself.

Richard moved from El Paso to Los Angeles and immediately took a liking to downtown LA, specifically the Main Street area near the Cecil Hotel. He felt at home here among the downtrodden disenfranchised sector of the population. He gravitated to the dark alleyways and porn store marquees.

Violence poured out of him, animalistic and uncontrollable. While a .22 was his weapon of choice, he deferred to a blade fairly often because it brought you closer to the truth of death, a feeling that was sexual and almost spiritual. Some of his victims had gashes to their necks so deep they'd almost been decapitated.

Those who resisted him drew an especially inhuman ire. Maxine Zazzara, a confident attorney who fought back against Richard, angered the killer so much that he tried to cut her heart out. Thwarted by the thickness of the rib cage, he removed her eyes instead, keeping them as mementos.

"Be all that is evil, I, your humble servant, invoke Satan to be here and accept this offering."

When he returned to his room at the Cecil that night, he pulled the eyeballs from his pocket, which had absorbed most of the blood, and placed them on the bedside table.

"Eyes without a face . . ."

He genuflected to the sad face of the moon waning outside his window and Billy Idol's song, then laughed.

It *had* been written just for him.

SKID ROW

In 1989, a Los Angeles jury convicted Ramirez of thirteen counts of murder. The judge sentenced him to death.

Upon the conclusion of his trial, Ramirez held up his palm, tattooed with a pentagram, and stated to journalists, "Big deal. Death always went with the territory. See you in Disneyland."

After Ramirez, another serial killer, Jack Unterweger graced the "Suicide Hotel," using it as a base out of which to hunt and brutally murder prostitutes.

Other, less-prolific murderers, sought refuge there: In 1988, a man accused of killing his girlfriend in Huntington Beach was arrested at the Cecil; in 1995, a murder suspect named Eric Reed was found at the hotel after breaking out of a jail in Castaic. In 2003, there was another homicide at the Cecil. Shortly after noon on a Saturday, police found a man who looked to have been strangled to death in his room.

And the hotel continued to bait people at the end of their tether with the allure of painless oblivion. In the early 1990s, a drunk woman determined to jump from the 10th-floor window was talked down by legendary local officer Larry Soeltz.

Long-term residents, like the seventy-seven-year-old Saverio "Manny" Maniscalco and Michael Sadowe, who lived at the hotel for thirty years, called the building "The Suicide."

In all, at least sixteen people have committed suicide or been killed at the Cecil Hotel, many of them in gruesome fashion. In speaking with tenants there, I'm convinced the number is probably higher, as many crimes and deaths appear to have been covered up, misreported, or unreported completely.

One former tenant named Mike said he witnessed a lady jump out of the Cecil. She landed on the roof of a pawn shop and was still alive for a few moments when first responders arrived. One of them told Mike the lady was mumbling, "Why did you do this to me?"

The problems of the Cecil Hotel are, of course, greatly fueled by underlying systemic economic injustices that generate homelessness and poverty in the downtown Los Angeles area, which is home to Skid Row, regularly cited as containing the largest number of un-sheltered people in any U.S. city.

The origin of the homelessness problem in this area is hotly debated—as are the remedies—as downtown Los Angeles has had a growing poverty problem for over a century. As far back as the late 1800s, area newspapers have documented a preponderance of vagrants, itinerants, and drifters. The "deinstitutionalization" of the mentally ill in the latter half of the twentieth century, in concert with the government's failure to provide adequate social services, also played a role.

In 2006, Police Chief William J. Bratton began enforcing the "broken windows" campaign, which resulted in thousands of tickets being written for homeless people who violated petty laws such as jaywalking and littering with cigarette butts. Potentially successful plans, such as the county's proposal to invest $100 million into five regional homeless shelters, were rejected. In 2006, a bit of progress was made when the Jones agreement decriminalized sleeping on the sidewalk; of course, this resolution had the effect of exponentially increasing the number of homeless encampments.

The criminalization of homelessness also overlapped with the "reinstitutionalization" of mental illness. Author Stephen Hinshaw notes that the Los Angeles County Jail might as well be thought of as the country's largest mental facility, admitting around 150,000 people with mental disorders every year. People, he notes, who are without treatment plans and are susceptible to "drug trafficking, sexual exploitation, and recidivism."

The Cecil Hotel sits at the nexus of these troubled streets, where a cycle of poverty, drug addiction, and mental illness pumps through generations of tortured souls. Yet, when the gentrification of downtown finally transformed the area back into a moneymaker, new developers still sought to invest large amounts of money into hotels and bars marketed to college students, working professionals, and tourists.

When the Elisa Lam case went viral in 2013, the hotel's macabre past was litigated and highlighted for the entire world to see. Once again, the Cecil was known as a rotten flophouse, one of the most dangerous hotels in the world, haunted, and rife with corruption and crime.

Mysterious violence persisted at the hotel, meanwhile. In 2010 firefighter Charles Anthony MacDougall was stabbed inside the Cecil. He was about to receive the Paramedic of the Year Award when suddenly he was placed on administrative leave after police investigators found inconsistencies in his account. The story has essentially been buried. We may never know what MacDougall was really doing inside the hotel and what really happened to him. My request for information on the case was denied by the LAPD.

But seemingly no matter how many times the ownership changes hands, no matter what new policy change or renovation is ordered, no matter how much lipstick they put on the pig, the curse carries on. In 2015, the body of another suspected suicide victim was found on Main Street in front of the Cecil Hotel.

Or perhaps he was murdered. I don't know because the LAPD refused to disclose any information about that case either.

I drove into the Historic Core district and immediately felt the dark pulse, an almost magnetic pull, of the Cecil Hotel. Like a throughline, a raw nerve of the universe, had been exposed.

I imagined Elisa arriving here, likely with a misconception of the layout of Los Angeles. Most people who are unfamiliar with the city don't grasp how large and spread out it is. The Hollywood area, which contains some of LA's most iconic streets, is 7.5 miles from downtown; the nearest beach is 17.5 miles away and, due to perpetually congested traffic, takes at least an hour to reach by car, much longer by public transportation.

Pulling up to the Cecil Hotel, I stared up at its bulking mass. Its call to me, a susurration of overlapping whispers, had grown louder. *This is just in my imagination,* I told myself.

CHAPTER 9

The 14th Floor

WHEN ELISA ARRIVED HOME she expected to be greeted by her puppy. It was instinct, a neural pathway in her brain paved by the primal love forged between a human and a hound.

Two days earlier, he'd scampered out into the normally vacant street in her Barnaby neighborhood and was struck by a car. It was a freak accident, but the repercussions were eternal. The details were too gruesome to ponder, so she buried them deep inside.

This loss triggered memories of another death—her grandpa's. Elisa had been by his side for the last twenty-four hours of his life. The hospital granted the family their own private waiting room, which someone described (she couldn't remember who) as the nurses' way of letting you know death is imminent. It was the place where you said your good-byes. In the final hours the nurses explained to the family—with Elisa translating from English—that grandpa needed a respirator tube. She said yes on behalf of the family.

They put him on a dialysis machine, too. His skin color looked off, probably the result of his failing kidneys and liver. She was convinced the hospital made a mistake and marked the test wrong, causing the wrong tube to be used. Or had she misunderstood the nurse . . .

Her last words to him before he was brought to the ICU were "don't be scared." She sat by his bedside, holding his hand, squeezing it to let him know she was there. He squeezed back once. But soon he slipped into unconsciousness. She sat there with him, alone.

It was amazing to her, the thin line between life and death, the reality that we will all slip off into the ether someday.

Eventually the nurse nudged her and said, "I think you should tell your family to come in. He's going."

Elisa had clutched herself and cried as family members, nurses, and doctors rushed around her. At least he had seen her graduate high school. And years later, when she went to visit her grandma, all of grandpa's trinkets and documents were still laying around, and it was like he was still here. She kept his scarf.

Elisa went to the Vancouver mall to get out of the house and escape her haunting memories of grandpa and puppy.

She saw a comically dressed man, which was all the distraction she needed. "I'm sorry," she later wrote, "but a 50-year-old Asian man wearing a Paul Smith suit, a denim jacket, a mink stole, a Louis Vuitton backpack, Air Force Ones, and shutter shades—WHERE IS HE GOING? Does he work at an accounting firm run by Kanye West and a 10-year-old girl? Is he late for an appointment with Willy Wonka at the World Bank?"

Elisa wasn't normally so harsh, but she needed to let off steam.

Before Toronto, it was all she could do to stay awake. Three straight days of sleeping. Relatives came into town, and she slept right through it. Well, mostly. That would have been great. Unfortunately, she was awake long enough to get berated for not socializing. Her family just didn't understand that it was physically painful for her to sit at a table with other people. She did so with her boyfriend and his dad, and she had smiled and nodded her way through it.

It's like there was another person watching her. Judging her. Making her believe things about herself that weren't true. But it was just herself. She was both predator and prey. And sometimes it felt like she was running from someone—something—that pursued her as relentlessly as the Terminator.

Elisa wrote in her blog that she was hospitalized in a "mental ward" once: "a depressing hospital-colour painted place with bad food and donated furniture, an antiquated TV and incomplete puzzles . . . it reeks of hopelessness."

If she wanted more of that she would need to "subsist on a vegan diet of lentils and berries and chant Buddhist sutras for 6 hours a day . . .

"Yoga, meditation, drum circles, acupuncture etc. I will emerge as an earth goddess in touch with my spiritual self embracing my wholeness! HBO Enlightened!"

Elisa returned from Toronto with bronchial congestion, a cough, a sore throat, and her ever-present insomnia problem. She had traveled to get outside her comfort zone, to live life in the real world instead of the cocoon of curated identities and pleasures she had accumulated online.

Her social alienation was growing more acute, and to make matters worse, she was continually in the throes of alternating hypomanic episodes or periods of deep depression, during which she would hole up in her bed and excommunicate herself from the world.

She felt so alienated she read *The Loner's Manifesto*. Then she started hunting through the self-help sections of bookstores.

She saw some old friends, which she thought would make her feel better but actually made her feel worse. She saw a male friend with whom she'd once had a powerful platonic connection. Four years earlier she remembered waking up nestled in his arms. There was nothing romantic (all right, she might have harbored a crush at one point in high school), but their love ran deep. He counted as one of the only people in her life who directly asked her if she was depressed.

Now that connection was a distant memory. They weren't in high school anymore, they no longer saw each other every day. Now he was off doing great collegiate things like all her other friends, leaving her behind.

Oh well, she thought. "ALL LIVES END. ALL HEARTS ARE BROKEN. CARING IS NOT AN ADVANTAGE."

DRAWN TOWARD THE WINDOW

When I entered the lobby, I heard echoing laughter. The source: a drunk transient in the corner of the lounge. I checked in, noticing the same things others had described, the strange ornate decor of the lobby, the non-tenants milling about as though sizing up those who had come to stay. And behind the check-in desk of the lobby, which was once sheathed in protective glass, there were a dozen or so surveillance screens next to a stopped clock.

I wanted a room on the 14th floor, where Elisa's surveillance video was filmed and where the Night Stalker had lived, but evidently those rooms were reserved for permanent residents (making me wonder what Elisa had been doing up there). Instead, they gave me a room on the 5th floor, the same floor Elisa stayed on. Good enough.

I immediately noticed the nausea others have described. A claustrophobic dread that sticks to your every thought like the moisture of humid air adhering to your skin.

I checked into my room. It was a cramped hole with a window looking out onto Main Street.

I walked over to the window and looked out, recalling how many people had ended their lives by jumping from the higher floors. What an awful way to die. What horror. Many people who have jumped and somehow lived reported that their immediate thoughts upon being airborne were panicked regret, as though the sudden reality of having taken such a drastic step instantly cleared the fog of their despair. I've often thought of what the remainder of that fall would be like.

I started thinking of what it would be like if I opened my window, climbed up onto the sill and simply stepped off—then I shook my head and admonished myself. What the hell was I doing thinking something so awful?

I recalled that Natalie the psychic had that exact same experience upon checking into her room: She suddenly found herself transfixed with the window and thoughts of suicide, as though the hotel whispered a mortal invitation, a beautiful vision of falling in grace, anticipating ultimate freedom from pain and fear.

As I tried to relax and settle into my room, the feeling of dread and nausea intensified. *Ghostbusters* was on the TV.

I stood up and walked over to the door and put my eye up to the eyehole, taking in the ever-creepy bird's eye view of the hallway. I could hear murmuring voices, but no one was visible. My fear intensified. I felt restless, vulnerable, and endangered.

Dear God, I'm going to spend the night here? I thought. *Yes. And I've got work to do.*

I was looking for people who might know what happened to Elisa, obviously. But failing that, my goal in staying at the Cecil was to experience the hotel the same way Elisa did. Elisa had given virtually no attention to the paranormal. In all of her hundreds of pages of writings, not once did she ever reference ghosts, or hauntings, or possession, or anything in the esoteric paranormal realm. So unless it came to me, I would leave whatever entity that lived there alone.

I left my room and headed to the elevator, noting that even the hallways felt claustrophobic and surreal. There was something about the industrial piping that lined the ceiling and the soft cobalt glow that made me feel like I was inside some sentient mechanical structure.

Where was everyone? Since leaving the lobby, I hadn't seen one tenant.

I entered the elevator and looked at the button panel, remembering Elisa's frantic button-pushing from the footage. The upper corner contained the surveillance camera recording me and spread out before it was an azure sky and puffy white clouds painted on the ceiling.

It wasn't the only odd artistic license taken by the Cecil Hotel management. Elsewhere, some of the walls of the hotel contained strange images, like that of an enormous black dog looming over a city.

THE SECURITY GUARD

I stepped off onto the 14th floor.

The 14th floor of the Cecil Hotel is actually the thirteenth floor. The building does not have a "13th floor." This is not unusual. In fact, in a majority of cities a sizable percentage of hotels do not have a 13th floor due to persistent superstitions dating back centuries.

After watching the surveillance tape of Elisa so many times, it was surreal to be there in person looking down the very hallway. What the hell had spooked her so badly when she poked her head out to see if anybody was there? Had she heard someone or seen something? Or was she imagining something and working herself up into a frenzy over nothing?

To the left of the elevator, not far from where Elisa made her final exit, was a window leading to a fire escape. The window was closed and I was unable to open it. I was, however, able to get a clear look outside and was surprised at how precarious it looked. The rusted metal trellis and stair-ladder of the fire escape looked ancient and janky. Below was a long fatal fall.

I thought about Elisa's movements from different phases of the video and tried to match them up to the mirror. I physically reenacted some of her actions.

Suddenly I heard a toilet flush and jumped right out of my skin. I had forgotten about the shared bathroom in the hall, and the *ba-woosh* sound came out of nowhere. It also meant someone else was on the floor with me.

I waited. But no one came out.

I walked back over to the window and looked out. I remembered that Elisa had been sans glasses, which explained why she had to lean down and draw her face so close to the button panel. But that fact made it harder for me to believe that she had pushed open this window and climbed out onto a decades-old fire escape where all that separated her from a fourteen-floor fall was a single misstep.

Then again, maybe without her glasses she couldn't see how dangerous the fire escape was.

"What are you doing?" A voice suddenly rang out from past the elevator.

I jumped out of my skin again and then laughed amicably when I saw that a Cecil security guard was standing next to the bathroom. He had a walkie-talkie in his hand and was tucking his shirt in.

"I'm looking—at the fire escape."

"Are you a registered guest?"

"Yes."

"You're not allowed out there," he said.

"Well, unless there's a fire, right?"

He stared at me.

"I have no intention of going out there . . . unless there's a fire."

Since the man clearly wanted me to leave the 14th floor, I took the elevator down to the 10th floor and wandered around. I had hoped to interview some long-term residents. A registered sex offender, I had learned from an online database, lived on the 10th floor. He had appeared on a CNN news clip in which he lounged in his room describing the hotel. This news clip had been hyper-analyzed by conspiracy theorists, some of whom posited that this man was responsible for Elisa's death.

I loitered there for a bit, hoping someone would leave their room but none did.

My next course of action was to go to a nearby speakeasy, a vintage-themed dive bar, and try ascertaining whether it was the same one Elisa went to. It was a long shot. Even if it were the same one, the chances of anyone there remembering someone from several years earlier were extremely small. But sometimes you get lucky and the universe forgets to file away an old document.

My First Lead

"Fidelio," I said to the bouncer, remembering the password from the last time I was in town.

I felt like I was in the hipster version of *Mulholland Drive* (which, incidentally, features a shot of the Cecil Hotel) or *Eyes Wide Shut,* except inside there were not dozens of beautiful naked people wearing exotic masks but rather loose gaggles of mascara-and-sweat-drenched hipsters wearing fedoras, fishnets, and feathers, coming and going under a humid nimbus of cigarette smoke.

Through the haze, I saw occultnik artifacts hanging from the walls. Percussive jazz music, driven by a dissonant electronic off-beat, grew louder as I pushed my way past laughing drunk people who stood frozen, phones in hands, sharing versions of themselves warped by Instagram filters.

I get anxious in crowds, always have. It's a combination of claustrophobia and social anxiety. Unless I'm drunk or otherwise high, I get anxious. In her posts, Elisa suggests the same.

I got a couple drinks and listened to the jazz, but the din of music and voices prevented me from asking random questions of strangers.

The only place that was quiet was outside, so I slipped back out the side door, where the bouncer sat on a stool in the darkness. I hovered near him, the blue glow from my e-cigarette lighting my feet as I walked in small, jittery circles.

Finally, I asked him, "Excuse me, sir. Kind of a random question but do you know anyone at the Cecil Hotel?"

After a pause, he responded, "Oh, that sketchy place over on Main? That the place where they found the girl on the roof?"

"Yes, sir. Crazy case. I'm writing about it. Trying to find people who live there or worked there."

"I know someone who works at the Biltmore," he said, typing into his phone. "Let me see if she knows anyone."

We talked a little while longer and I stuck around, hoping the bouncer would get a response. And for about an hour and a half, I dizzily struck up conversations in the speakeasy, checking back with him every thirty minutes.

Finally, I couldn't take it anymore and I was walking away from the speakeasy, when suddenly the bouncer called out, "Hey! I got a number for you . . ."

He handed me a small slip of paper.

"Her name is Tina, she might know someone."

"Cool, thanks, man."

It was the first, but not the last, time I would receive information from a bouncer. And next time, the info would be shocking.

Night Terror

Back at the Cecil that night, I couldn't sleep. This insomnia was different from anything I'd ever experienced. I'll just put it like this: The Cecil Hotel felt like it had a mind of its own, as though it were aware I had come there to study it and was therefore playing mind games with me, using its dark faculties to disarm me, neutralize me with fear.

I don't usually get paranoid. I generally do not lay in bed convinced someone is going to break into my room and kill me in my sleep. Nor do I usually feel like the walls of a room are watching me. But that's what it felt like in the Cecil. When footsteps echoed down the hallway, I froze in terror. Once, I couldn't take it any longer and bolted to the eyehole to watch as a figure walked past. I sensed that he would suddenly stop and turn his head to look at me, which would have certainly given me a heart attack.

When I finally did fall asleep, my dream centered around Elisa. In it, I was watching her in a small room from a bird's-eye view and she was aware that I was watching her and writing about her. She was also aware that she was dead. As I wrote about her, she began writing about me, but I couldn't decipher the handwriting. She composed somehow with a combination of pen, typewriter, and brain, some strange organic contraption right out of *Naked Lunch*.

Toward the end of the dream, she turned her head slowly up and to the right to look at me. Her eyes were missing, like one of Ramirez's victims, and in their place were eyeholes from the hotel's doors. While I observed her in bird's-eye view, she could see me in telephoto closeness, could peer into my eyes and soul and discern my intentions and motives, which I wordlessly swore to her were pure.

THE MOST FRIGHTENING EYES I'VE EVER SEEN

In the morning, I felt a terrific urge to get the hell out of the building as quickly as possible. I wanted coffee and an omelette, so I planned to head to the nearby Margarita's, the restaurant Richard Ramirez had frequented. But as my legs deposited me onto Main Street, I noticed that there was a young woman standing on the sidewalk, staring up at one of the windows of the upper floors.

I remembered my college experience at Santa Cruz—which happens to have been Elisa's next planned stop after LA—and the figure staring at the balcony where a young man ended his life with a shotgun.

There was something else about the young woman that struck me. Her jacket wasn't exactly the same as Elisa's, but it was red and it concealed her face. The young woman stood in the middle of the sidewalk, compelling annoyed passersby and pedestrians to walk around her as she gazed, hands in jacket pockets, up at the Cecil.

I recalled the popular photograph taken by a teenage boy several years ago, which shows a wispy apparition in the shape of a human hovering in the window of the Cecil Hotel. I couldn't help but wonder if it was connected with how many people have committed suicide by jumping out of the building's windows, or with the morbid feeling of being drawn to the window that both myself and others experienced.

Is that what the woman in red was sensing? I asked myself. Or is she the embodiment of one of the jumpers, nostalgically revisiting ground zero of her exit from the material world? Or is it just a random person staring at a building?

There was only one way to find out. I started toward her, but she abruptly turned and headed swiftly down Main in the opposite direction.

I decided to check out Pershing Square, where the Pigeon Lady fed birds before she was brutally murdered inside her room at the Cecil. I crossed Main and navigated through throngs of disheveled people toward Spring Street. I passed The Last Bookstore, where manager Katie Orphan had reported one of the last known conversation with Elisa, and then zig-zagged for a few more blocks.

The Pershing Square block has undergone multiple renovations in the last few decades, shedding real-growth palm trees for fakes. It remains as a sleeping ground for the homeless.

Suddenly, the woman in red ascended a narrow flight of concrete stairs and entered the purple pillars of the Square. For a split second, she turned her head back, but I couldn't tell if she saw me. It felt, strangely, that she had led me here somehow. And when she reached the top of the stairs she ran into a tall, menacing man with shaggy black hair, who appeared to have been waiting for her.

She stopped in her tracks, looking up at him. Then they hugged and I could tell that she was whispering something to him, at which point his eyes trailed up and fixated on me. I was horribly confused. This woman, decked in red, had been staring up at the Cecil before disappearing and reappearing at my next destination, and seemed to be aware of me and passed this info along to a man who eerily resembled Richard Ramirez. I remembered the eyes from old photographs.

I backed away and tried to casually shuffle off down the road with my hands in my pockets. Ten seconds later, I glanced back and the man still stood staring at me with the most frightening eyes I'd ever seen—beastly and black as coal. But now the woman in red was gone, nowhere to be seen.

I felt flabbergasted by this experience for days. I still get chills when I think about those eyes and the mysterious red sparrow that presaged them.

CHAPTER 10
The Autopsy

THE ORIGINAL AUTOPSY OF ELISA LAM was written on February 27, 2013, shortly after her death. However, the coroner had stated that it was inconclusive and that further tests would need to be conducted to determine how Elisa died. It took over six months for the coroner's office to complete what is normally done in six to nine weeks.

Finally, on June 19, forensic pathologist Yulai Wang finally signed off on the cause of death and on the twenty-first, after all the delays, mysteries, conspiracy theories, and feverish forum frenzy, the LAPD and LA County Coroner's Department was ready to tell the public what had happened to Elisa Lam.

By the time they released the full autopsy, postmortem, and toxicology report, I had read so many of Elisa's posts I felt like she was a friend of mine. That's why it was weird to read about her brain, the very brain from which the posts had originated, weighing 1,100 grams and looking dusky gray, her cerebral hemispheres symmetrical.

I took it all in with the same cognitive filtering applied when recalling a dream. Certain figments and details would call out to me: the green hue of her body, marbling on parts of her leg, the head and face bloated with bulging eyes, skin slippage and her scalp skin and hair sloughing with the slightest touch. It was hard to read. How do coroners do what they do?

Most of it wasn't so grisly. In fact, much of these reports are clinical and difficult to understand if you're not an expert. Later, when actually speaking to a forensics expert, I would learn how important it is to have analysis done by someone who actually knows what they're talking about. But for the time being, I was left on my own, along with all of the other web denizens, to trust the findings and conclusions of the LAPD and Coroner's Department.

I remember a distinct sense of electricity running through me at the prospect of finally getting some insight on the cause of her death. It's hard to say why I had become so attached to the case.

After nearly six months and multiple delays, the LAPD presumably hoped to put the fire out by releasing the full autopsy, toxicology, and postmortem report.

CLOTHING

We know that Lam's body was found naked and that her clothes were floating in the tank with her. The autopsy finally confirmed what these clothes were: a pair of black men's shorts, a large green shirt with an "Alexander Keith's India Pale Ale" logo, a shirt with a deer logo, sandals, her extra-small red-hooded sweatshirt, and black lace-trimmed underwear.

A section of the Criminalist Report discussing evidence collection seems to have been written from the point of view of either Detective Stearns or Tennelle:

> The body had reportedly been recovered along with the clothing and a wristwatch after being submerged in a hotel water supply tank for many days. Sand and small, flat, whitish and fragile flecks of unknown material were on or throughout all the clothing, and several dark hairs or fibers at least several inches in length were noted on a couple of the garments.

The Investigator's Report notes an interview with Sarah Lam, Elisa's sister, who says Elisa had no suicidal ideations.

PHYSICAL EXAMINATION

The external examination noted a one-inch scar on the right knee and quarter-inch abrasion on the left knee. Beyond these, there were no signs of external injuries. No contusions, hemorrhages, bruises, or needle punctures. There were no signs of trauma to her neck. There were no wrist scars, no evidence of self-harm.

INTERNAL EXAMINATION

Soft tissues taken from Elisa's larynx showed no signs of hemorrhage. Same with her hyoid bone and thyroid cartilage. One anomaly that did turn up is signs of a Focal erythema of the thyroid. This condition is found in about 40 percent of women and usually takes years to diagnose. It is also not typically associated with strangulation or a physical injury.

Elisa's cardiovascular, hepatobiliary, and gastrointestinal systems were all normal. There was no trauma to her genitals, but Elisa had had anal bleeding as a result of prolapse. The explanation I would later find for this is that after death, your body has no immunity so the bacteria breeds exponentially and deteriorates the body's cells. This creates a gas that expands and bursts organs and innards out of the body. Pretty grim stuff, but not considered a sign of sexual assault—at least by the LA County Coroner's Department.

Elisa's respiratory passages contained secretions with a brownish mucosa, which is usually created after death. Her chest pleural cavities contained dark brown fluid, 300 cc on the right and 200 cc on the left. Her abdominal cavities contained no fluid collection.

TOXICOLOGY

Elisa was known to have taken prescription medications, but, according to the toxicology, not all those medications had been taken by her recently. A screen of her heart blood as well as results from her liver, indicated to coroners Ed Winter and Yulai Wang the following:

- Venlafaxine (antidepressant) was present in the blood in her heart and in her liver enzymes.
- Bupropion (antidepressant) metabolites were present in the blood in her heart and in her liver enzymes (but not the drug itself, meaning that she had probably taken it recently but not the day she died).

- Quetiapine (antipsychotic) & its metabolites were not detected in any quantity in the blood from Elisa's heart.
- Lamotrigine (mood stabilizer) was found in such small amounts in the blood from Elisa's heart that it's debatable it was even there ("quantity not sufficient"); however, Lamotrigine was found in trace amounts in her liver enzymes. This suggests Elisa took this medication recently, but not the day she died.
- Bile ethanol (alcohol) results: 0.02 g percent (normal).
- Ethanol (alcohol) was not detected in any quantity in the blood from her heart, meaning Elisa had not consumed any alcoholic beverages the day she died.
- Toxicology report conclusively establishes there were no illicit drugs in Elisa's system whatsoever. They tested the blood in her heart for marijuana, cocaine, MDMA, barbiturates, opiates, and amphetamines—all came up "not detected," meaning she hadn't even taken the Dexedrine (prescription amphetamine/stimulant) recently.

No illicit drugs, no alcohol. The toxicology report did not test for date-rape drugs like Rohypnol (roofies), GHB, or Ketamine.

Then I found what I had been looking for: the cause of death. It turned out it was sitting there right on the first two pages of the autopsy, which, in my anxious excitement, I had scrolled past. It's probably a good thing I missed it, as it likely would have distracted me from the rest.

The Investigator's Narrative Body Examination noted moderate decomposition and declared that "rigor mortis was resolved" and "liver mortis was fixed." And: "There was no obvious evidence of trauma seen."

> *EVIDENCE OF EXTERNAL TRAUMATIC INJURY: none*
> *EVIDENCE OF INTERNAL INJURY: none*
> *OPINION: The decedent died as a result of drowning. A complete autopsy examination showed no sign of trauma*

and toxicology did not show acute drug or alcohol intoxica-
tion. Decedent had a history of bipolar disorder for which
she was prescribed medication. Toxicology studies were
performed for the presence of these drugs. However, quanti-
tation in the blood was not performed due to limited sample
availability. Therefore, interpretation is limited. Police in-
vestigation did not show evidence of foul play. A full review
of the circumstances of the case and appropriate consulta-
tion do not support intent to harm oneself. The manner of
death is classified as accident.

From the anatomic findings and pertinent history, death
was ascribed to: DROWNING

Other conditions contributing but not related to cause of
death: BIPOLAR DISORDER

LAPD's Cause of Death

So there it was. No foul play. Elisa accessed the roof on her own, took off her clothes, climbed into the tank and drowned. After six months of anticipation, the official coroner's report turned the most mysterious case of the century into a tragic, inexplicable accident.

In notes from his on-scene investigation, Detective Tennelle says Elisa was last seen on January 31. However, in a witness statement, Tennelle says Elisa was last known to be alive on February 1. Since her time of death is not known but believed to have been around midnight, this could account for the discrepancy.

In a later civil court deposition, Detective Wallace Tennelle told lawyers, "I think she went through the door," likely referring to the main rooftop entrance ascending up from the 14th floor. It's an odd statement because this is the door that was supposed to have had an alarm that would immediately alert hotel staff if opened. If Elisa walked through this door, as the detective believes, it means either: A) The alarm was not working or B) A hotel employee deactivated it so that Elisa could walk through.

The statement by Tennelle is important and we shall revisit it.

Tennelle offered further evaluation: "My opinion is that [Elisa] fell off her medication, and in her state, she happened to find her way onto the roof, got into the tank of water . . . At the time, I think that water tank was maybe full. But as people used the tank, used water, unknown to her, the level was dropping to a point where she could no longer reach out and escape, and she died that way."

I spent many hours imagining this manner of death, which in some ways is worse than being murdered. Upon climbing into the tank, Elisa would have realized fairly quickly that the interior had no notches or handles, nothing by which to gain leverage. If the water level dropped, or was already low enough that she could not reach the top, she would have been forced to tread water, as it was high enough that her toes could not touch the bottom.

The interior was also quite likely dark, possibly pitch black. Elisa may have been treading water in the tank for hours. Her yells for help would likely have been muddled by the cistern, and, at least according to the police explanation, she was alone on the roof. There was no one to hear her. There was nothing she could do.

In desperation and exhaustion, she may have removed her clothes to shed as much weight as possible so that she could continue to tread water until someone rescued her. Or perhaps she thought she could use her clothes to clog the tank's pipes and force a maintenance worker to check on it; or she hoped to raise the water levels of the tank so that she could reach the top and escape.

It is also possible that Elisa removed her clothes because she had hypothermia from the water, a condition that can, paradoxically, cause people to feel overheated. Or, perhaps Elisa had simply intended to do some skinny dipping and forgot to take her clothes off until she got inside.

It was impossible to say for certain why Elisa may have climbed into the tank or what state of mind she was in. But if she drowned in the water tank, there's no reason to think it happened immediately. I shudder to imagine her desperation and despair.

Flipping back through the autopsy, I noticed something else interesting. At some point between June 19 and June 21, when the report was released to the public, an important page of the medical report was amended. The cause of death, which was originally marked COULD NOT BE DETERMINED, was scratched out, initialed, and dated; the box to the left of ACCIDENT was then marked, initialed, and dated. I wondered what they could have discovered in those few days to concretely prove that her death was an accident.

Tennelle offered his reasoning for ruling out homicide: "My partner and I tried to figure out how somebody could have put her in there, and it's difficult for someone to have been able to do that and not leave prints, not leave DNA or anything like that. So she climbed in on her own."

Unsurprisingly, not everyone believed the conclusions reached by the police. More important, not everyone agreed with the coroners' analysis of the autopsy. But for the LAPD, the case was closed.

At the time, it occurred to me that the release of the autopsy might have marked the end of my true-crime investigation. After all, what is true crime without the crime?

However, as it turned out, for the websleuth community, the investigation was just getting started. And the autopsy, the very document that the LAPD hoped would close the books on the case, only raised more questions.

In time, I would develop an alternative interpretation of Elisa's cause of death. By that point, my life and my investigation into the case—which became one in the same—were turned completely upside down.

PART 2
SEROTONIN AND SYNCHRONICITY

"That's the effect of living backwards," the Queen said kindly: "it always makes one a little giddy at first—"

"Living backwards!" Alice repeated in great astonishment. "I never heard of such a thing!"

"—but there's one great advantage in it, that one's memory works both ways."

"I'm sure MINE only works one way," Alice remarked. "I can't remember things before they happen."

"It's a poor sort of memory that only works backwards," the Queen remarked.
—LEWIS CARROLL, *Alice in Wonderland*

CHAPTER 11

The Art of the Meltdown

IN JUNE 2014, I DISSOLVED MY RELATIONSHIP with my girlfriend. That's really the most diplomatic way I can phrase it. We'd bickered like starved hyenas for years but always with a sense of some shared mission. That mission ended in calamitous ruin.

I compounded the situation by doing something really stupid. I decided that the reason it had all gone wrong was a deficiency on my part, a lack of psychological purity that had driven us apart. I convinced myself that the right course of action was to go off all my psychiatric meds and find "the true me."

Over the next month, my ex and I each looked for new housing arrangements in San Diego while sharing our apartment. The situation rendered me physically nauseous on an hourly basis. Meanwhile, I tapered off Prozac, Wellbutrin, and Strattera, reverse engineering the neurochemical grid of my mind as though I was HAL in *2001,* singing "Daisy" as a human astronaut disassembled my cognitive units.

I chopped my pills in half, in slivers, carefully twisting the bicameral halves of the plastic capsules, methodically reducing the number of granules and orbs I would feed my brain. It felt like I was evacuating a baby from a war zone in a hot-air balloon. While I starved myself of neurotransmitters, my ex dated a fifty-three-year-old activist who lived in his van. I will henceforth refer to him affectionately as the Anarchist.

I drove to Albuquerque to visit my parents, a trip designed to stagger and limit the times at which my ex and I both required the shelter of our apartment, which in the summer months had turned into a sweltering hive of murdered love.

On my way home I sporadically vacated the freeway, crossing multiple lanes to reach exit ramps so that I could pull over at rest stops and have panic attacks and nervous breakdowns.

At the same time as I discontinued the medley of pharmaceuticals and antidepressants that had kept me stable for years, I began consuming large amounts of prescription painkillers. This obviously should have registered as being antithetical to finding "the true me," but I nevertheless armed myself with a grenade strap full of them. Because nothing says freedom from pills—like pills.

When the apartment lease finally expired, I threw most of my possessions in a dumpster. I dragged my furniture, appliances, and amenities out to the alley and left them to be pilfered.

I lived in my work office, sleeping on a $150 cot from REI. As the final vestiges of the antidepressants disappeared from my brain chemistry, and the trauma of the breakup seeped into my muscle memory, I turned into little more than an exposed nerve with eyeballs. I cried constantly, listened to Nine Inch Nail's *The Fragile* and Elliot Smith's *From a Basement on the Hill* on loop, and read morbid crime reports to convince myself there was worse pain than what I was experiencing.

During the day, I distracted myself with more Vicodin, SEO, and true-crime blurbs. I excused myself from work meetings to lay down on the floor of the rec room and hyperventilate with the lights off. At night, I brushed my teeth in the employee bathroom, steering clear of the hallway where the custodians serviced the building, dragged the cot back out and slithered back into my hole.

I didn't eat much. Over the next two years, with no appetite and no SSRIs, which typically cause five to thirty pounds of weight gain, I became fairly emaciated.

Much has been written about the "zaps" that accompany discontinuation of SSRIs. These are supposedly highly unpleasant sensations describing as feeling like a jolt of electricity in the brain. In my long career of going on and off antidepressants, I've never experienced a zap.

What I did experience was suicidal ideation, something I don't talk about with doctors but that I've nevertheless decided to divulge here. As the pain intensified, my conscious and unconscious mind began colluding to hatch exit strategies. It felt automatic. Like some biological red light was blinking, warning me that my submarine was descending to dangerous depths.

My research into the history of the Cecil Hotel may have deposited the raw imagery of suicide in my subconscious and now, intermittently throughout the day, my mind hit the space bar on grainy visions of men and women jumping from windowsills, their dresses and ties flapping in the air.

THE SIMULATION IS GLITCHING

My mind started to play tricks on me. One night, as I crawled into my cot in the corner of my tiny office, I heard what sounded like footsteps coming from the floor above. I stopped and listened, turning off my fan (I can't sleep without it, even in the winter). There were multiple other businesses who shared the office building out of which my company worked. But it was midnight.

While I had never heard someone there that late before, it was completely reasonable that someone had to finish up a late-night project. It could have also been a custodial worker, though they usually finished up several hours earlier.

Nevertheless, the building started to unnerve me, further confining me to my cot.

I began to have exceedingly strange dreams, too. One night I dreamt that reality was a simulation. In the dream, one of the simulation designers communicated to me through shadow puppets that I did live in a simulation but that I should stop worrying about it. It felt like a thinly veiled threat.

And I was registering what I can only call glitches. Even in my delirium, I knew that this was almost certainly the result of withdrawal from the antidepressants. Digital artifacting, pixels randomly conspiring to look like faces. Audio blips during music that resembled demons chirping. Seeing the same people over and over again on the street, as though reality were trapped in a loop.

Even though I stabilized somewhat in the coming year, the glitches were replaced by synchronicities. Highly charged words, phrases, and actions echoed all around me, on the radio, on billboards, etched into bathroom stalls. And the more I researched the case, the more intense the synchronicities got.

I dreamt of Elisa again. Once more, she was aware that I was investigating her case. In fact, she was on her computer, researching my research, posting about it on Tumblr. In another dream, Elisa seemed to be falling in a black vacuum, her limbs and hair suspended while she mouthed words of caution to me in slowed silence. Dream Elisa always wore her red hoodie.

The footsteps returned at odd intervals. The pace of the footsteps sometimes quickened to a scampering, as though a child were running through the hallway. It was certainly possible, I told myself, that an employee was finishing up some work and had brought their child along.

But at midnight? It was always at midnight.

I didn't like leaving the office and entering the hallways at night because I wanted to conceal the fact that I was sleeping there. While I could pass off some encounters, it would be hard to explain brushing my teeth in my pajamas in the employee bathroom.

But the sounds started to legitimately unnerve me. *Was someone else living in the building at night?*

One night I changed into normal clothes, crept into the dark hallway, proceeded to the elevator and pressed the button for the floor above. When I got there, I peeked out first to look down the hallway.

Nothing. None of the lights in any of the offices were on.

Suddenly I remembered that some of my colleagues had taken to putting a piece of plastic in a back-entrance door to make it easier to get inside on a whim. Is it possible that one of the many transients passing through the alleyway behind the building had seen them do that and used the open door to get access?

But what about the running sound? A chill went through me. As a child, I had a particular fear of the sound of something scampering quickly through the darkness outside my room. Now, years later, that fear manifested into reality.

I was about to abandon my inquiry and return to my cot when I heard a clicking sound at the end of the hallway, where the glow of the red *Exit* sign cast the only light.

Summoning my hydrocodone courage, I traversed the hallway like a character in one of the *Alien* movies.

When I reached the exit, I pushed open the door and emerged into a staircase that led to the roof. *This is really dumb,* I told myself, as I ascended the stairs. *Seriously, this is really dumb.* I pushed open the door to the roof.

Our office was probably the tallest building in the area and so there wasn't much surrounding light. The roof was almost entirely feature-less. I could see the outline of a couple maintenance contraptions.

I went to the edge and looked over. There was a row of spikes twinkling in the moonlight. "Bird control" or "roost modification," erected by city officials and building owners to protect private prop-erty. The spikes looked like long needles that might be used to medi-cate an elephant. There were hundreds of them, extending out a foot from the ledge.

I was not planning to jump—not consciously, at least—but I viv-idly imagined nicking myself on the spikes or impaling myself and having to wait for the police to come rescue me while hanging in agony. In addition to preventing pigeons from roosting, the bird-control spikes might serve as a suicide deterrent as well.

This is what's known as a happy accident.

I went back to the door to the stairwell. It was locked.

"Oh fuck you, God!" I yelled with a chortle of rage. Nothing infu-riates me more than when I am sabotaged by my own erratic behav-ior, which is God's fault, of course.

I paced and started to panic. The situation wasn't life-threatening. I could have lasted the night up there, but how the hell would I ex-plain having to be rescued off the roof in my pajamas? *"I heard footsteps while laying in my cot."*

Suddenly, I remembered that on a Friday night of drunken de-bauchery after work, some of my colleagues had scaled a narrow passage connecting the roof to a vestibule-like platform of windows outside our office.

I realized that my situation seemed eerily analogous to Elisa's.

If one follows the "psychiatric accidental death" explanation to its logical conclusion, Elisa died because of a perfect storm of ailments converging—mania (possibly a "mixed state"); withdrawal from meds; delusions; and possibly hallucinations—which convinced her to climb into the water tank.

This explanation was beginning to make more sense to me. After reading the autopsy and then experiencing my own nervous breakdown and its attendant "glitches," it became clear to me how easily a normal situation can turn into a complete nightmare in only a few quick steps.

I hopped down onto the passageway and shuffled sideways toward the open-air vestibule-type structure. Below me was a fatal fall. But I made it.

Now let's hope one of the windows is open, I thought.

Later, I would recall my experience after reading a news story about a young woman, Jamie Minor, who, after demonstrating "erratic behavior" on surveillance video, tried to sneak back into her work office but got trapped in a large ventilation shaft. She had no way out of the shaft and likely died after days of dehydration. One of the more horrifying deaths by misadventure. Friends and family later confirmed Minor had been suffering from bipolar disorder.

The window was open, fortunately. I climbed through and slithered back into my cot.

SUICIDAL IDEATION

Much debate has taken place regarding whether Elisa's death was a suicide. After all, she was a diagnosed depressive with bipolar disorder. Around 80 percent of bipolar patients contemplate suicide, compared with only one in twelve of people in the general population. New data suggests that between 25 percent and 60 percent of those with bipolar attempt suicide at some point. Between 4 percent and 19 percent succeed, making suicide the number one cause of premature death for those with the illness.

However, suicide by drowning is rare, representing only about 1 percent of successful attempts in 2012 (compared to approximately 50 percent by firearm; 25 percent by suffocation/hanging; 16 percent by poisoning/pills). Many who consider the suicide question in this case ask why Elisa wouldn't have just jumped off the roof. It was right there in front of her, as opposed to the water tanks, which were tall and difficult to access.

The Cecil Hotel is infamous for its suicides, so much so that locals call it the "Suicide Hotel." And it's especially well known for its jumping suicides. But jumping suicides are actually almost as rare as drowning, constituting just over 2 percent of victims.

But was Elisa suicidal? We know she suffered severe depression and bipolar disorder, but suicidality, chronic suicidal ideation, is a bit more complex.

Elisa wrote in her blog:

> *There is no physical manifestation of my "illness." Would I become psychotic and want to off myself? I know I wouldn't do anything rash like actually jump off a bridge. I'm too much of a coward. Instead I'll just lie in my bed and let the days pass by. That's my physical manifestation, sleeping for days in bed.*

Elisa, even while denying that she would ever consider suicide, mentions psychosis as a possible factor that could change her mind. On November 2, 2011, Elisa wrote the following on Tumblr:

> *Suicide is not an option for me but in the last 96 hours I have considered it to be a possibility multiple times. I am just that disappointed with the human race.*

A few days earlier, on Halloween, she explained the reason in a post.

> *Exhaustion:*
> *I've never been this physically and emotionally exhausted. I've cried more tears than I can handle. My eyes are so swollen. My throat is hoarse. The bones in my body ache. I've had only 2 hours of sleep.*

What is significant here is that she had described the previous day as one of her best days in months. She said she nailed a job interview, found a box of aged French books for only $30, bought a snowboard, and watched *Drive*, one of her favorite movies. That she could fluctuate from such a high to suicidal thoughts in only a couple days underscores the volatility of bipolar disorder and the irrational nature of its mood swings.

However, at this point, it's unclear whether Elisa had even been diagnosed with bipolar disorder. The date of that diagnosis is uncertain. In a post in which she lists and describes her medications, she casually mentions a bipolar med.

"The other one is lamotrigine because apparently I'm bipolar as well?" she wrote.

Her full list of prescribed medications, accompanied by a photo of each of her different pills laid out, is as follows: Effexor, Wellbutrin, Dexedrine, Seroquel, and Lamotrigine.

Though stimulants can be helpful for some bipolar patients, many psychiatrists and general practitioners with experience in psychopharmacology raise their eyebrows at the suggestion of combining an amphetamine, such as Dexedrine, with bipolar meds. In fact, many medical professionals view it as dangerous. After all, if a patient is bipolar, particularly a patient like Elisa who had episodes of severe hypomania, why would you be prescribing a medication that activates the brain and could trigger mania and cycling?

Additionally, Wellbutrin is sometimes thought to be a problematic drug for people with bipolar because of its activating, stimulant-like effect. Other doctors think Wellbutrin can be a "secret weapon" against bipolar. The general consensus is that a patient experiencing severe hypomanic episodes should not be taking an antidepressant without also taking a mood stabilizer or a drug specifically for bipolar. This may have been the case with Elisa, whose autopsy shows the presence of Wellbutrin and Effexor but virtually no remnants of Lamotrigine or Seroquel.

It is thus possible to reasonably conclude that Elisa was experiencing severe hypomania, mania, or a "mixed episode" during the elevator surveillance footage. She may have even been experiencing psychosis. But does mania or psychosis necessarily lead to suicide? Or death by misadventure? Is there overlap?

By the next year, Elisa's struggle with depression and bipolar was continuing to take a psychological toll.

I just don't see my depression having a legitimate support. No I don't self-harm. No I'm not in an abusive relationship in fact my boyfriend is in many ways, perfect for me and a nicer, sweeter more supportive guy could I have met and I'm very lucky I did. Sure I think about suicide but I don't want to kill myself and unless I become schizophrenic I don't think I will kill myself.

Elisa may not have been aware of the overlapping symptoms shared by schizophrenia and severe bipolar disorder. Because bipolar disorder can induce psychosis, including hallucinations and delusion, it is often confused with schizophrenia. In his book *Another Kind of Madness,* Stephen Hinshaw wrote that his father was misdiagnosed as schizophrenic for decades before doctors finally identified the problem as bipolar disorder.

That Elisa went off her mood stabilizer meds, perhaps abruptly, speaks to the possibility that the psychosis she may have experienced the night she was recorded in the elevator would have felt like schizophrenic symptoms. Thus, one cannot rule out that Elisa followed through with her vow of taking her own life at the perceived onset of schizophrenia.

It is just as likely that a severe hallucination or delusion convinced Elisa that she needed to hide in a dark, quiet spot. It wasn't until she hit the water that she realized she could not reach the top and there was no way to climb out.

HALLUCINATIONS

Did Elisa hallucinate something that made her take refuge in the water tank? Bipolar disorder can cause hallucinations and psychosis. Many people with bipolar disorder report that they are able to experience hallucinations while understanding that they are not real. Others can not make that distinction.

In her blogs, Elisa references a dizzy tunnel-vision sensation and a variety of physical ailments related to her illness, but she does not once describe a hallucination.

In her hypomanic rants, though, she certainly displays the signs of having extremely powerful delusional thoughts. And on the day she disappeared, she was off her mood stabilizer and bipolar meds. This may have triggered an unusually strong manic episode that may have included hallucinations.

Some examples of hallucinations reported by people with bipolar include the following:

- Seeing faces in random patterns, like wallpaper, rust stains, etc.
- "Shadow persons," often caught in peripheral glimpses.
- Dark demons that cuddle beside them in bed, breathing on their neck.
- Static men, with skin like the static from a TV.
- Someone running by really fast—(one Redditor reported frequently seeing a person in a white hoodie).
- Someone standing at a distance and watching them.
- "a sentient melting photograph" [fascinating description I found on Reddit].
- People whispering or singing, sometimes urging one to take a certain action.
- Train whistles when there's no train around.
- Humanoid creatures or monsters.
- Thoughts and inner dialogue becoming unbearably loud.
- Hypnagogic hallucinations, which occur during the transition to sleep.
- Hearing distinct voices in white noise or static.
- False memories.
- Shapes of varying colors that float around and shift.
- Phosphenes, seeing images behind closed eyes.

We task our brains, the most mysterious biological organ on the planet, with transforming raw sensory data into a usable format that we experience as our senses of sight, sound, smell, hearing, and touch. Sometimes, however, our minds show us fragments of a world that is not there. The visions can be truly horrifying for people who experience them.

IT WORSENS

The extent to which hypomania disrupted Elisa's life is massively under-reported in most articles and comment threads about the case. Her bipolar disorder seemed to worsen over the course of 2011 and 2012. It is, of course, possible that she simply began to recognize the symptoms more and more readily acknowledge and examine the extent to which it was affecting her life.

Bipolar disorder can easily be confused as depression until the hypomanic episodes become evident. Elisa suggests that for years she was rendered bedridden with crippling depression. But the hypomanic episodes seem to have intensified in the years of her writing. When she starts her college courses, more and more of her posts are incoherent stream of conscious diatribes written in all-caps. In many of these posts she acknowledged that she had not slept in twenty-four hours or more and hashtags them #hypomania. She wrote posts entitled "Adventures in Hypomania."

On June 1, she wrote a lengthy testimonial to her hypomanic episode:

> *For your viewing pleasure . . . my current adventure in hypomania*
>
> *I haven't slept in 24+ hours . . . Ok google let's see [how] you define hypomania*
>
> - *Inflated self-esteem or grandiosity (MY SELF-ESTEEM CAN HANDLE ANYTHING!!!)*
> - *More talkative than usual or pressure to keep talking I AM SENDING INTENSIVE MULTITEXTS ABOUT RANDOM THINGS TO FRIENDS!!! ALSO I AM WRITING A LOT ABOUT MYSELF AND PUTTING IT ON THE INTERNET*
> - *Distractibility (e.g., attention too easily drawn to*

> *unimportant or irrelevant external stimuli) . . . in math*
> *class I wasn't paying attention because I was working*
> *on my BRILLIANT EXTRAORDINARY IDEA and*
> *sketching madly . . .*
> • *Increase in goal-directed activity (either socially,*
>   *at work or school, or sexually) or psychomotor*
>   *agitation . . . I WILL DO ALL THE THINGS I HAVE*
>   *PUT OFF BECAUSE I CAN DO THIS I AM BATMAN.*
> • *Excessive involvement in pleasurable activities that*
>   *have a high potential for painful consequences (e.g.,*
>   *the person engages in unrestrained buying sprees,*
>   *sexual indiscretions, or foolish business investments).*
>   *This has yet to happen to me but OH BOY I LOOK*
>   *FORWARD TO WHEN I DO!!!!*

> *I'm not psychotic enough that I will jump off a bridge to*
> *test this brilliant, spectacular theory I have in [my] head.*

This post, which extends on in considerable length and grows more intense and incoherent, clearly suggests hypomania. Among the many aspects we could point out here, let's note that in one passage she acknowledges experiencing psychomotor agitation as well as the temptation to indulge in certain activities with a high potential for negative consequences.

The hypomania seems to have lasted for days, during which time she was hardly sleeping at all. Then, on June 13, she posted: "I'm sleeping a lot to avoid facing the fact I am a horrible student and may not be suited for university."

It seems she had finally crashed.

On October 26, Elisa wrote a sequel to her hypomania series, "Adventures in hypomania Part II," another rant in mostly capital letters in which she excitedly embraces her bipolar condition. It is also interesting to note that in the hashtags of this post she mentioned having run out of sleeping pills. Is she talking about prescription sleeping pills? If so, this is an additional prescription that has gone unreported. If this prescription was Ambien, it's possible that the lucid sleepwalking scenario, discussed by websleuths like John Lordan, may be worth considering.

By September 17, 2012, Elisa was terrified of her mental illness. The mood disorder component of bipolar was exhausting her, and she found herself angry and agitated much of the time. In a post from that day, we also see the return of suicidal ideation.

> *I want to kill myself*
> *it scares me so much that I am thinking about it because this is the lowest point to reach*
> *I've never ever attempted to kill myself*
> *I'm too much of a coward*
> *but I see no purpose in living anymore*
> *I'm waiting for this to pass and tomorrow it will hopefully be gone*
> *This is horrible but the reality is that if I want to be taken seriously, I will need to actually attempt suicide. My psychiaderp seems tired of my tears and I'm tired of dealing with me. It is up to me whether or not I want to change my situation she says.*

Once again, we see an obvious suggestion of suicidal ideation. Of additional importance is Elisa's characterization of her psychiatrist, who she believed is weary of treating her. Elisa would write elsewhere about her disdain for the triage system of Canadian healthcare, which she felt made it difficult to convince doctors of her suicidal risk. The only way to really do that, she believes, is to actually attempt suicide.

SEXUAL ASSAULT AS A MENTAL ILLNESS TRIGGER

Another troubling question worth considering is whether Elisa's psychiatric problems were triggered by a sexual assault trauma. It is widely believed that both severe bipolar disorder and depression can be set into motion by traumatic events. This is even more common in people who have a genetic predisposition toward mental illness.

I have not seen any other analysis of the following posts and they may be an important unreported aspect of the psychiatric dimension of this case.

Sexual assault is one of the most well-established traumatic events that can trigger mental illness. In fact, one study concluded that "80 percent of teenage girls" who are sexually assaulted experience mental illness afterward, sometimes for many years into adulthood. Was Elisa sexually assaulted at some point in her life? She addresses the issue twice in her blogs, directly yet paradoxically.

On September 1, 2012, Elisa wrote:

> *No I haven't been raped or abused. No I've never OD'd because I'm not addicted to anything. No I've never had an eating disorder. No I don't self-harm.*

This would seem to directly answer the question. However, a couple months later (perhaps after receiving more therapy?), she essentially contradicted herself and suggested she was a sexual assault victim:

> This theoretical trauma could also have been avoided, of course, if I'd never blogged at all. If I hadn't fallen in love with writing when I was six. If I'd developed a talent for something else. If I'd been born male. If I'd not been born at all—shit, if I'd only had the foresight not to be born at all, *I wouldn't have been raped when I was 17, either.* Seriously poor planning on my part–everyone knows the more invisible a woman is, the safer she is. You can't get more invisible than not existing!

One cannot conclude from these two statements alone whether Elisa was raped or not because she contradicts herself on it. The context of the posts does not clarify whether this was a real or imagined scenario. She uses the word "theoretical" once but then makes a very specific reference to being raped when she was 17. The overall psychological ambiguity may be more telling. The medical community commonly states that rape victims will often deny—even to themselves—that they were assaulted for years, sometimes decades.

If Elisa was a rape victim, it is a distinct possibility that the trauma of this triggered her years of depression or worsened it considerably. Later, as we assess the evidence for whether Elisa was the victim of a sexual predator prior to her death, it's important to keep in mind that she may have already been a victim before ever stepping foot in the Cecil. This could explain her enhanced state of alarm in the surveillance tape.

CASE CLOSED?

Many have questioned whether Elisa's bipolar disorder triggered full-blown psychosis. I've seen online debates between people who declare themselves to be on the spectrum of bipolar disorder disagreeing pretty intensely about whether the illness could manifest the symptoms Elisa was exhibiting, or whether it is even possible that a manic state could cause such a state of delusion as to convince someone to climb into a water tank.

One long account I read struck me as particularly relevant. In it, a person who identified as bipolar said he was "prone to acute manic episodes, and have experienced everything from mild hypomanic states to delusional mania that ended in full-on violent psychosis that landed [him] in jail."

As he watched the elevator surveillance, this man saw echoes of his own behavior during "mixed states." Using his own manic episodes as comparison, he argued that every one of Elisa's actions would have been logically justified in her mind.

"In my bipolar episodes," he wrote, "I went on shopping sprees and bought hundreds of Nerf toys, cosmetics (I'm male) and other weird random crap, decided to go on a cross-country bus trip to meet the President, dyed my hair and got tattoos, tried to legally change my name, believed I was on missions from God, etc."

One psychologist argued that Elisa's behavior in the surveillance tape is not particularly strange and does not seem like a psychotic break.

Another commenter wrote: "[It's] important to note that even if she was bipolar and symptomatic, she still could have been murdered. It just makes her an easy target. It also makes it more likely that her death would be written off as an accident."

In other words, Elisa experiencing a severe manic or psychotic break *and* being the victim of foul play are not mutually exclusive.

A large number of posters had begun to share their experiences with mental illness, depression, and bipolar disorder. Sites like Reddit and Websleuths ended up becoming de facto crowdsourcing platforms for identifying the symptoms of mental illness.

The question that had to be answered was could bipolar disorder cause such aberrant judgment as to lead someone to climb into a water tank on the dark roof of a hotel?

One woman, a moderator for the subreddit Unsolved Mysteries, took to Reddit to write out her thoughts on the case. Sam Oliver, or username hammy_sammy, started a thread entitled "Resolved: Elisa Lam (long, link heavy)" in which she described why she thought the case was solved.

Sam argued that in the absence of any evidence of foul play, the only logical conclusion was that Elisa climbed into the tank during a manic episode. "The symptoms of her mania—impulsiveness, sense of heightened abilities, hallucinations—would reasonably lead her to climb in the tank and shut the lid," Sam wrote. "God knows what she might have been hallucinating that motivated her to climb in that tank and shut it."

Sam also shared her own experience with mental illness, stating that about five years earlier she had suffered three psychotic breaks for which she was hospitalized for six weeks at a time. She wanted to offer an interpretation of the case from a "patient's perspective" that took the reality of mental illness into account. Very strange, irrational actions result from mania and psychosis. They can lead to deaths that look suspicious.

"[T]he case of Elisa Lam is not a mystery," she wrote. "It's a tragedy."

My interest in bipolar disorder resulted to some extent from the fact that it runs in my family. My aunt Jill had it. My memories of

Jill are of a sweet, vivacious woman who would cackle for hours with my mom. Despite this cackling, for years after her death I had struggled to comprehend that she had a mental illness.

This was also the case for several close friends of mine. Bipolar disorder took a significant toll on their lives, nearly causing death in some cases.

It seemed incredible to me that an illness native to so many people could be so misunderstood. Over two million Americans have it. To look at the larger picture, one in four American adults experience the effects of a mental illness in a given year. During that same time around the world, according to the World Health Organization (WHO), 800,000 people die from suicide. Yet how many conversations do you hear about these issues? If it weren't for the occasional celebrity suicide, we might not ever hear about it on the news or in social-media chatter.

A final bit of irony, in 2014, a writer/director team announced they were developing a horror movie based on the Elisa Lam case. The film was called *The Bringing*. They sold an option to the script to Sony for a six-figure advance, drawing the ire of the public, who charged them with exploitation.

I wondered if the people who were mad were aware that the vast majority of the online videos and blogs devoted to the subject were monetized with Google Adsense. Every time they clicked on one of these articles or videos, they were essentially feeding an industry that was financially gaining from the case and Elisa's death.

The plans for *The Bringing* were announced in March 2014, only days before World Bipolar Awareness Day.

CHAPTER 12

David and Yinna Lam vs. the Cecil Hotel

BY THE SUMMER OF 2015, I was on the verge of abandoning the case for good. The police had shut down their investigation and refused to comment on any aspect of it whatsoever. The Cecil Hotel also refused to comment.

My state of mind had worsened considerably, and I needed a change of pace. I packed up what remaining possessions had survived the purge of my apartment and drove to the East Mountains of Albuquerque, New Mexico, to live with my parents and work there remotely.

In 2015, Elisa's parents, David and Yinna, who hadn't made any public statements regarding the case, sued the Cecil Hotel for criminal negligence.

The lawsuit, filed by the Lam family attorneys, maintained that the Cecil Hotel bore criminal responsibility for Elisa's death because of the safety conditions on the roof. This lawsuit was important because it likely meant that the LAPD detectives would have to reveal some of their investigation notes. Such disclosures could include information regarding whether any witnesses or suspects were questioned.

The civil trial was set for February 2016 in Los Angeles superior court. I planned to be in attendance.

GETTING SICKER

Elisa hadn't slept in forty-eight hours. During that time, she left her room twice. In fact, she only left her bed three times. Twice to use the bathroom and sneak into the kitchen to scavenge for food and once to plug in the battery charger to her laptop.

Things had been good for a minute. Elisa's first major paper at the University of British Columbia was about Buddhism in China. She was confident in her abilities. She had a boyfriend she adored, who made her feel all the things rock ballad love songs talk about. The last time she had confessed her love to someone, it didn't work out so well; the guy saw her as more of a bro. But this time was different. Maybe she'd finally turned a corner.

He had "beautiful, intelligent eyes," and his relaxed body language had a way of neutralizing the pain and anger that sometimes consumed her. He was a computer science major and extremely smart about technical stuff. He knew how to work RAM graphic cards and load Starcraft games and fix her eternally shoddy computer and, most important, would calmly listen to her freak out for six hours, all the while saying, "It's ok. Computers are fixable."

Of course, he didn't know—and perhaps even Elisa didn't know—that what she was really freaking out about was her own mind, the faulty wiring of the graphics card within. But she imagined he was assuaging her fears over that, too. *It's ok. Brain chemistry is fixable. It's just like a computer. Right?*

But despite this great thing in her life and her excitement over college, the illness controlled her. And it wasn't long before it began to affect her life in every way.

It felt like her mind was deteriorating. She had tried multiple antidepressants before but they hadn't really worked. Her symptoms were like a game of whack-a-mole: When she treated one element, another would pop out; and when she went to treat that symptom, the original would return, with reinforcements. It was maddening and virtually impossible to describe to her family doctor, who was compassionate but confused.

Sometimes she wanted to run away, take a trip somewhere. But she knew that first she needed to get her shit together.

She was struggling to keep up with her course load. In December 2011, she had to withdraw from two courses, which devastated her.

Then she overslept one day and missed an exam that was worth 10 percent of her grade in another course.

The reason she overslept, paradoxically, was insomnia. For several nights prior to the day she missed her exam, she barely slept at all. She had stayed up all night on the Internet, primarily Tumblr.

When she looked back over what she had written, it was clear that something was wrong. There were multi-page diatribes in all caps about the most random subjects, an all-night binge of free association. It felt euphoric at the time. But when she crashed, she crashed hard. And the result was a major blow to her grade.

She considered banning herself from the Internet because it seemed to be fanning the flame of her ADD and mania, but then she realized her Internet use was an effect, not a cause. And, in many ways, Tumblr was helping her. She needed the Internet. She used Tumblr to record her life and, in the process of externalizing her inner chaos, to try and bring some order to it.

She had also found a small community of anonymous Tumblrs who shared some of her problems, namely loneliness. To one she wrote, "Pain and loneliness is universal" and she didn't know if she was convincing him or herself.

Elisa enjoyed writing. She loved the feeling of giving form to the inchoate thoughts rattling around in her head. By pressing publish, she was making visible an internal reality that was hard for her to articulate in conversation. Maybe someday someone would understand what she was going through.

After a particularly bad depressive spell that had left her bedridden and incommunicado for days, a Tumblr anon, fearing that something terrible had happened to her, asked what was going on. She assured her disembodied friend that she was just trying to spend less time online.

But Elisa needed medical help, and she knew it. She had convinced herself for so many years that she could handle the peculiarities of her brain chemistry. But the reality is she was losing control.

She could be at the top and it would come along and sink her to the bottom; and once she was at the bottom, it could scoop her up and take her to the top. It was almost as if someone was experimenting with her head. The illness—seemingly treatment resistant with constantly changing, multiplying symptoms—was now an even bigger part of her life, and she obsessed over it. Feared it. Wrote about it.

If she didn't get her shit together soon, she was going to have to drop out of school. She had already taken a six-month academic break the year before and she scolded herself for accomplishing nothing during that time. It seemed like her "most prized organ" didn't even work anymore. It was under attack by some condition that seemed to adapt, mutate, contort itself to fit in her life no matter if things were good or bad.

This was when she knew it was time to get serious about treatment. The illness was slowly but surely destroying her life. It was time to see a real psychiatrist. And if that didn't cut it, she had heard good things about electronic-convulsive treatment (ECT).

THE CIVIL LAWSUIT

On November 3, 2015, the Lam family attorneys, Thomas J. Johnston and Brian F. Needelman filed a motion at the Stanley Mosk Courthouse in Los Angeles accusing the Cecil Hotel of Negligence Causing Wrongful Death.

"As a result of Defendant's negligence, Plaintiffs [David and Yinna Lam] have suffered the loss of their daughter's love, companionship, comfort, care, and affection . . . [they] have incurred economic loss, including funeral and burial expenses."

Among other other things, the lawsuit alleged the Cecil Hotel management did not properly monitor access to the roof and water cisterns.

In response, attorneys for the Cecil Hotel stated that the "Decedent [Elisa Lam] was herself negligent and careless." Further, the defense actually named the plaintiffs themselves, Elisa's parents, as being negligent.

The Lam family attorneys had to file a special motion because they had sued the Cecil Hotel instead of the Stay On Main, which is what the Cecil Hotel Management had legally changed the building's name to after the media attention from the case. After nearly a century of bad reputation, the Cecil Hotel management was finally attempting to clean up its act . . . by changing its name.

In other deposition testimony, General Manager Amy Price confirmed that Elisa had checked into a shared dormitory room, 506B, on January 28 and was booked to check out three days later on February 1st. The hotel received complaints, Price stated, from Elisa's roommates about her strange behavior and on the 31st, Elisa was moved to a private room on the same floor.

Price further stated that the water cisterns run on a gravity operated system whereby water is pumped from a main water line at street level. The tanks, situated on the northern border of the hotel, are "difficult to access" and restricted from guests. Both Price and Chief Engineer Pedro Tovar stated that the only ways to access the roof are three exterior fire escapes and an interior staircase connecting the 15th floor to the roof. The door is equipped with an alarm that, if activated, issues a loud sound on the 14th and 15th floors and at the front desk.

According to hotel management, this alarm was not activated at any point in January or February 2013.

Price said she was not aware of any guest trespassing on the hotel roof. Pedro Tovar, who had worked for the hotel for thirty years, described the difficulty of accessing the water tanks.

"The tanks are on a platform approximately 4 feet above the roof," he attested. "To access the tanks, someone would have to climb a ladder up the platform, and then squeeze through the tanks and plumbing equipment to reach another ladder and climb up the side of the 10-foot-tall tank. The tanks are fully covered though each has a heavy metal lid that is approximately 18" by 18"."

Tovar further stated that he accompanied LAPD investigators and the K-9 unit on their search of every floor and the roof. Tovar said they searched the roof but nobody climbed the water tanks and looked inside them. This is an important detail because it confirms that investigators spent time on the roof with the K-9 unit. Let's consider that there are conflicting reports as to whether the lid of the tank in which Elisa was found was open or closed. Santiago Lopez, the maintenance worker who discovered the body, stated the lid was open.

In the pre-trial hearings, the Lam family attorneys entered into evidence the declaration of Brad P. Avrit, a licensed civil engineer, in opposition to the Cecil Hotel lawyers' Motion for Summary Judgment.

Avrit's analysis led him to conclude that the rooftop area of the Cecil Hotel presented a danger to its tenants, especially given that it was evident that tenants and guests had accessed the roof over the years and left graffiti behind. He said the hatch door of the water tanks were "not secured via any locking mechanism" and that the hotel could not have been certain that only trained personnel would access the tanks.

"Once a person, whether intentionally or inadvertently, were to go into the subject rooftop water tank," Avrit stated, "there were no grab bars, access ladder, etc., essentially creating a confined space in which there were no reasonable means of safe exit available."

The insecure nature of the water tank hatches also "created a potential safety hazard to all occupants of the building, in allowing for intentional contamination of the water supply being utilized by all guest rooms."

Further, Avrit noted three critical points that shed light on the rooftop situation: one, that the water tanks were accessible by a wooden ladder that was in place at the time of the accident; two, that there were no surveillance cameras in place at the access points of the roof; and three, it is quite possible that the stairwell door alarm was not working properly.

One of John Lordan's biggest problems—and mine—involved the fact that no scent was picked up on the roof. It only takes a single touch for DNA to be transferred and its scent sticks around for weeks. Yet, the LAPD appears to have discovered no trace evidence. No fingerprints, no scent.

John calls this "a big glaring hole." How do you rule out foul play if you can't determine the path she took on the roof? And if you can't establish with trace evidence that she walked up there and touched things with her hands, how can you even be sure she moved up there on her own accord?

You can't rule out foul play just because there's no obvious body trauma, John stated. Elisa could have been led to the roof at gunpoint. Or she could have died from a more accidental manslaughter scenario and been carried there.

What's even more incomprehensible is that once the detectives were on the roof, they did not search the tanks. To understand how absurd that is, you have to take a look at the roof and realize that there's virtually nothing else up there. There's the utility room and the tanks—that's it. By this point, four or five days from the time she disappeared, there's no way it would not have occurred to investigators that they were likely looking for a corpse.

It makes you wonder, John brazenly stated in a video, whether the LAPD investigated the roof at all.

Instead what we have, he points out, is a circular loop of logic— almost a tautology—between the investigators and the coroners: The detectives say that the death was an accident based on the coroner's findings; and the coroners say the death was an accident based largely on what the investigators say.

The conspiracy side of John just couldn't help but find it weird that the three principal witnesses in the deposition statements continually repeated that the LAPD did not check the water tanks. It sounded to him like people being coached and helping each other out.

John was definitely right about at least one thing. If there was any chance of new information coming out, it was from this civil case. I made a vow at that point to be at the trial.

I thought about whether Elisa's parents would be there or not. It pained me to think of them, to imagine the nightmare they were going through. Though I wanted to speak with them, to hear their thoughts about what may have happened to Elisa, I did not want to bother them. Despite the thousands upon thousands of news articles and videos about the case, there was not one interview with the parents or Elisa's sister.

But I couldn't help but wonder whether the family believed Elisa's death was an accident. It was so rare in these true-crime cases for the victim's family to not voice their opinion on what happened. It lent another veil of mystery to the case, in addition to the silence of the hotel and the LAPD.

As if on cue, I saw a comment on a YouTube thread, by a user named Mark, who wrote: "I have heard from the family. I know what happened to Elisa. This was not an accident. That's what they want you to think. I wanted the family to know what I know, they deserve that. This case must be reopened."

I shook my head. Another day, another bizarre claim. But I sent a message to the user and said I wanted to talk to him.

I left the garage, where my whiteboard of thoughts about the case glowed from a green LED, and entered the hallway. My mother, who I thought had gone to bed, stood in her white nightgown staring at a framed photo. Though it was dark and I could not see her face, hands or feet, the gown picked up the moonlight and shimmered like some spectral shape, at certain angles almost warping into iridescent gossamer. I once told my mom that the gown made her look like a ghost.

"It's the ghost," I said, momentarily startling her. Then she cackled.

"I thought you were asleep," she said.

"I thought you were, too."

I walked over to my mom and gave her a hug.

"Are you working on the case?" she asked.

I imagined how devastated she would be if something happened to me, something horrible, like what happened to Elisa. She might not make it. She would fall apart; there would be no consoling her. This kind of loss has no human quantification. Then I thought about that loss becoming an international spectacle, with millions of people writing about me and making videos with my face, turning me into a ghoulish meme on the Internet.

Just more poison to their souls. I wanted to give it up, to not feed this industry of predatory true crime, which increasingly resembled a zero-sum game where tragedy equaled views, subscribers, and dollars. But I couldn't back down now. I felt to the depth of my soul that there was something more here.

"Yes," I responded.

CHAPTER 13

Friends and Enemies of Occam's Razor

THE SKY DUMPED SEVERAL FEET OF SNOW that winter, and for almost two weeks we remained indoors. Occasionally I would go for a walk to smoke my e-cigarette and get some air. But I spent most of my time in my room, reading. Though I considered myself done with the Lam case, I couldn't help but continue tracking some of the articles, forums, and comment threads still popping up online.

I stayed up until ungodly hours reading the newest conspiracy theories on the case, following the strangest breadcrumbs down the most unlikely of rabbit holes. As my depression worsened and diversified, some of the more extreme conspiracy theories became a perverse form of therapy.

I knew it was wrong, that it trivialized a tragedy, and while I didn't believe any of them, I was fascinated by the depth and granularity of the world-building involved. Many of them were variations on popular conspiracies, updated for the modern era, which tapped into ancient anxieties, archetypes, and pathologies.

MIND CONTROL, SATANIC CULTS, AND OTHER CONVERSATION STARTERS

The extreme end of the conspiracy spectrum in this case features some astonishingly disturbing ideas, made even more disturbing by the level of detail underpinning them. There is conspiracy around the Invisible Light Agency (ILA), an enigmatic, probably defunct, company whose Google maps address places it inside or next to the Cecil Hotel. Conspiracists usually tie this in with Elisa's tweet about a new invisibility cloak technology to make the argument that Elisa was the subject of some sinister experiment involving an invisible assailant.

Most of the conspiracies are variations on a couple themes, namely that (1) a secret cabal used the Cecil Hotel for nefarious purposes and (2) some kind of experiment, ritual, or sacrifice took place, and Elisa became unwittingly ensnared in it.

The secret cabal variable often features the Illuminati (more recently referred to as the New World Order, the Globalists, or the Deep State), satanic cults, Masonic secret societies, paramilitary black-ops groups, snuff filmmakers, and various combinations therein. The experiment variable ranges from occult sacrifices and satanic rituals to mind control psychological operations (psyops), clandestine technology proofs of concept, and false-flag bio-war attacks.

The most detailed conspiracy may be that the tuberculosis outbreak going on in downtown LA at that time was a false-flag biological experiment. Elisa was either the viral host (conspiracists point to her post in which she says she has the flu) in a population-control scheme or the perfect patsy for a bio-war attack waged by the government on its own people and then blamed on a domestic or international terrorist organization. And the fact that the tuberculosis test was actually named LAM-ELISA meant, of course, that the news headline of Elisa Lam's death would be a media-embedded signal to other operatives that the project was underway.

Other notable details from these conspiracies:

- Since witchcraft celebrates a "holy" day on February 1st and Elisa disappeared at midnight of that day, she must have been a human-sacrifice victim for a satanic gathering at the Cecil Hotel to celebrate Imbolc. And the mysterious black hairs found on Elisa's body during the autopsy prove this.
- A satanic cabal of elites organized a snuff film and conscripted high-ranking LAPD members to be involved, thus protecting them legally. A more "ma n' pop"-minded conspiracist thinks it was a low budget "found footage" or indie horror film by a run-of-the-mill psychopath.

One of the more noxious, and surprisingly frequent, conspiracies suggests the Elisa in the surveillance video was an imposter Elisa, a "crisis actor." The crisis actor concept has become popular in the last decade within some conspiracy circles, especially in response to school shootings. The basic idea is that the government hires operatives to play victims and their family members pretend to be sad in order to push propaganda into the mainstream media narrative.

I personally can't imagine a more vile accusation to make against someone who has lost a loved one than to say that loved one never existed in the first place. It's as though you would rob them of even their memories of that person.

A more light-hearted conspiracy posits that Elisa was playing the "Elevator Game," an urban legend that pressing a certain sequence of buttons in an elevator will allow you to access alternate dimensions and contact the beings who dwell there.

My favorite conspiracy (it's actually more of a synchronicity) involves none other than the godfather of occultists, Aleister Crowley. Apparently, in 1889, he wrote a poem while staying at the prestigious Hotel Cecil in London, after which the Los Angeles Cecil was named. The poem is entitled *Jephtha*, after a figure in the early Jewish text by Pseudo-Philo. Jeptha has a daughter named Seila, who is a symbolic human sacrifice. *Seila*, of course, is an anagram for *Elisa*.

The beginning of them poem reads:

– Let my LAMp, at midnight hour,
– BEEN SEEN IN SOME HIGHLY TOWER
– Where I may oft outwatch the Bear
– The spirit of Plato, to unfold.
– What Worlds, or what vast Regions hold
– The immortal mind that hath forsook
– HER MANSION IN THE FLESHY NOOK.

Conspiracists remark that this poem seems to be about a human sacrifice whose name is an anagram for Elisa; it takes place at midnight (almost the exact time Elisa supposedly went missing) and the sacrifice is "fleshy" in a "highly tower." This would seem to describe Elisa being found naked in a water tank on top of the hotel.

The kicker is that Crowley developed an entire philosophical system of thought, known as Thelema, which revolves entirely around an interdimensional alien or demon named—wait for it—LAM.

The Most Absurd Conspiracy Theory in History

Earlier, I mentioned seeing a comment in a forum thread in which a user by the name of Mark claimed to have direct evidence of what happened to Elisa. He claimed to "know what happened, how it happened" and more. He even claimed to be in contact with her parents about discussing a course of action.

I sent Mark a message telling him I would like to speak with him, and he responded with his phone number. We texted a bit before the call. He identified himself as a sixty-two-year-old man and talked up his credentials by saying he had worked on about thirty cold cases and had solved more than half of them, doing so in only a few hours and without even leaving his house.

A couple days later, I called him and for the first five minutes or so, Mark seemed to be reasonable and knowledgeable of the case. He also seemed to be genuinely passionate about it.

Mark said that his revelations of what happened to Elisa resulted only from close inspection of the surveillance tape. He used a special web tool that allowed him to zoom in super close on the pixels.

At some point in the conversation, Mark's rhetoric took a marked departure as he started referring to what was really going on in the elevator. He claimed that with the assistance of his tool he could see "a combination of belts and clamps" that kept "[Elisa's] entire body bound such that it stays firm instead of limbs flopping around. They put a strap over the top of her head to hold it steady."

Elisa is dead in the surveillance video, Mark said. A group of men are using pulleys and straps to manipulate her movements like a puppet.

Mark kept talking but my eyes glazed over. Was this a joke? Was he trolling me?

As he continued, I realized he wasn't kidding. He actually believed what he was saying: The surveillance video was a performance to make people think she lost her mind; she was already dead and her murderers were part of a satanic cult who used Elisa for a ritual sacrifice.

"I know you don't believe me," Mark said. "Trust me, I know what it sounds like. Most people think I'm crazy. But you gotta think outside the box. There's a lot more going on in this reality than most people can handle."

"Mark. I, uh . . ." I started to respond and then stopped. There was nothing to say.

It seems as though the Elisa Lam case taps into a raw anxiety, an exposed nerve that drives people to need to understand the unknown and explain the irrational.

As someone who self-identified as a conspiracy theorist for over a decade, I found myself troubled by the conspiracy theories in the Lam case. These ideas hurt the case, damaging the relationship between websleuths and law enforcement and stigmatizing the victim. But it went beyond that. There was something bigger going on here. But in my current state, I couldn't figure it out.

IS THERE A BAR AT ROCK BOTTOM?

In February of that year I drove from Albuquerque to Lake Tahoe for the wedding of two close friends of mine. Prior to leaving, my mother (a legendary worry-wart) continually questioned my plan to drive alone into an area that could easily be covered in ice. But I bought chains for my tires and ensured her it was safe. She was aware of my psychological problems but did not know the severity of it, nor did my dad.

It occured to me how similar my situation was to Elisa's. Struggling with psychiatric problems on the cusp of a solo trip.

On the way, my mood worsened and I self-medicated with painkillers. Some ice fell but I drove through it without stopping to put chains on my tires—because I'm a rebel.

On the day of the wedding itself, I mixed alcohol, painkillers,

Xanax, and marijuana. After the wedding, during a late-night party I blacked out but was apparently still physically walking around. I woke up the next day with a vague, horrified feeling that I had done something wrong. It turns out I had heckled a few speakers. My speech, in which I evidently referenced "galaxies" several times, had been weird. And at some point in the night I knocked a chair over.

I apologized profusely and was forgiven. But I was mortified. Then I realized I had missed calls on my phone. One of them a number I didn't recognize and the others . . . my mother and sister. Uh oh. In horror I realized I had neglected to call my mom and tell her I was ok. She'd spent two nights thinking I was dead. I called her, and the moment she heard my voice she burst into tears. I felt awful.

Then I called my sister and she was disappointed in me. Unfortunately, she'd been left to field the neurotic calls from my mother wondering if her only son was buried in ice.

I drove home more disappointed in myself than I've ever been in my entire life. Depression and drug abuse were slowly unraveling me, straining friendships, encumbering my family, turning me into something I no longer recognized. I've experienced intense phases of depression before, but nothing like this.

There was another storyline here that I was struggling to put into words. There was something different about my mind. A mutation was occurring.

A few hours outside of Albuquerque, I entered a thick snowstorm that eliminated all visibility. A white fog descended and engulfed everything. Before it registered that I should slow down, I hit a patch of black ice, and my car surged into a high-speed 360-degree spin in the middle of the freeway.

In suspended motion, I braced for the end. This is it. The life of Jake cutting off mid-sentence. Back to the primordial ether. Back to the Source—whatever I was before I was born.

If there had been other vehicles on the road, it most surely would have been the end. But my car came to a rest angled diagonally across three lanes of the freeway.

I had lost control. Literally and figuratively. Completely and totally. I sat there lost in a fog, nearly equidistant between family and friends and yet with no direction or plan as to how to get back on track.

Where did I belong? The answer, in my current state, was nowhere. It was the one thing I knew for certain.

THE UFO CONFERENCE

I briefly considered going to Peru for an Ayahuasca clinic after reading about how the psychedelic can help depression by paving new neural pathways. New research on psilocybin (mushrooms) and ketamine made an even stronger link. But I thought about the possibility of me totally freaking out on Ayahuasca and instead opted for a conference in the Joshua Tree desert.

A couple days before I left, I went on a walk in the woods with my parents. While reminiscing about our late Beagles, Dominique and Collette, I spotted something ahead of us, a piece of paper in the middle of the deserted trail. I picked it up and gazed upon a coloring book image of a ghost in a flying saucer, a partially colored-in kids' illustration of a UFO.

We hadn't seen a single other person, yet here was this artifact deposited conspicuously in the middle of the trail before us. And I marveled at the synchronicity—because, you see, the next day I was set to depart for my Joshua Tree event, which was: a UFO conference.

Contact in the Desert started as exactly what you would expect from the UFO desert in the middle of the Joshua Tree desert—a fringe gathering of conspiracy theorists, UFOlogists, and paranormal researchers that almost borders on cult-like.

This year the desert floor at 29 Palms reached blistering temperatures as high as 113. The speaker list was a who's who of the fringe field, including George Noory, Giorgio Tsoukalis, Jim Marrs, Stanton Friedman, Erich Van Daniken, Linda Moulton Howe, David Wilcock, Richard Dolan, Daniel Sheehan, Clyde Lewis, Travis Walton, and David Paulides.

I immediately looked for Clyde Lewis and found him sitting behind the Ground Zero merch booth. Beside him, his producer, Ron

Patton, energetically engaged with some fans. I introduced myself and told him I'd been a long-time fan of his. Then I casually mentioned how some of his shows touched upon the case I was working on.

"What case is that?" he asked.

"The Elisa Lam case," I responded, casually.

His eyes lit up, as I knew they would, and we went down the rabbit hole together. By the end, he told me he wanted me to be a guest on the show.

As the sun set over Joshua Tree, an incredible purplish crimson glow bathed the land, casting shadows over the vast tableau of yucca trees that turned into psychedelic Samurai frozen in their final battlefield death gasp. The temperature dropped, breaking the heat, and my father and I wandered out into the trees, discussing the limits of human knowledge. My father is much more of a skeptic than myself when it comes to conspiracy theories, especially paranormal activity. We'd had countless arguments over the JFK assassination.

We ate edibles and gazed at the trees. I took pictures of him in his turtle-like hat and asked him when he was going to finish his Vietnam novel. He'd once told me the Vietnam War was a great hole in American history.

"Never," he said.

I guess the hole had grown larger.

I told him the story of the previous year, when I had attended the conference with Jared, my college-roommate-turned-lifelong-partner-in-creative-neurosis. We'd come to the same section of the desert, across the highway from the lecture halls. Jared took pictures in the "golden hour," the short window of time between dusk and night when a beautiful, almost otherworldly glow redefines the landscape.

He was looking through his pictures later when, suddenly, he said, "What in the hell?" and motioned for me to come over.

I looked at the picture. In the sky above the desert where we stood, a small orblike shape hung in the sky over us. He scrolled to the next picture: The orb was there too, though its position had changed slightly; and in the following half dozen pictures, the orb remained, moving in a semi-circle above us.

We looked at each other and then looked up. A few moments passed during which the two of us entertained the notion that we may have been under surveillance by a UFO, or at least a government drone.

I recalled Steven Greer, a well-known UFO whistleblower, who conducted a meditation at Vero Beach in 2016. He told his adherents that UFOs would soon appear as they guided and welcomed the visitors with pure consciousness. Suddenly, an ember orblike light appeared in the sky above the ocean; a few moments later, a second orb appeared, illuminating the sky with a lambent glow. The people in attendance gasped in shock.

"Let's welcome them," Greer said to his adherents.

"So you really believe this stuff?" my dad asked after I told him the story.

"I'm not sure. In a universe this big and absurd, our conception of reality will always be limited and flawed."

"You've heard of Occam's Razor, right?"

I groaned. I hate Occam's Razor.

I recalled journalist Josh Dean, who wrote one of the better articles about the Elisa Lam case, telling me that he was only able to get one response from the LAPD regarding the case and it was from Detective Tim Marcia.

"Good detectives," Marcia said, "operate under this principle: Occam's Razor—'Other things being equal, a simpler explanation is better than a more complex one.' In other words, when you hear hoofbeats, think horses, not zebras. Once the horses are eliminated, then move on to the zebras . . ."

I recalled what happened a week after Jared photographed the orb in the sky. He was looking through other pictures of random things around his house when he saw the orb again but this time overlaid against a wall.

The orb was not a UFO but rather a digital artifact inside his camera.

And some debunkers claim there was a naval training exercise called COMPUTEX going on near Vero Beach when Greer summoned his spiritual UFOs, though, to be fair, I haven't seen a single report confirming that.

Occam's Razor, once again, makes its move.

The Cemetery Synchronicity

Back at the conference, a voice called to me out of the din of conversations. It was Ron. He stood beside what looked at first like a post-goth rock-star couple.

"I was just talking about you," Ron said. "They're working on the Elisa Lam case, too."

"They" were Frank and Genevieve, a married paranormal researcher team. I remembered instantly that they had been on Ground Zero with Clyde Lewis talking about the synchronicities of the case.

Genevieve is Chinese-American and speaks with a slight but crisp British accent; she has dark green hair and blue eyeliner. Frank is Salvadoran whose parents fled here in the 1980s to escape the horrific violence of the CIA-fomented right-wing revolution there.

"Oh, have you heard about the cemetery synchronicity?" Genevieve asked me with a smile.

"What is that?"

Apparently, The Last Bookstore, they explained, hired a registrant privacy company that manages its website. The registrant company's business address is a PO Box on Canada Way in Burnaby, a suburb in Vancouver. Burnaby happens to be where Elisa and her family lived. Additionally, and this is really the kicker, the postal/zip code listed on the Last Bookstore's registrant info shows up in Google Maps as being located within the Forest Lawn Cemetery, the same cemetery where Elisa was buried.

"What in the actual hell . . ."

I looked this up and it's real. It's certainly possible that someone is running an elaborate prank (which, given the hysteria over the case, wouldn't surprise me), but the base-level info is factual.

MISSING 411 AND AN UNEXPECTED CONNECTION

The next day I attended David Paulides' presentation. Paulides is a former cop who is on a crusade to document thousands of mysterious disappearances around the country.

In his *Missing 411* books, Paulides notes recurring characteristics to these cases. In many of them, the person had just been seen by a friend and disappeared very quickly, sometimes in close proximity to a group. Sometimes their voices are heard faintly, as though they are there but concealed in some way. One child who disappeared was seen briefly at the top of a high cliff that he couldn't have possibly reached on his own.

Frequently, bloodhounds are unable to pick up a scent and, in many cases, bodies are found in conspicuous areas that have already been searched many times.

In the course of his work, Paulides assessed around 2,000 cases and found eerie similarities and patterns: The disappearances are clustered in twenty-eight distinct areas; the victims are usually found in water or national parks; the cause of death is either anomalous or difficult to ascertain, even by trained coroners; sometimes victims are found conspicuously laid out in spots that were searched multiple times by investigators.

About eighty minutes into the presentation, I realized in horror that I hadn't urinated in at least ten hours. My bladder was full to bursting as I sat at the back of the conference hall. I drink a lot of water anyway, but in the hot desert environs I was a veritable porpoise.

I side-shuffled down the row of sitting people and was about to reach the exit when suddenly I heard a familiar name . . .

"Canadian tourist, Elisa Lam . . ."

I stopped and looked up. Paulides was discussing the Lam case. I couldn't believe it. What did Elisa have to do with disappearances in national parks?

He started going over some of the basics of the case but I couldn't concentrate because of the ten-pound medicine ball of urine throbbing against my pelvis. As much I as desperately wanted to stay and listen, I had to leave.

By the time I got back, the conference hall had let out, and the crowd dispersed. I made my way back over to the merch area. About 15 minutes later, I saw Paulides, satchel in hand, return to his booth, where his books lay stacked on a table. When I came moseying around, he gave me an uninterested once-over, gulped some water, and checked his phone. Then he pointed to the table of his books.

I bought the volume where he discusses the Lam case and immediately flipped through to that section.

Paulides says that Coast to Coast AM host George Knapp predicted that the harrowing phenomenon described in the first five *Missing 411* books would eventually move to the city. Sure enough, it did. In Paulides' sixth book, *Missing 411: A Sobering Coincidence,* he covers cases in which people inexplicably vanish from crowded areas, buildings, bars—some of them heavily alarmed and surveilled.

In this book, Paulides devotes about ten pages to the Elisa Lam case, calling it "one of the most mysterious disappearances [he has] ever investigated."

What shocked me is reading that many of the characteristics of the Lam case, which I considered to be random and arbitrary, turned out to fit into some of the profiles Paulides had established in previous books. In other words, as extraordinary and unusual as the Elisa Lam case is, he believes it is part of a pattern.

Many of the cases involved surveillance footage being captured shortly before the person's disappearance but not revealing how the person got from point A to point B. Many of the cases featured inconclusive autopsies in which accidental drowning is attributed but not proven.

Kevin Gannon and D. Lee Gilbertson, a retired police officer and criminologist respectively, analyzed many of these cases and about a dozen other suspicious drowning cases and wrote about them in their book *Case Studies in Drowning Forensics.* Paulides references their analysis throughout his work.

After surmising that many of the victims were in fact murdered, Gannon and Gilbertson come to a chilling and controversial conclusion regarding these cases, which they believe may be connected to the Smiley Face Killer murders: "They cannot be touched. They cannot be caught. They are superior. This is the collective mentality of an organization of killers."

A majority of the parents in these cases suspect murder and have begged for additional autopsies and independent analysis. Many of these parents are adamant that the death of their loved one was neither an accident or suicide and that local law enforcement are using the designation of "accidental drowning" to forego further investigation.

I have problems with some of Paulides' analysis, and his followers often jump to extraordinary, uncorroborated conclusions, ranging from alien abductions to Bigfoot and cannibal cults. But Paulides' perspective regarding the efforts of law enforcement agencies to distort, conceal, and whitewash the results of missing persons and homicide investigations is spot-on.

Paulides poses an important question: "Can anything positive come from not telling the public the absolute truth about a death? . . . After the trial," he continues, "it should be made available to the public."

Paulides, who is himself a former cop, concludes by asserting that police departments sometimes distort information and investigation conclusions for the sake of placating worried community members.

CHAPTER 14
Inbound Train

I WAS TORN. Assuming Elisa's death had to have been a homicide ignores the complex nature of psychiatric conditions. People who claimed there's no chance Elisa could have climbed in on her own, for example, demonstrated a poor understanding of the variability of hypomania and psychosis.

On the other hand, chalking it all up to mental illness runs the risk of scapegoating a condition that millions of people safely live with every day. And to ignore the many suspicious anomalies in the case risked depriving Elisa of justice. What if she *had* been the victim of a predator? What an awful thing to be murdered and then posthumously branded with such an ignominious identity.

As the train passed through the dark desert planes of Arizona, I recalled that earlier that year a man on psychedelics ran into the Burning Man while on psychedelics and died. It was the same year, another friend of mine had done the exact same thing in a different setting and sustained life-threatening injuries.

I have many friends and loved ones who abstain from psychiatric pharmaceuticals despite having clear symptoms of illnesses. In some cases, these symptoms have caused severe manic episodes, debilitating and life-threatening injuries, and even suicide attempts. The refusal to take meds is not always rooted in philosophy, but certainly the denial of the existence of mental illness sometimes takes the form of a spiritual discipline, a belief that with self-actualization one can control and eliminate one's own negative thought patterns.

Some argue that psychiatric illness doesn't even exist in the first place, that society is pathologizing what are genuine, if sometimes eccentric, expressions of human consciousness marooned in a sick society.

One of my friends, who had nearly died a few years earlier, told me some kind of energy healer cured his bipolar disorder with hypnotism. I worried about this and we debated the issue. I'm sympathetic to the belief that many pathologies are reactions to society and open to the belief that the human mind can write new source code for itself. I also see virtue in rebelling against the homogenization of social behavior and consensus reality. But there's a slippery slope there that must be acknowledged.

I opened Elisa's blog document again. This time I wasn't looking for evidence of a killer (that would have to wait a few months). I wanted to put myself in the mind of Elisa and figure out how she got to that rooftop.

MANSLAUGHTER

Perhaps the surveillance tape showed her after an encounter with some men or women at the hotel during which she had either smoked something or been accidentally dosed with something. Toxicology showed no illicit drugs but it did not test for GHB or any number of other "date rape" drugs. It's worth considering whether Elisa was dosed with a date rape drug when you consider that something like GHB can produce strange behavior and hallucinations. It is also often used for the purposes of rendering a partner unable to fight back or remember a sexual assault. Elisa was found naked in the water tank, and her clothes were with her, floating in the water.

I have wondered more than once whether Elisa's death was voluntary manslaughter after an attempted date rape. Perhaps Elisa made new friends, or met up with online friends in person for the first time. Perhaps she befriended a hotel tenant or employee. A person or persons dosed Elisa and because she was still on a couple meds, it didn't slow her down as much as it might normally have. But it did cause her to exhibit unusual behavior, which we saw a glimpse of in the surveillance video. "Date rape" drugs, like Rohypnol, slow down the central nervous system and can cause dizziness, impaired judgement, loss of motor control (which might, in some circumstances, look like psychomotor agitation), confusion, and even excitability.

Perhaps the drug was just kicking in when we saw her. After she left the view of the elevator surveillance, she restlessly made her way to the roof just as the full effects of her dose kicked in. Her "new friends," who had kept an eye on her and followed her through the hotel, then joined Elisa on the roof, where they found her lying down, one side of her clothes covered in a sand-like gravel spread across the surface of the roof (if you remember, the autopsy says there was a "sand-like particulate" on her clothes).

Elisa, who was by then completely still, had also stopped breathing. After removing her clothes, the men realized Elisa was dead or close to death. They panicked. Looking around the roof, they realized there was no way to transport Elisa's body back into the hotel without someone seeing. Their only option was to conceal the body on the roof. But where?

They spotted the water tanks. By the time anyone found her, they'd be in a different state. Except for the employee, who might have reasoned differently; or the tenant, who perhaps viewed this as revenge against a hotel rumored to be considering kicking out low-income residents.

Or maybe it was an online follower, someone with an unhealthy infatuation who read Elisa's travel-itinerary post, and decided to try and meet her in person.

THE KILLER'S SHOE

Websleuth Marcel F messaged me his thoughts on Elisa's mysterious death. He'd tried unsuccessfully to get the case looked at by politicians, the American Embassy in Calgary; he even contacted the RCMP and tried to get the attention of Prime Minister Justin Trudeau.

Marcel, after analyzing the surveillance video, believes you can actually see the killer's shoe for a fraction of a second right at the moment before Elisa disappears from the frame.

"I profoundly believe there is a two-toned black and white shoe in the footage . . ." Marcel wrote. "According to my breakdown of her last movements, her hair is grabbed, and then she is forced to step around someone. Her foot movements are, two left shuffles, one right step, a left step over someone, and then her right leg swings around, as the right leg is seen in the video."

I studied these frames in slow-mo over and over again. The moment Marcel refers to as revealing the "two-toned black and white shoe" of the killer looks to me like Elisa's foot juxtaposed against the floor at an odd angle. But I could be wrong.

Psycho #5

January 25, 2013. The train to Southern California lurched almost imperceptibly into motion. For a moment, she felt disoriented. A sense of weightlessness in a 10,000-ton kinetic machine. Then the vertigo set in. And the tunnel vision of a scene that wasn't all there—artifacting, imprecise patchwork, like reality itself was shifting and reshuffling based on the movement of her head. These were her latest symptoms.

Perfectly geometric beams of dusk sunlight streamed through the windows, intersecting and merging at odd angles, illuminating random body parts, tufts of hair and bald spots. The sides of passengers' faces glowed as they turned to talk and laugh, grab things, settle in for the overnight trip. They seemed so calm and happy, so balanced. In the flow.

Elisa was most certainly not in the flow. In fact, the only time she felt in the flow was during an episode. High price to pay for a few hours of clarity and confidence.

Right now, she needed electricity or she would die. Not literally, but almost. She needed Internet access, and her shitty laptop wouldn't run without being plugged in at all times. She hated her computer, but it was the only beast that could take her into the cyberworld. If she was able to get a full-time promotion at the Pacific National Exhibition (PNE), maybe she could upgrade.

Internet, I need you, she thought. She was quite open about her emotional dependence on Tumblr.

Elisa had broken up with her boyfriend right after getting back from Toronto. Or, more accurately, he had broken up with her. Officially, he worded it as wanting a "break," which according to her sister meant he wasn't happy in the relationship but didn't want to send her into a downward spiral of even worse depression.

She rifled into her bag and pulled out her laptop. After logging into the Amtrak wi-fi, she brought up the admin page for her blog Ether Fields and, remembering a recent reunion with old friends, started a new post:

> . . . *Evidence that I do have amazing beautiful things in my life and even though everyone is busy and going off doing great things, they do care about me. I'm not a professional depressed person. I am so much more than that and these people are my reminders that I am very lucky. Life is long and difficult and people will always be stupid and complain. But it is worth it so long as you have special moments. There will be lots of these moments in the future and there have been a lot in the past. So what if everything is shit and all the plans have gone to hell. If I ask for help, someone might even be willing to spare a hand. Thank you friends, family and tumblr.*

A rush of endorphins, serotonin, and dopamine—the first and most primal drugs—danced around in her head. She felt the joy coming, rising up from within her. A pulse of positivity that streaked through her and lit up a thousand thoughts.

And, looking around the train, she realized that she loved everyone aboard. This was the angle, this was her path to self-actualization. All success and triumph stemmed from that core principle of joy and gratitude in the moment. With hard work and patience, she could be a famous blogger someday. She could do whatever she wanted.

"If only I could bottle this excess happiness for the future."

It was her secret weapon, and no one would be able to stop her. This was the jaw-dropping secret that all the greats had discovered long ago: Embrace the chaos and stand for love in its midst. This is exactly what she had wanted, to escape from the stale prison of her daily experience and do something new, something completely un-precedented. To hell with school, to hell with the naysayers.

This was the start of her West Coast Tour, her prison break. She didn't even know exactly where she was going. Most likely San Di-ego, Santa Cruz. Possibly Los Angeles. It didn't matter, as long as it was outside of her room in Vancouver.

She opened two new browser windows. Once she had added a few images to the post, she published it and then blasted it out on Twitter and Tumblr. She reblogged and retweeted several other posts.

"Bless the internet," she wrote. "All those who wish to find a way to express their sadness can go there and feel less alone."

The final crimson rays of the falling sun disappeared.

A man seated several rows up suddenly turned his head and made eye contact with her. It didn't last long, but it was enough to set into motion the realization of a fear she'd ignored for days. It had to do with the very Internet she so adored. Suddenly she was appalled at the fact that she'd posted her travel itinerary, her destinations, and even the dates.

How many guys had messaged her out of the blue on Tumblr? she thought. Her paranoia over online followers searching for her in real life had never been more pronounced.

Why had the man looked this way? she thought. She retraced the last few hours, searching the files of her mind for the moments when she selected that particular train car. Images of that man now sur-faced, and the look of his eyes, the nuance of his gaze, felt familiar. Had he followed her to this car? Had he followed her online?

She felt a familiar pin prick of anxiety and then multiple pricks. The panic rushed in over her like a wave, overwhelming, debilitat-ing. She sat in a train, yet in her mind she was marooned in the froth of a stormy sea on a moonless night.

She took her only lifeline. Opening up her laptop, she started a new post on Tumblr and let the fear spill into expression.

Half of brain: Why am I using my real name? . . . What kind of a narcissistic twit am I anyway to think my little voice will add anything useful to the blogosphere? . . . What if there are already crazies out there Googling me? They could find out where I live in ten seconds . . .

Other half of brain: All I'm doing is *publishing writing under my own name*—i.e., the thing I've wanted to do most in the world since I was six . . . Why should some imagined psycho stop me from doing what I love and taking credit for it? . . . Isn't this all moot until I have more than four readers?

First half of brain: . . . That imagined psycho might turn out to be real and come after me . . . That psycho could be number five.

If the internet ever figures out that I exist, you can be damn sure I'll hear that and worse. And if it escalates into something truly frightening, one of the first things people will say is that it could have been avoided if I hadn't been so stupid as to blog under my own name, to make it *so easy* for people to hurt me.

She looked up. The man wasn't looking at her—but that's because the man wasn't there. He was missing from his seat!

Her eyes darted around the train. Fortunately, she was in the very last row of the cabin, so he couldn't possibly be behind her, though she checked anyway. She scanned the inside of the train as the discordant metal scrapes emanating from the tracks grew into a shrieking roar.

She closed her eyes. *"Psycho #5" is supposed to be fictional,* she thought.

Stay in the flow, she told herself. It was hard. Winning an argument with your own brain chemistry takes everything you've got.

I laid on one of the seats in the observation deck, crashing after three hours of reading Elisa's blogs about her depression. Like a dog jealous for the attention of his owner, my depression lumbered in and sat on me. I compared it to hers. I read more of her back and forths with Tumblr users who commiserated with her illness. It made me feel better, and I drifted to sleep as the train passed silently through blackness.

A Ruling in the Civil Case

My train pulled into Union Station shortly after 11 A.M. and I rushed over to the Stanley Mosk Courthouse. The online court record stated that the day's hearing would commence at 9 A.M. but, I hoped, surely some preliminary motions might delay things a bit.

After walking through the court metal detector, I approached the information desk and made eye contact with an attendant behind the kiosk.

"I'm here to attend the civil case of David Lam vs. Cecil Hotel, case number BC521927," I stated.

The woman diverted her eyes to the computer screen on the kiosk desk and chattered off some words on the keyboard. She frowned and looked back at me.

"I'm sorry, it appears that Judge Howard Halm dismissed this case last week."

The Family Speaks (Via Lawyer)

The ruling infuriated me. It wasn't just that I had needlessly taken a twenty-four-hour train trip. The civil trial promised to expose a significant amount of information through the discovery process. The detectives, who up until that point, had refused to answer even the most basic questions about the case, could very well have been legally mandated to describe pertinent details from their investigation notes.

Later that night, I discovered that John Lordan made a Brain-Scratch video the previous week about the dismissal of the case. He actually attended the final hearing and took notes about the proceedings, I noted as an admonishment to myself.

The plaintiff's primary argument, Lordan stated, was that the roof had constituted a mortal danger to Elisa and to other guests because the water cistern—which he likened to a grain silo that is legally required to be locked when not in use—was not locked and had no internal mechanism by which someone could climb out once inside. The water tanks at the Cecil Hotel were an accident waiting to happen.

The judge apparently then stated that the lid weighed twenty pounds, was not hinged, and was removable. A lock by itself, he argued, would therefore not have secured the tanks. In his video, Lordan said he'd wanted to jump out of his seat at that point. First of all, there are ways to securely lock an unhinged removable lid. More important, Lordan believed there were other issues at play here than just whether the tanks were locked.

The fact that there was graffiti, as well as multiple reports of drinking on the roof, shows that getting up there was not prohibitively difficult. Yet the plaintiff did not seize upon this line of attack and instead only stressed the fact that the cistern remained unlocked, which left the hotel's water supply vulnerable to contamination or poisoning.

Johnston, the plaintiff's lead attorney, seemed nervous, John said. Once again narrowing in on the accessibility of the tanks, he noted that since Elisa's death the hotel has added locks.

Representing the only public statement on behalf of the Lam family regarding Elisa's death, Johnston stated the following: "The case speaks to the horrors of mental illness . . . Elisa Lam was not killed by a boogey man or a haunted hotel. She fell off her medication, had a psychotic break, accessed the roof, found the water tank and died."

Then, after virtually no further deliberation, the judge granted the defense's motion and threw the case out. A jury would not get to hear the case, and the LAPD would not be required to release any additional evidence or information.

Another websleuth investigating the case, Paul Brevik, was in attendance. Paul had made some videos (now taken down) about the case on a YouTube Channel called Lepprocommunist. He believed the police explanation, that Elisa's death was an accident caused by mental illness. For him, the statement by the Lam family attorneys was the ultimate confirmation.

He and John discussed the case. Even John, who was more inclined to believe in foul play, pointed out that the attorney's statement was "about as close as a firm answer as we're going to get unless we get a confession."

John disagreed with the judge, calling the decision overreach. "Twelve minds would have been better than one," he said.

John closed the video saying it may very well be his last on the case. He said it was emotional for him and that it broke his heart.

"There's a pit of emptiness in my stomach."

So far, the case for Elisa's death being a tragic accident continued to strengthen. Now it appeared that even the family did not believe Elisa was the victim of homicide.

However, as much as I wanted to move on with my life, there was something that still felt off. And then I received a very unexpected phone call, one that ultimately became the birth of our documentary about the case. The voice on the other end was sheepish and inflected with a Canadian accent.

"It's Joe," he said.

"Joe who?"

"Joe Elwell. You sent me a message a few months ago. Sorry it took so long." After a short awkward pause, he finally spelled it out for me, "I was friends with Elisa. And there's no way in hell her death was an accident."

CHAPTER 15

A World with Evil

ELISA DISAPPEARED TWO DAYS BEFORE Joe's thirty-fifth birthday. But he didn't find out what happened to her until weeks later, when his former supervisor and friend messaged him on Facebook. Joe had recently made a big change, relocating from Vancouver, British Columbia, to Hamilton, Ontario, 3,100 miles away. He was launching his own company, a for-hire security service, and felt the thrill of entrepreneurship coursing through him for the first time.

All around, Joe was a happier person, having finally processed and discarded some of the childhood psychological trauma that held him back for years.

But then he heard the Facebook ping.

"Something's happened to Elisa," Mary wrote, after a short intro message.

She told him about the water tank, the surveillance video from the elevator. Incredulous, he looked it up online . . . and felt his happiness melt away in moments.

After their online chat ended, Joe forced himself to watch the video and read a couple of articles about the case. He had to lay on the floor, sick to his stomach.

He remembered years earlier meeting Elisa for the first time. When Joe clocked into work that day, Mary had mentioned there was a new hire slated to begin. It was still early in the season at the Pacific National Exhibition, but the pressure to get things in order for the approaching seventeen-day surge of festival-goers was already high.

Before working at the PNE, Joe felt like a fly on the wall, merely observing life going on around him. Now he felt comfortable talking to strangers. What he found is that when you're no longer afraid of the people around you, a new universe opens up. New stories appear before you and, like streams merging to form a river, your life becomes part of a larger narrative.

His previous job had been much different. He worked security for the air ambulance elevator for emergency paramedics at Vancouver General Hospital. He'd escorted paramedics in a small elevator with gurney-ridden patients clinging to life. Horrific injuries. One time it was a man overdosing on PCP who needed a cloth held over his eyes; if it slipped off for even a moment, the man screamed, "Don't let me see the light!" as though the overhead fluorescents were incinerating his skin.

The hospital had one of the biggest morgues in the region and he provided security for that, too. It was, in a way, ironic to provide security for the dead. He'd been happy to get away from that job and into something where he was dealing with people who were healthy, excited and, well, alive.

As he had made his rounds at the PNE grounds, he stopped for a moment and checked his cell phone. When he looked up, he saw a young woman with a huge backpack up ahead. She looked slightly lost. The kind of lost where you're in the right place but still have no idea where to go. He saw that a lot here.

Joe approached her. "Hi, can I help you with something?"

The young woman turned to him. She was pretty, with expressive eyes and a vibrant smile that poured across her face after an initial moment of confusion.

"Oh hi," she said. "Yes, I'm here for my first day of work. I'm supposed to report to Mary, but I have no idea where she is."

"I can take you to Mary. She's just back this way," Joe said.

"Oh, thank you so much!"

They began walking and talking. Joe learned that she was an

undergraduate studying at the University of British Columbia. She had a wide range of interests and Joe got the feeling that there was great passion boiling under the surface of Elisa's demeanor. She seemed hungry, a quality he liked to see in young people—or, people younger than himself, people who weren't yet jaded by life and ground down to the bone by stress and cynicism.

Joe turned back for a moment. There was something about the young woman, something in her eyes, her smile, a glimmer in her eye, that made Joe want to spill his soul to her. But, given that he didn't even know her name yet, he decided just to extend his hand and introduce himself.

"I'm Joe, by the way" he said.

"Hey, Joe. I'm Elisa."

Joe and Elisa befriended each other and over the course of several years shared their summers together at the PNE. There was indeed something special about Elisa. She would walk in and light up the room with her smile. She made people feel at ease; she acknowledged everyone around her. She evinced a deep empathy for people, even those she didn't know. The Elisa Lam Joe knew loved life, loved participating and being involved. She was brave, a mover, a shaker.

She was so good with people that Joe had spoken with PNE management about giving her more work. He believed she was an asset to the company and could help people. She had an organic compassion for those around her. She had a bright future ahead of her.

Joe remembered all the schoolbooks she brought with her so she could study on her breaks, though she always made time to goof around and laugh.

He remembered the last time he saw Elisa, shortly before he left the company. She was walking up the ramp, walking toward her supervisor, and he waved at her, got her attention; she looked up and waved back, grinning broadly. Their final good-bye was a distant hello.

His time working in a morgue, his memories of securing an enclosed room filled with chambers of bodies, triggered a conjuring of an image in his head—something he didn't want to see or think about but that he couldn't control. Elisa laying in the morgue, awaiting her autopsy, the last physical contact with a human she would ever have before her earthly remains were committed back to the elements of nature.

We all live and die on this planet confronting our own mortality, Joe thought. But Elisa was taken far too soon. Her energy was stolen from this world.

He sat up from the floor with a jolt, as though awakened from a falling nightmare. Who—what—had taken his friend from him? At that moment, Joe decided he would get involved.

Soon after speaking with Joe, I decided I would get *more* involved. I decided to pursue a documentary about the case, enlisting Jared as my co-director. Many websleuths viewed the case as unsolvable, but I wanted to come at it from multiple angles, addressing not only the psychiatric angle but the sociological obsession. And, of course, I still held out hope that new evidence could be unearthed that might help solve the seemingly intractable mystery of Elisa's death. One thing was for certain, it would not be a typical true-crime journey.

NEW SURVEILLANCE FOOTAGE

Websleuths asked why there was no additional surveillance from the lobby, other hallways, the sidewalk outside the hotel, all of which are surveilled?

If it was important for us to see a grainy, pixelated video of Elisa in the elevator that night, why was it not important for us to see other footage of her?

It turned out there *was* additional footage, which Tennelle corroborated with a disturbing new disclosure that poured gasoline on the websleuth forums.

"We did see her come in with two gentlemen. She had—they had a box, gave it to her," he said. "She went up into her—to the elevator. We never saw them again on video."

Who were these two men? How did they know Elisa? Were they questioned by the police?

Maybe they took her to dinner and the box was leftovers. Did they see her again?

I called the hotel and asked to speak to Amy Price, the general manager.

"Hello, Ms. Price. I hope you're having a lovely day. I wanted to speak with you about the Elisa Lam case. I understand that this must be a sensitive issue but now that the civil case is over, would you be able to answer a couple of questions?"

"No comment," she said.

"In all likelihood, the hotel was not responsible for Elisa's death and all the conspiracy theories are wrong. If you simply cleared up a couple of issues, I think it would go a long way."

"No comment."

"Can you comment on why you have no comment?"

"No . . . I mean, no comment."

I called back a few minutes later and assumed a slightly different voice. I asked the front desk manager whether the hotel was hiring.

"I don't think so," she said. "The hotel is actually about to close for renovations."

The grin I wore at the thought of infiltrating the hotel as a bell-hop instantaneously turned into a horrified grimace. Aw no, aw no, I looked it up and sure enough the Cecil Hotel was slated to close indefinitely for renovations.

If we were going to make a documentary about the case, we needed footage from inside the hotel. And we had, uh, one week to trebuchet our asses down there and get it.

WEBSLEUTH WITCH HUNT

As I planned my travels, websleuths honed in on new people they deemed suspects. One of them was a musician with the cognomen "Morbid." His real name is Pablo.

The whole fiasco started, Pablo told me, when he received a mes-sage from his friend, telling him he needed to check out a news clip about him on YouTube. Pablo clicked on the YouTube link and went to 2:56 in the video, as instructed, where there were a few shots of him from a music video he produced and directed in 2009 while visiting San Diego.

The video was for his band Death of Desire, since renamed Dynasty of Darkness, and in it, Pablo plays an alter-ego character of himself named Morbid; he looks like a shorter, slightly stockier version of Marilyn Manson mixed with a Rob Zombie character.

The news clip was from a Taiwanese news channel, which had downloaded clips from his video and used them to suggest that Morbid killed Elisa Lam. Pablo was shocked. Like a nightmare played in fast forward, his mind raced to put the pieces together while watching the full video.

The previous year, in February 2012, almost a year to the day of Elisa's death, he stayed in the Cecil Hotel. While there, he recorded a video of himself laying in bed, talking about himself and his band. In the background was a picture of some iconic imagery, including a picture of the Black Dahlia, and featured prominently in the video are Morbid's arms, which are sleeved with gothic tattoos.

It just so happens that Morbid has another band, called Slitwrist, for which he had done another music video that featured an artistically rendered scene of a girl lying dead in a forest. One of the band's songs has lyrics about someone dead and slumbering in the ocean where no one can hear them scream. Then he ruminates on escaping to China.

These are the breadcrumbs some very irresponsible "websleuths" (though I hesitate to use that designation) used to manufacture a theory that Morbid killed Elisa. He tracked one of them, a woman from Hong Kong, who had seemingly made it her life's mission to harass him. She had accessed his FB page and downloaded Pablo's personal photos and posts, then circulated them on forums in order to "prove" he was Elisa's killer.

There were dozens more doing this, and they filled up the threads of Elisa Lam tribute pages, Facebook threads, Reddit and Websleuth forums, and YouTube videos. Many of these posts went viral.

Morbid soon began receiving hundreds of messages from people on YouTube and other platforms. They called him a murderer and threatened to kill him.

Later, the name of another target, Dillon Kroe, began to surface in the forums. Apparently, the man wore a black trench coat, lived near the Cecil Hotel and had drawn a portrait of Elisa. This was somehow enough information for people to sketch together a scenario in which he was Elisa's stalker.

Then, Kroe abruptly deleted the portrait image from his social-media accounts, which further fueled the suspicions. On a lark, I looked at his social-media accounts on Instagram and Tumblr and saw that he followed Elisa on these platforms. Moreover, on several of Elisa's posts, Dillon had left a heart symbol comment. A minority of websleuths, practicing sloppy, arguably libelous speculation, publicly surmised that Kroe and Elisa met online prior to her trip and had planned to meet up while she was in town.

As with Morbid, I reached out to Dillon over Facebook to clarify things: "Hey forgive me for a random question from a stranger, but did you paint something related to the Elisa Lam case a couple years ago? Your name came up in a comment thread for a case I'm writing about."

He responded quickly: "Hi Jake. Yes, I did. Unfortunately, I cannot answer anything regarding Elisa Lam or the Cecil Hotel at this time. Good luck on your book!"

"Thank you. I'm a bit puzzled by your response. You can't discuss a painting you made?"

He repeated himself, this time in even more blatant legalese. "Due to confidential subject matter, I cannot in any regard comment or make a statement about anything relating to or about Elisa Lam or the Cecil Hotel (Stay At Main) at this time."

My first guess was that like Morbid, Kroe had been harassed online by some of the websleuths and had either filed a cease-and-desist order against someone, or had conferred with a lawyer on how to address people who asked him about the case.

Kroe is a talented artist. As I looked through his portfolio, I was impressed. The portrait of Elisa, which was hard to find because Kroe had seemingly scrubbed it from all his pages, featured a strange mark on her forehead. I was interested in the backstory of the painting but would have to wait to learn more.

DISTURBING VIDEOS

My flight to LA was scheduled for 6 A.M., which meant I wouldn't sleep that night. I drank and sleuthed instead.

I discovered the YouTube account of a Norwegian websleuth named Wilhelm Werner Winther, who appeared to be obsessed with the Lam case. But the nature of his obsession marked a new phase in my investigation.

His first video, posted on June 13, 2015, featured piano music with children singing in the background. A series of still images, annotated with explanations, diagrams, quotes by Elisa, and photoshopped tribute images of Elisa.

Right from the start, his content gets controversial and disturbing. A still image of a Cecil Hotel hallway is photoshopped with an arrow pointing down it, declaring: "The last official observation of Elisa, January 31st, 2013, she walked this way at 11:58 P.M.—with a pistol pointed at her."

The next image features a diagram of a body in a tank with the metrics (240 cm by 82.5 cm). The text reads: "When Elisa was dropped into water tank by her murderer – Mr B.O. (the graffitist 'Booger') – the sudden pressure change created a pipeline interaction described by hotel tenants as a loud 'bang' . . . Feb 01 2013 at 00:20 AM)."

The bang Winther referred to likely came from tenant Bernard Diaz, who reported a loud sound coming from the floor above him, which would have been the floor Elisa was moved to on the night she disappeared.

I had no idea who Mr. Booger was, but apparently Winther believed he had identified the killer. He then analyzed the graffiti on the roof, claiming that one of the graffiti symbols scrawled on the water cistern where Elisa's body was found is an Egyptian hieroglyph from 2100 BCE that means "women enclosed in cylindrical structure."

Winther knew the case extremely well, down to some of the most obscure details that only someone who has meticulously researched it would. For example, in the next video, he addressed the "sand-like particulate" that is buried deep in the autopsy and never explained.

But his analysis took a dark turn. In video after video after video (there are over a dozen devoted to the case), Winther described in graphic detail the "sodomizing and subsequent killing of Elisa Lam . . ." One section included a picture of a skull and a medieval torture device he claimed was taken by Elisa's murderer.

His next video and several subsequent videos from the following year contained images from inside the lobby of the Cecil Hotel that show part of the face of a young Asian woman that Winther claimed was Elisa. The implication here is that these are leaked images from the days Elisa checked into the hotel. One of them shows her outside the Cecil with two other young Asian woman, ostensibly the roommates who later complained about Elisa's bizarre behavior and requested that hotel management move her to a different room.

Of course, it's extremely unlikely the young woman in the images is actually Elisa, which means Winther either sourced the photos online or traveled to the Cecil at a later time and photographed young Asian women inside and outside the hotel.

I messaged Winther about the case and his claims of Elisa's murder.

"The rape were [sic] videotaped by Elisa's would-be abductors/killers," he responded. "We can't reveal our modi operandi or expose personnel on our side in this case. To the extent the USA already has been punished for the official corruption obstructing formal justice in Elisa's case, it's impossible to give further details. What we can say, however, is that failure to provide a formal solution will cost the lives of millions of Americans . . . because they won't have access to 100 percent effective anticancer drugs."

This went on and on. Another elaborate conspiracy. What was it about this case that triggered so much detailed hysteria?

I was still curious as to whether he had gone to the Cecil. I asked him.

"Yeah—and Elisa has visited me in Norway in 2012."

Exhibition

Joe flew to Vancouver to participate in our documentary. We met up with him right as the 2016 Pacific National Exhibition (PNE) got underway. This was where he and Elisa had worked together for years. The timing was an incredible coincidence and added to the emotional resonance of our time with him.

Joe wanted to let the world know who Elisa was as a person. Her humanity had been covered up in the sensationalism of the case.

But his portrait of Elisa differed from mine. Joe never saw a depressed side to Elisa, had not read her blogs, and seemed skeptical of the mental illness narrative.

After the sun had set, we boarded the fairground's Ferris wheel with our cameras. Streaks of purple wispy clouds were still backlit by the afterglow of dusk.

I casually reminded him once that people will often hide their depression in public, only exhibiting symptoms unconsciously. He agreed with this and, to my surprise, stated that he had struggled with his own depression for years.

"Everybody has a side of them that they don't present to the public," Joe admitted.

His depression, he believed, stemmed from the trauma of his parents getting divorced when he was five years old. He tried to repress this feeling but it was too raw and real to ignore.

As we reached the top of the Ferris wheel, a cold breeze blew in from the ocean. The panoramic glow of the amusement park rides below made for a dizzying spectacle. It was a weird moment, sitting with Joe so high in the night sky, watching him occasionally stare into the distance in silence. Then he would remember something, smile, and start talking again.

Presently, his eyes glazed over and he seemed lost. He shook his head. "What was she doing on that roof that night? It haunts me—it keeps me up at night."

As we entered the fairgrounds, the hustle and bustle reminded me of the most recent book I'd read, *The Devil in the White City,* which chronicled and compared the simultaneous construction of

the historic Chicago fair—then the biggest civic project ever undertaken—and the killings by H. H. Holmes, generally considered one
of the first serial killers. Holmes used the fair to lure young women
to his nearby mansion, which he constructed for the express purpose
of torturing and killing.

By contrasting humanity at its entrepreneurial best, striving to
outdo itself in all manners of architecture, and humanity at its worst,
the book shows the duality, the bipolarity, of the human mind, inspired by both angels and demons.

Serial murder of this magnitude of evil was so completely un-
heard of and shocking at the time that it literally pre-dated the term
"serial killer." The modern diagnosis of "psychopath" was similarly
unborn. That such evil could exist in the human mind as a matter
of neuropathy was so alien to people, they didn't even have the language for it.

If it turned out that Elisa wasn't killed, it may be another instance
of humans not having the language to describe something, not being
able to conceptualize the reality and power of mental illness.

A LITTLE TASTE OF HELL

Joe recalled that when he learned about the additional surveillance
of Elisa entering the hotel with two men, he became determined to
question the LAPD about their investigation. This was prior to the
release of the autopsy, after which Stearns and Tennelle closed the
case. For weeks, Joe had been trying to get in contact with one of
the LAPD detectives working on the case. He had already spoken
to an RMCP agent, who hadn't been very helpful but had at least
empathized with him.

Joe couldn't shake his suspicion that there was still more to the
story than was being told. In general, he felt there was an unseen
world of corruption and evil behind the curtain of our everyday reality. He didn't believe in conspiracy theories, he believed in conspiracy reality.

There had to be some explanation for Elisa's behavior in the
surveillance tape and her subsequent demise. The Elisa he knew

wouldn't have wandered onto that roof and climbed into that tank. The Elisa he knew was a bright light in a world of darkness.

Then, Joe saw something else online that got his mind racing. The controversial celebrity Tila Tequila had posted a shocking message on Twitter about Elisa.

No stranger to bizarre online posts, Tila had previously advocated for both the Flat Earth and Hollow Earth theories—an oddly paradoxical viewpoint. She believed in a vast alien conspiracy and an Illuminati base on the moon. She once posted that she had already died seven times. Her most controversial activity involved anti-semitic statements and gestures that drew outrage online. She later blamed some of these statements on her own history of mental illness, claiming that in March 2012 she was suicidal and had to check into rehab.

Her newest tweet read, "I know who killed Elisa Lam. I believe I am the only person on this entire planet who knows what happened. I have just kept my mouth shut because there is a lot more to it and of course . . . cases like this . . . I just did not want to draw any attention to myself but I know exactly why they did it and yes it was indeed a ritualistic murder. Just like Paul Walker's."

Joe wasn't willing to completely write off someone claiming that Elisa had been ritualistically murdered. Stranger things have happened.

When Joe finally got Detective Stearns on the phone, back when the case was still open, he said to him, "I just want to make sure the department is doing its due diligence. Are you interrogating hotel employees or guests? Somebody has to know something."

"This is still an ongoing investigation, Joe. I agree that it is a very strange case, and tragic. The parents have lawyers assisting them and, rest assured, everyone is doing their due diligence."

"So you agree that it was likely a homicide?"

"It's certainly possible."

"*Possible. It's possible.* Okay, well, I just—I . . . demand justice for Elisa. You hear me, sir? And this is just a little taste of the hell you're going to deal with if you and your boys don't figure it out."

It struck me that Joe may have an emotional connection to the homicide narrative in the case. In the intensity of his despair for the loss of a friend, homicide allowed him to villainize an external antagonist, an embodiment of Evil borrowing human skin. Joe believed in Evil. He was a born-again Christian, in fact. A world with Evil made sense to him. A world in which friends died from accidents resulting from mental illness did not.

CHAPTER 16
Dark Synchronicity

I DREAMT OF ELISA AGAIN. Usually, my dreams are incoherent scrambles in which faces of people I've known might momentarily materialize. Lately, though, my dreams developed a narrative structure. This time Elisa appeared as the *Stranger Things* character Eleven, wading through the dismal realm of the Upside Down. She wore her red hoodie and near the end of the dream, she climbed the final flight of stair to reach the roof of the Cecil.

A blurry man opened a door for her and she emerged onto the roof, where the ashy detritus of the alternate dimension hung suspended in the night air.

Another man awaited her arrival. A tall man with shaggy black hair.

In the dream, I climbed up the fire escape of the Cecil, high above the city. Some winged demon hovered nearby, taunting me. When I reached the top, I stole a glimpse of Elisa approaching the strange man.

Suddenly the man's head jerked to look right at me and I recognized those horrifying eyes of the figure at Pershing Square. The fright shocked me so much that I lost my balance on the rails of the fire escape and I fell. The winged demon laughed hysterically at me as I plunged and then—

I sat straight up in my bed with a panicked grunt.

DOWN THE RABBIT HOLE

Later that evening, a percussive beat drove the frenzied roar of a melody laced with police sirens, helicopters, the shriek of some metallic Mothra, and a loudspeaker voice beseeching humans to "Give up . . . give up!" It's both the opening anthem of *Ground Zero with Clyde Lewis* and a serviceable paean to the coming apocalypse.

"Tonight our guest on Ground Zero is Jake Anderson, who has spent the last three years immersed in one of the most mysterious cases of all time." Clyde's brassy baritone voice boomed over the airwaves. "I met this guy at Contact in the Desert and we started talking about the Cecil Hotel, which I've been fascinated with for years, and it turned out that Jake wanted to make a documentary about the place and this case."

I sat across from him in the studio, waiting to go down the rabbit hole with my favorite radio host. In a way, Clyde's show is like an interactive museum of rabbit holes. If conspiracy theories and parapsychology are part of a theatrical play, his show revels in the staging and production of the play, the stuff that goes on behind the curtains.

"I've always been fascinated by that place," Clyde said. "In fact, I really want to do an investigation there because it seems like there is a residual haunting going on. Something evil is there. Generation after generation of people seem to experience the effects of trauma there. You spent the night there, Jake, what was it like?"

"I was nauseous from the moment I walked in the door, Clyde," I said, genuinely on edge about my impending return. "You know, I like to play the skeptic's role sometimes, but it definitely feels like there's something going on there."

I was conflicted. In my heart, I felt that this case was much more about the disconnect people have with regards to mental illness. Foul play was about as conspiratorial as I could go without feeling like I was aiding in the stigmatization. I'd posted two fairly benign articles on *The Ghost Diaries* about some of the creepy aspects of the case, but I felt immense guilt for not drawing attention to the mental illness component.

But Clyde's core audience didn't want to hear about serotonin and mood disorders. They wanted to hear about the supernatural spirits that lived inside the Cecil Hotel.

And here's where my real conflict came in: Even though I wanted to focus on mental illness and how it can warp reality far more powerfully than a demon, I was no longer sure there wasn't really something unexplainable going on at the Cecil. The belief stemmed from a combination of my visit to the hotel and the strange (precognitive?) dreams and synchronicities I'd experienced since.

My seventeen-year-old rationalist self was appalled at what I had become—a mentally unstable thirty-five-year-old man entertaining the idea of paranormal activity—but what did my seventeen-year-old self know? He hadn't been broken yet.

I didn't believe in sentient ghosts or demons, but I was starting to seriously consider the idea that paranormal activity is a kind of open-ended information transfer, feedback loops of data generated by consciousness, left like time capsules, notes tucked into library books, waiting to be discovered.

As crazy as it sounds, there's decades of evidence, championed by reputable physicists, that strongly suggests a link between human consciousness and the quantum core of our universe.

It starts with the shocking conclusions of quantum mechanics in the early twentieth century that have been corroborated over and over up until the present day. These experiments, which confounded the greatest scientific minds, show that at the subatomic realm there is no fixed objective reality without a human observer. If you drill in to the very core of the particles that make up matter and energy, there is only potential and probability—no concrete solid states—*until* human consciousness observes it and collapses the potential into certainty.

The other discovery that baffled scientists was that particles could communicate information to each other instantaneously across space/time. This non-local interaction violated Einstein's General Theory of Relativity and drove him bonkers. Ultimately, he was forced to concede the truth of quantum mechanics and conferred upon the non-locality phenomenon the now-famous appellation "spooky action at a distance."

The "single particle double-slit experiment," uncertainty principle, and quantum entanglement are too complex for the space we have here. I bring them up as a foundational premise for the unexplained but powerful connection between consciousness and reality.

There are several other important theories/experiments that began to impact my thinking about the Cecil Hotel and what could be going on there:

- *Orchestrated Objective Reduction*, or Orch-OR. Renowned theoretical physicist Roger Penrose and anaesthesiologist Stuart Hameroff advanced the theory that consciousness is not a purely neurological phenomenon but rather arises as part of a synergistic quantum process embedded in microtubules. They suggest minds can leave imprints, residual information. In January 2014, Japanese researchers detected quantum vibrations in microtubules, providing important corroboration for this theory.
- *Global Consciousness Project.* A series of experiments took place at Princeton in the 1990s, where scientists launched PEAR (The Princeton Engineering Anomalies Research). The researchers there compiled a book called *Margins of Reality*, in which they describe how the human mind can have a small but mathematically significant effect on random number generators. The PEAR team eventually launched an even larger initiative, one that still exists today, called The Global Consciousness Project. This project collates ongoing statistical data showing that the intentions of a human observer can create order in random number systems.
- *Retroactive Precognition.* A few years ago, social psychologist Daryl J. Bem produced strong evidence for the controversial ESP concept known as "retroactive precognition." In his paper, entitled "Feeling the Future," Bem described a series of experiments suggesting that people are more likely to remember something in the present if they commit it to memory in the future. Let me

state that again: According to Bem, you are more likely to remember something right now if you memorize it tomorrow.

- *Synchronicity.* Legendary psychoanalyst Carl Jung developed the concept of synchronicity, which he defined as "acausal parallelism," a web of seemingly random coincidences connecting subjective experience with external events. Jung, one of the few renowned scientists to give serious scientific consideration to parapsychology—which assisted in the collapse of his friendship with Freud—also believed "spirits" are the unconscious projection of psychological complexes. Also known as thought-forms, or tulpas (a concept originating in early Indian Buddhism), the physical embodiment of a thought or feeling.

Given these ideas, let's reconsider the nature of ghosts, possessions and hauntings at the Cecil. Could such activity be data from the emotional states and thoughts left behind by people who died there traumatically? What kind of informational impressions might we expect? Intimations of shape, snatches of dialogue and out of place sounds, unusual and disturbing thought patterns, sudden, indirect movements and changes in temperature—in other words, the kinds of experiences reported by people who have paranormal encounters.

But what really freaks me out is that if what Bem says is correct and present cognition can affect the past, does that mean people may be "haunted" by the future? Could your thoughts now, as you read, affect my writing of this book? Could our analysis of Elisa now have affected her in the past? I started to imagine that in the surveillance video, Elisa sensed us, perhaps even me; she felt the presence of future observation.

Clyde was into it, all of it. "It sounds like there is definitely some residual haunting going on. Generation after generation after generation, you see some kind of imprint, a quantum signature, picking up on these intuitive mumblings from the past."

During the commercial break, Clyde was giddy. "Wes Craven told me that when Freddy Krueger made it to the big screen, he was truly convinced that the spirit of the fictional character had possessed the serial killer Richard Ramirez. Seriously, he had to get therapy."

"I read that Unterweger loved the movie *Silence of the Lambs.*"

Clyde's eyes lit up. "Really . . . maybe he's a tulpa of Hannibal, just like Ramirez is to Freddy Krueger."

"Stranger things have happened," I said.

After the break, Clyde talked more about synchronicities and thought-forms. Comparing it to the *Dark Water* synchronicities in the Lam case, he brought up the film *Rosemary's Baby* as an example of predictive programming. Director Roman Polanski's wife was killed by Manson's family in a ritualistic slaughter eerily similar to the satanic sacrifice in the film.

Are these just random patterns in the static? Our minds projecting meaning onto chaos? Or is there some structure to it all?

The callers gave me yet another reminder of how the Lam case was in the zeitgeist, something that had burrowed into the collective unconscious.

One of the callers surprised me by suddenly bringing up the show *Stranger Things.* It wasn't only that I had just uttered the words "stranger things" to Clyde in a different context, the caller referenced the show's "Upside Down" alternate dimension, wondering if that could be involved in the Lam case.

While, on its face, the connection was absurd, I had only recently had a dream where Elisa was in the Upside Down. These are the kinds of strange synchronicities that stalked me through the entire investigation.

TALK THERAPY

Needless to say, after my Ground Zero appearance I needed to see my therapist. I hesitate to even call him a therapist; he's a psychiatrist, which means he prescribes drugs. For quality talk therapy, you have to find a specialist, though I did have one therapist at Kaiser who made a good faith effort to tap into some of my thought patterns.

One of the biggest problems in mental health is that the rise of pharmapsychology has marked a simultaneous decrease in talk therapy. Without understanding how your past fuels your thought patterns and how your thought patterns fuel your behavior, all the meds can do is maintain an acceptable level of functionality. There's no curative power there, only maintenance. You're bailing water out of a floundering ship.

This goes for other holistic healing as well. Exercise, meditation, nutritious diet, positive thinking, self-love, reciprocal relationships, kinship with nature, etc. are all believed to help carve your neural pathways into patterns of healthy behavior.

There are two major forms of talk therapy, cognitive-behavioral therapy (CBT) and interpersonal therapy (IPT).

CBT is sometimes referred to as a "psychodynamic therapy" that focuses on emotional responses to external triggers. The premise is that thought patterns can be destructive and that through "learned optimism" and neutralizing "automatic thoughts," the mind can actually change its own reality. Essentially, you learn to control your own thoughts and emotions, creating more beneficial patterns.

IPT focuses more on the present. Instead of working to identify negative triggers from the past, the therapist helps the patient develop strategies for day-to-day life. This includes assessing current relationships, grief, stressful transitions, and isolation. IPT helps the patient establish goals and steps toward attaining those goals. Instead of trying to change the underlying depression, the therapy builds around it so that its effects are minimized.

Some people respond very well to talk therapy. In fact, in patients for whom it is curative, talk therapy has actually been shown to have much of the same effects on the brain as medication. This was demonstrated by assessing a patient's sleep electroencephalogram (EEG). The reason for this is a mystery, as is depression and mental illness itself. While serotonin—one of nature's most basic building blocks in species development—and neurotransmitters are involved, simple addition and subtraction of its quantities in the brain have not been shown to necessarily equate more or less depression. The receptor theory, whereby drugs target the brain's ability to absorb neurotransmitters, has similarly not conclusively solved the problem.

Depression and related mental illnesses seem rather to be a synergistic phenomenon that involves genetic predisposition, traumatic history, psycho-social dynamics, and other factors.

That talk therapy can cause the same biological changes on the brain as medication, Andrew Solomon says in his book *The Noonday Demon*, might suggest to some that medication is bunk, but the reality is rather that there are multiple ways to positively change neural activity in the brain.

Talk therapy has its own problematic idiosyncrasies. For one, choice of therapist is crucial. One study showed that conversations with English professors could be just as beneficial as sessions with professional therapists, seemingly implying that emotional connection is of primary importance when it comes to therapy.

"Should We All Take a Little Bit of Lithium?"

No matter who's sitting across from me, explaining one's depression is similar, I imagine, to describing color to a blind person. One thing I can say is that depression is *not* sadness. Sadness is more like a form of nostalgia, apprehension over absence or injustice. There is a human ambition to sadness, a warrant for some future where there exists a right and wrong. Sadness has almost a sweetness to it, a charming quality. People write poems and songs about sadness. It inspires Hallmark get-well cards and wistful apologies. There is an economy to it.

Depression is an entirely different beast. Depression wrangles your mind, squeezing, crushing, choking, surgically removing your identity. In the depths of a major depressive spell, you no longer feel human, you no longer remember what it feels like to be you. Depression is thus beyond sadness. It makes you pray for sadness.

But it wasn't just depression and this was the part that was so difficult for me to articulate. I was beginning to think there was something more going on inside me.

The base-level sensation was an amalgam of despair, panic, and claustrophobia. Not a normal claustrophobia that has a relation to confined spaces, but rather a vertical terror that spiked through all other cognitive and emotional levels, pinning them together in a single affected tier. It doesn't matter where I am. I could be in a wide-open territory. Claustrophobia in fields, in outer space, as abstract and esoteric as loneliness in crowds, just the raw existential damage we accumulate.

The feeling is a panicked fight-or-flight response ripped out of its normal evolutionary cycle. It's like I missed my life, or that my life has passed me by, or that someone else is me and experiencing my family, my joy, my destiny. It's like waking up to realize you slept through your entire life, or waking up to find out you've been completely replaced. The doppelgänger is in your head, a version of you—a perfect happy version—that got kicked out of the multiverse for impersonating you, and God had the locks changed.

The morning sunlight streaming in the window, the sound of children laughing and riding their bikes, the fact that it is Saturday morning and the birds are chirping, these external realities rush into you and crash into your face. The anxiety, the memory of the dream you had the night before in which you bared your soul to everyone you've ever known, and now they're all gone and you're stuck here, unable to flee, trapped with yourself in this wretched timeline where everything has gone wrong.

You want to make pancakes for your wife and kids but suddenly realize they don't exist. There's a glitch in the matrix, and you're nostalgic for a Saturday morning that's taking place in another universe.

I race out into the living room, hoping by some miracle that a new space will feel more reasonable. But I see through the window that cars are driving across the sun-baked bridge to go to the beach. The happy people, who are fulfilled with their lives—who are exactly where they should be—are taking trips with their families and friends. They are creating and absorbing the experiential legacy that will one day nurture them and allow them to know they lived their lives. They're in the right universe.

I go back to sleep, climbing back into the dreamworld—the dimension where things fall my way, where I don't sabotage myself, where maybe I can catch a glimpse of my wife, kids, dog, and white picket fence—where I long to stay.

This is what I have trouble explaining to a doctor.

"I'm tired." I started to tear up, my voice cracking. I had never done this in front of a doctor. "I'm just so tired of not knowing what's wrong with me. This illness—I've been battling for fifteen years. I'm just, *fucking*, sick of it."

He nodded, soberly, printed out a one-page article, and handed it to me. To my surprise, the title was "Should We All Take a Little Bit of Lithium?"

I didn't tell him about the synchronicities (unless you're lucky enough to have Jung as your primary, what is a psychiatrist going to say about that?) but I did mention my upcoming trip as a source of anxiety.

"Traveling always makes me anxious, especially Los Angeles," I said. "But the hotel I'm visiting is known for serial killers, suicides, and murders. It may be haunted, too."

"Why in the *hell* are you going there?" My doctor, who I'd never heard swear, asked with genuine concern.

"I have to. I'm—I'm investigating it. Hopefully, it doesn't destroy, uh, kill me."

I laughed. He did not.

CHAPTER 17

The Last Bookstore

I PREPARED FOR MY RETURN to the Cecil Hotel, arranging for a drone operator to photograph the exterior. I also doubled-down on research, looking for any of the latest information. I can't imagine that there's ever been a case that is so popular for which so little is known.

What was Elisa doing on the 14th floor? Her room, though it had changed, was on the 5th floor. The upper floors are supposedly where the long-term residents live. Why was Elisa up there?

And speaking of her changed room, who were the supposed roommates that had complained of her behavior? Had the police questioned them? It seemed almost unbelievable that with a case this popular, no one had ever spoken to these roommates?

What was the apocryphal story of the allegedly disturbing postcard sent by Elisa to an "Amanda"? This was an online rumor that websleuths claimed had originated from the cousin himself. But there was no additional info about it.

What was Elisa doing on January 26 and 27? She was in LA but hadn't yet checked in to the Cecil. Who did she stay with? In attempting to retrace Elisa's steps, the question I kept returning to was whether Elisa had intended to meet someone in Los Angeles.

Some online commenters had questioned why Elisa was wearing men's shorts several sizes too big for her. Not exactly characteristic of a fashionista while in Los Angeles, they observed. One insensitive commenter even floated the idea that such a garment looked "post-coital."

THE TIMESTAMP MAP

One websleuth I met online had gone to great lengths to try and retrace Elisa's movements in Southern California. I met Robin on a forum thread for the website Crisis Forums, where a number of websleuths were still toiling away on the case, desperately looking for any clue, any thread of a yarn that could be pulled on.

Like me, Robin had been studying Elisa's blogs. But his work was less focused on the content of Elisa's posts than the frequency, time, location, and device information. Using the metadata provided by the source code of her social-media pages, he had developed a unique kind of digital forensics, which he called a "timestamp map."

By studying the metadata of Elisa's posts, he determined that (1) Elisa was on Tumblr pretty much every day without fail for two years prior to her West Coast tour and (2) Her most common time of activity was late at night. (3) Elisa definitely arrived at the Cecil Hotel on the twenty-eighth, not the twenty-sixth, as some believed. (4) Elisa did not use her laptop for any Tumblr posts for 2.5 days before her disappearance. (5) She did not use her Blackberry for Tumblr posts because she had lost her phone, and possibly another phone while in San Diego

In his day by day breakdown of Elisa's posts, Robin distinguishes between queued posts and non-queued posts. Tumblr allows you to schedule when you're going to post something and it appears Elisa used this feature quite a bit. [This would also explain Elisa's posthumous posts, though it doesn't make them any less eerie.] A queued post does not signify where or when Elisa was when that post was published; a non-queued post does.

Robin's map shows Elisa arriving in San Diego on the twenty-fourth after a missed flight that kept her up almost all night. As a result, she slept most of the day, which we know because she posted about it from her hostel. On either the twenty-fifth or twenty-sixth, she went to the San Diego zoo.

Robin believes that Elisa didn't arrive in Los Angeles until the twenty-eighth. Therefore, he says, Elisa's post about "creepers" on

The Cecil Hotel (renamed Stay on Main), in downtown Los Angeles, has a notorious history.
Many suicides, murders, and mysterious deaths have taken place there.
Serial killers Richard Ramirez and Jack Unterweger lived there during their murder sprees.
Photo by Jared Salas.

The Cecil's management has refused to comment on the Elisa Lam case,
but some residents believe hotel employees may have been involved in her death.
Photo by Ryan Washburn.

The Cecil Hotel, which opened in 1927, is said to be haunted.
Management has announced plans to build a pool and a bar on the roof where Elisa died.
Photo by Jared Salas.

Downtown Los Angeles, an area that is both the "Wall Street of the West"
and host to one of the largest populations of homeless people in the world.
Photo by Ryan Washburn.

A surprising number of people have jumped to their deaths from the upper windows of the Cecil Hotel. Visible *(on the right)* is one of the fire escapes Elisa may have climbed to access the roof.
Photo by Ryan Washburn.

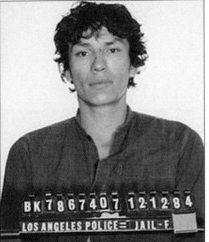

BK 7867407 121284
LOS ANGELES POLICE = JAIL-F

Richard Ramirez, known as the Night Stalker, who terrorized Los Angeles in the late 1980s with over a dozen brutal murders, was a Cecil Hotel resident

SPECIAL
Daily Police Bulletin

Issued Daily Except Saturday Sunday & Holidays by Police Printing Bureau

For Circulation Among Police Officers Exclusively

OFFICIAL PUBLICATION OF POLICE DEPARTMENT, CITY OF LOS ANGELES, CALIFORNIA

CHIEF'S OFFICE, City Hall (Phone Michigan 5211—Connecting all Stations and Depts.)   C. B. HORRALL, Chief of Police

Vol. 40   Tuesday, January 21, 1947   No. 14

WANTED INFORMATION ON ELIZABETH SHORT
Between Dates January 9 and 15, 1947

Description: Female, American, 22 years, 5 ft. 6 in., 118 lbs., black hair, green eyes, very attractive, bad lower teeth, finger nails chewed to quick. This subject found brutally murdered, body severed and mutilated January 15, 1947, at 39th and Norton.

Subject on whom information wanted last seen January 9, 1947 when she got out of car at Biltmore Hotel. At that time she was wearing black suit, no collar on coat, probably Cardigan style, white fluffy blouse, black suede high-heeled shoes, nylon stockings, white gloves full-length beige coat, carried black plastic handbag (2 handles) 12 x 8, in which she had black address book. Subject readily makes friends with both sexes and frequented cocktail bars and night spots. On leaving car she went into lobby of the Biltmore, and was last seen there.

Inquiry should be made at all hotels, motels, apartment houses, cocktail bars and lounges, night clubs to ascertain whereabouts of victim between dates mentioned. In conversations subject readily identified herself as Elizabeth or "Beth" Short.

Attention Officers H. H. Hansen and F. A. Brown, Homicide Detail.

KINDLY NOTIFY C. B. HORRALL, CHIEF OF POLICE, LOS ANGELES, CALIFORNIA.

Elizabeth Short, known as "the Black Dahlia," was found brutally murdered only blocks from the Cecil Hotel. It is rumored that she had a drink at the Cecil the night she was killed.

A drone image shows the water tanks and utility room on the roof
of the Cecil as well as the side and rear fire escapes.

The utility room on the roof, with its own staircase and ladder.
It is possible that Elisa—or her killer—
climbed on top of this structure to access the water tanks.
Photos by Ryan Washburn.

The roof of the Cecil Hotel had four water cisterns. Approximately two weeks after Elisa disappeared, her corpse was found in the rear right tank. *Photos by Ryan Washburn.*

It is still unknown how Elisa accessed the roof without setting off an alarm,
and how and why she ended up in the water tank.
LAPD detectives concluded that Elisa climbed into the tank
by accident due to complications from bipolar disorder.
Photo by Ryan Washburn.

Firefighters used lasers to cut a hole in the side of the water tank
so that they could remove Elisa's body.
Photo by Jonathan Alcorn / Reuters Pictures.

A view of one of the hallways in the Cecil Hotel. Some previous tenants describe its hallways as the sites of hard drug use, prostitution, murder, sexual assault, and paranormal activity.
Photo above by Ryan Washburn; (left) still from author's documentary.

The elevator arrives at the 14th floor, where the surveillance footage of Elisa Lam was filmed and where serial killer Richard Ramirez lived in the 1980s.
Photo by author.

Stills from the notorious surveillance video recorded inside the Cecil Hotel on Elisa's last night. Elisa acts erratically and at times appears to be hiding from someone. This was the only surveillance footage released even though detectives later acknowledged the existence of additional footage of Elisa entering the Cecil Hotel with two men.

Analysis of the distorted timecode in the lower left indicates the video may have been tampered with.

Websleuth Cody Fry believes the footage was slowed down
and that nearly a minute was removed.

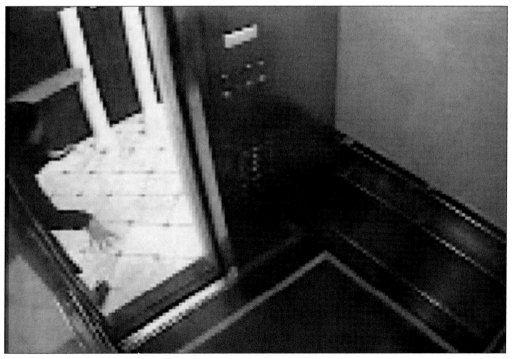

Toward the end of the video, the minute in the timecode changes twice in 7 seconds.
Was evidence of Elisa's killer destroyed?

Re-creation of Elisa in downtown LA. A few days before she disappeared,
Elisa posted online that she had been harassed by "creepers."
Photo by Jason Lee.

A homeless encampment only blocks from the Cecil Hotel.
One anonymous source reported a statement from an off-duty cop claiming
that some of Elisa's belongings were found in a dumpster on Skid Row.
Photo by Jared Salas.

One of the last public sightings of Elisa was at The Last Bookstore, only a few blocks from the Cecil Hotel. There are conflicting reports about her behavior there.

On the same block as the Cecil Hotel is the restaurant Margarita's Place, where serial killer Richard Ramirez often dined in the 1980s.
Photos by Jared Salas.

Joe Elwell was friends with Elisa Lam for several years. After conducting his own investigation, he believes Elisa was murdered and that the LAPD is covering it up.
Photo by author.

Joe returned to Vancouver, Canada, Elisa's hometown, to gather evidence.
Photo by Jason Lee.

Websleuth John Lordan runs the popular true-crime YouTube channel BrainScratch. John spent years investigating the Elisa Lam case and believes that either the LAPD or the Cecil Hotel management may be concealing what really happened to her.
Photo by author.

A page of Elisa's autopsy report containing one of the many anomalies John Lordan points out in his Brainscratch videos. Here we see that the coroner has made a hasty last-minute change: He has scratched out "could not be determined" and instead marked "accident" without explaining what evidence changed his mind.

Clyde Lewis is a popular radio host whose nightly program, *Ground Zero*, explores conspiracy theories and concepts like synchronicity. Clyde believes Elisa may have been possessed.

Clyde Lewis also hosts monthly in-person lectures and Q&As at the Ground Zero lounge, where he discusses government and corporate corruption, propaganda, and health issues.
Photos by author.

Joni Mayhan is an author and paranormal researcher who has visited the Cecil Hotel. She says dark entities from the past may have preyed on Elisa. *Photo by author.*

Image of the Cecil Hotel lobby taken by psychic medium Natalie Davis, who stayed at the hotel the very same nights in 2013 as Elisa did. She shares a disturbing account of her stay. *Photo by Natalie Davis.*

Dr. John Hiserodt is a board-certified pathologist with 20 years' experience in forensics and has worked as a coroner in both the public and private sectors. In his professional analysis, the autopsy of Elisa Lam does not establish accidental drowning as the cause of death. He believes it is more likely that Elisa died before entering the water tank. *Photo by author.*

MISSING

Elisa Lam

Elisa Lam, 21, from Vancouver, B.C. was traveling in Southern California when she went missing. She was last seen at The Cecile Hotel in downtown Los Angeles.

Lam is described as an Asian woman of Chinese descent. She has black hair, brown eyes and stands 5 feet 4 inches tall. She weighs about 115 pounds. Lam is fluent in English and also speaks Cantonese.

Anyone with information about Lam's whereabouts is asked to call police at (213) 486-6890 or (877) 527-3247. Anonymous tips can be called in at (800) 222-8477.

 Missing Persons of America
Missing Persons of America on Facebook

the twenty-sixth was referring to the area around her San Diego hostel, possibly in Little Italy.

Her Speakeasy visit would also have been a San Diego venture. Robin says that on the twenty-sixth at 11:31 P.M., Elisa wrote a non-queued post about how the Italian and Mexican guys come at her strong, calling them "creepers." It then appears that she went to a midnight Speakeasy show for a couple hours. She tweeted about it at 12:57 A.M. using her Blackberry. So at some point between 1 A.M. and 2:30 A.M. when she returned to her hostel, she lost her Blackberry. Her next post, at 3:50 A.M. was with her laptop, when she posted that she had lost her phone.

Robin believes she traveled via bus to Los Angeles on the twenty-eighth and arrived at the Cecil Hotel in the late afternoon when it was getting dark.

Robin even had a theory as to why Elisa was in LA. Or at least he was aware of one of the activities Elisa was excited about there. Evidently, Elisa attended a taping of the Conan O'Brien show. In fact, there is video of her sitting in the crowd. Robin stated that she attended this taping on January 30, when Dr. Sanjay Gupta, a neurosurgeon, was a guest. Elisa follows Gupta on Twitter, and Robin supposes that she was interested in the neuroscience of mental illness.

Her last non-queued post was on the twenty-ninth. On this day, in the late afternoon, Elisa went out and bought gifts at The Last Bookstore. This was the last time she would be seen outside of the hotel. Two and a half days later she was filmed in the elevator, whereafter she disappeared.

THE LAST (KNOWN) PERSON TO SPEAK WITH ELISA

The Last Bookstore used to be a bank. Its walls are lined with ornate marble, and the rooms the books are stored in are old vaults, complete with pressured locking doors. Some of the hallways veer into curving labyrinthine sections, with a tunnel made of hardbacks. They used one of the old bank vaults to house a few genres. They have a section for vinyl records, too.

The manager of The Last Bookstore, Katie Orphan, made headlines when she reported that she had spoken with Elisa on the day she vanished. This was widely reported to be the last conversation with Elisa and the last sighting of her outside of the hotel.

Katie told reporters that Elisa was "very outgoing, very lively, very friendly." Their conversation was apparently pretty surface level, though, centering around whether her purchases would be too cumbersome for the remainder of her trip. "It seemed like she had plans to return home, plans to give things to her family members and reconnect with them."

Orphan, like so many others, did not have a good feeling about the case. "The fact that it doesn't feel like a very satisfying conclusion to her story, I think, has helped keep it fresh in my mind. But it also just seems almost a dismissive way of looking at her death and just saying: 'Well, it was an accident and we're done.' . . . Mysteries like this should not remain unsolved."

But Orphan, it turns out, was not the only person who had an encounter with Elisa at The Last Bookstore.

In the course of our investigation, we found a man named Tosh Berman who spoke with Elisa at The Last Bookstore on January 31, 2013.

Tosh Berman, an LA native born and raised, lives in Silverlake but frequently goes downtown. He likes the mixture of cultures and ethnicities there, the bustle of working-class denizens, students, tourists, and homeless people all bouncing off each other. But most of all he loves the eclectic architecture.

However, there is at least one part of downtown that Tosh avoids: Broadway and 5th, a couple blocks from the Cecil Hotel, which he calls the Gates of Hell. He says the intersection and neighboring blocks are well-known for weird occurrences, car accidents, disturbed transients and a general dark energy. When he walks through the area, he says, his spider senses are activated.

On January 31, 2013, Tosh journeyed downtown to present some books to the public for his press TamTam Books. He had time to kill, so he browsed for vinyl records at The Last Bookstore. The vinyl vault was mostly empty except for him, another man, and a young woman he later identified as Elisa Lam. Elisa had a stack of records and, like Tosh, was browsing for more.

But, contrary to manager Katie Orphan's description, Tosh noticed something peculiar about Elisa. Though she was friendly, her disarmed, unguarded demeanor unnerved him.

Elisa asked him which album would be better, a Herb Alpert or a Miles Davis. This bothered him as a music lover, he joked, but as the conversation went on, he began to sense an affectation to Elisa that was both aggressive and desperate. He got the feeling that Elisa needed to communicate. While the other guy in the room avoided her and wandered off, Tosh remained and spoke to her. But Elisa's behavior became more erratic and Tosh sensed that she was psychologically disturbed.

"I was worried because she seemed mentally unwell. It was alarming how open she was with me, too open for a stranger in downtown LA. You have to be careful," he said.

Tosh found her appealing at first but her behavior made him uncomfortable. She never asked him his taste in music, he said, disappointed. She didn't ask about his life. It was more like she was talking *at* him.

"It felt like a medicine issue, like a manic phase . . . and I didn't want to get involved, didn't want to be in her world or sucked into her internal landscape."

Finally, he politely said good-bye and left.

Weeks later, when he saw the surveillance tape on the news, he was shocked. But Tosh couldn't recognize Elisa by the person in the elevator footage, couldn't even determine the ethnicity. He only recognized her after the local news showed a picture of Elisa wearing a scarf, the same scarf she had been wearing at The Last Bookstore.

Tosh described the footage as compelling but creepy, as it seemed like Elisa was fluctuating between many moods. Tosh, remembering how Elisa acted in person, feels she was seeing things in her own head. He didn't get the feeling that someone else was outside the elevator. Elisa was, once again, painfully alone.

"It's almost more scary to me that no one was chasing her. I was more afraid of her than what could be outside the elevator."

A friend of his with law-enforcement connections told him to contact the police and he did, leaving a message for a detective. But no one ever returned his call. Here was a man who had conversed with the victim on the day she disappeared, and the police did not question him at all.

But Tosh says the way she was acting in the elevator footage was not on display earlier that day when he saw her. However, he had found it odd that she was communicating so openly with a stranger. He felt she endangered herself and could have easily been manipulated, exploited, and possibly physical harmed.

"It felt like I had a power over her, like I could have easily invited her for a drink, and it bothered me because mentally I don't think she was prepared to be talking to strangers alone in a dangerous city in her state."

He was particularly surprised by the interview with Orphan because his perception was so different. While she struck Tosh as a fundamentally nice and interesting young woman, Elisa seemed to be in a disturbed state of mind and was a danger to herself.

Overall, the case is haunting and mesmerizing for Tosh.

"It's like *Twin Peaks* or a David Lynch narrative," Tosh said. "It's dreamlike. Most stories have a beginning, middle, and an end. This story just has these bizarre circumstances that are unexplained. It's still unclear what happened to her."

Did she climb up the ladder to the water tank herself? he wonders. Or did someone put her over their shoulder and carry her up there? They're both improbable, neither makes sense. Part of the weird fascination of this case, he believes, is the non-narrative nature of the mystery. There's no sense that this story will ever have resolution and that disturbs and entices people on a fundamental level.

Tosh then noted, in a statement that I wasn't sure what to make of, that he felt he had a certain power over Elisa and could have "invited her over for a drink."

This brings us to an important point related to the connection between mental illness and predation. Young women with mental illnesses are more vulnerable to crime. That Elisa had bipolar disorder and may have suffered a psychotic episode while at the Cecil Hotel does not preclude homicide or some kind of foul play being involved as well. The two are not mutually exclusive.

Predators target people who are vulnerable and alone. Someone who may be less likely to be believed when she claims someone is following her—such as Elisa, who it seems had developed a reputation as a troublesome guest within the hotel—is an even more ideal target for the strategic predator.

The question of what danger Elisa faced is one of the central investigations here and is a two-part question. To what extent was Elisa endangered by sexual predators, drug abusers, or violent transients or locals outside the hotel and inside the hotel (possibly even employed by or affiliated with the hotel)? This question would take some time to answer.

The second part of the question was: To what extent was Elisa a danger to herself because of her worsening mental state? She describes the problem pretty explicitly in her blogs:

"I'm fine if I don't open my mouth but as soon as I do and start talking, I can get in trouble," she wrote. "My mouth is my downfall and it will get me in trouble. I already do so many stupid things. I have troubles knowing where the boundaries are."

Elsewhere, she wrote: "I take things too far and I have no filter, little self-control and that's something I have to work on."

While traveling, Elisa seemed to feel especially socially inept. She wrote a post about it called "How to meet people (and possibly make friends) in TWO easy steps!"

Her plan, which she probably jokingly said she researched during her weeklong stay in an Ontario hostel on December 6, 2012, called for the following: "1. You go up to them and SHOUT talk very quickly with a maniacal smile. 2. And then run away."

Despite her social alienation, Elisa seemed determined to overcome it and meet new people. She expressed a strong desire to have a group of friends. But this desire conflicted with an intense anxiety she feels as well as a fear of "creepers." She refers to creepers approaching her days before she disappeared but this wasn't the first time, nor was it the first time she openly discussed the idea of being stalked.

"Thanks to the internet we record our lives and put it on some stage for creepers to stalk and follow so they can stop thinking about their own troubles for a moment and escape into someone else's."

This is a double-edged comment: She fears online followers turning into real-life stalkers; and she also recognizes that the Internet she loves so much turns into escapism.

"The INTERNET IS FULL OF PEDOPHILES," she writes. "They'll suddenly pop out of nowhere and try to attack you."

This falls in line with what she blogged on January 10, 2013, only twenty-one days before her disappearance: "If you're a young girl and an older attractive man notices you and is chatting you up, he wants to have sex with you. It really is that simple and sad."

Robin, the websleuth from England who analyzed Elisa's digital forensics trail, does not believe Elisa was in Los Angeles to meet anyone, nor does he even believe Elisa met with a potential suitor. Robin thinks Elisa's demise was an inside job.

WHY WAS ELISA ON THE 14TH FLOOR?

After the bookstore, we do not have a direct chronology of what happened next. In fact, this is the million-dollar question. But Robin has a hypothesis. And what happened to Elisa was no accident, he says.

Based on his digital analysis of Elisa's Internet habits, Robin believes Elisa was severely restless and agitated while at the Cecil. He does not think she was having a psychotic breakdown, though manic symptoms from (then untreated) bipolar disorder may have exasperated her restlessness.

When speculating on what "bizarre" behavior she may have been exhibiting that caused her roommates to request a room change, he imagines she was pacing around the room while they tried to sleep. This was a young woman who was used to Internet activity every day prior to coming to Los Angeles and suddenly has no phone and her laptop is getting a bad wifi connection. Therefore, she can't use the Internet unless she is in the lobby. She was a creature of habit and accustomed to reblogging before going to sleep. So she is restless, frustrated, lonely, and having trouble sleeping.

Robin thinks Elisa would have been especially confused when she returned from The Last Bookstore on the 31st, her last day, to learn she had been moved to a different room. He thinks she may have napped in her new room until about nine or ten o'clock at night.

Upon waking up, she was more disconcerted and alienated than ever. She had no entertainment and it was probably too late to go down to the lobby or the neighborhood surrounding the hotel, which would have been dangerous.

She got frustrated and in her restless state decided she wanted to walk around the hotel and explore. Robin thinks it's also possible she intended to call her family (which was a daily habit of hers) from the lobby. Regardless, she left her room with her room key, which indicates she planned to return.

At some point during her exploration of the hotel, she ran into security. This could have happened in the lobby or elsewhere in the hotel. The security guards, Robin notes, would have been aware of Elisa's entire situation. They knew she was a solo traveler and was essentially alone in a city she knew virtually nothing about; they knew she had been displaying questionable behavior and had been moved to her own room (in fact, said security guards may have accompanied her to the new room); and they would have known she was wandering around the hotel based on the surveillance feed from the 14th floor.

After the events of the surveillance video, Elisa may have run into one or more of the hotel's security staff, who asked if she wanted to see the roof. Again, they knew she was acting "strange" and that she was alone. In many ways, she was an optimal victim. The security guard escorted her to the roof, deactivated the alarm and held the door open for her. These actions are critical because it means Elisa was able to access the roof without setting off the alarm and she did not leave any DNA behind on the door.

Robin also notes that it makes sense that Elisa was accompanied or guided to the roof. She did not know anything about the layout of the hotel, and it was dark and treacherous. I've always had a difficult time imagining Elisa scaling the fire escape on the side of the building. But if she took the main-roof entrance, how was the alarm not triggered?

The accompaniment theory takes care of this. The security guard would have known the layout of the roof and would have had a flashlight. Robin notes that it's improbable that Elisa would have navigated through a dark rooftop to climb a random tank (that she would not have known anything about) by herself. Elisa, in her bored and restless state, would have been interested in the roof and would have been more likely to trust a stranger in a security uniform than a random stranger. She may have already established a rapport with this security guard from her stay at the hotel.

The security guard escorted her up to the roof (perhaps with a guest, a friend, or another employee) and showed her the view of downtown Los Angeles. Maybe this security guard—perhaps the one referenced by multiple guests as seeming predatory—regularly tried to seduce women on the roof; maybe not. At this point, Robin says, there's a couple of different ways things could have played out.

The security guard may have presented the situation as a favor. "You've been causing us some trouble." Or: "There, I showed you the roof . . . now what are you going to do for me?"

This man may have made a move on Elisa and freaked her out; they may have started to embrace; he may have outright attempted to force her to do something . . . but Robin thinks that they were either interrupted by something or Elisa realized what was happening and wanted to leave. The security guard may have ordered her to take her clothes off. However it played out, the security guard did not want Elisa coming back from the roof. Maybe he was worried she would report his advances. Or maybe she passed out from being drugged.

The security guard, Robin believes, ordered Elisa to get in the tank. Or he may have put her in himself. Or, and this is me thinking here, perhaps she tried to hide from someone on the roof—in the water tank—and then realized she couldn't get out.

Either way, Robin believes Elisa was still alive when she entered the cistern.

This theory does not go so far as to state Elisa was actually raped (which independent coroners have stated is not ruled out by the autopsy). Robin thinks the act was interrupted in such a way as to cause the security guard to panic. That Elisa may have been alive in the tank for hours has always been a chilling hypothesis. Robin believes it's also possible that the water was cold enough to cause Elisa to go into shock and render her unconscious (a merciful twist in an otherwise horrifying scenario).

The security guard theory, Robin says, is the most logical one if you think about motive and opportunity. All the anomalies of the case revolve around contingencies that the security guards would have direct involvement in: the ability to deactivate the alarmed door; access to and knowledge of the roof; access to and knowledge of the surveillance system; and access to and knowledge of Elisa's specific situation in the hotel, including her vulnerable behavior and room change.

Additionally, and perhaps most crucially, they would likely have been the first people dispatched to look for Elisa when she did not check out the next morning. This would have given him (or them) ample time to edit the surveillance footage, dispose of any evidence, delay the discovery of the body, and present a credible narrative of mental illness that would be corroborated by the surveillance video.

The only part of the theory that doesn't make sense to me is why the security guard would have left the cistern lid open. While it's possible this detail was misreported, the official narrative states that the lid was open when Santiago Lopez discovered the body. Of course, as my investigation continued, new information about Santiago would surface that would force me to question whether the hotel employee depositions in the civil case were 100 percent truthful.

Robin is hardly the first or only websleuth to suggest that the Cecil Hotel security guards may have been involved in Elisa's death. But is there any evidence for it? And is there evidence that Cecil Hotel employees have sexually harassed and/or assaulted guests?

Answering these questions triggered a new phase of my investigation, one in which I would find credible evidence of foul play and a cover-up.

CHAPTER 18

Return to the Cecil

As THE JOURNEY INTENSIFIED, my anxiety and mental condition worsened. And synchronicities arose with greater frequency. It's as if the hotel had dispatched thought-form sentries to sabotage me and prevent my return. It reminded me of in *The Shining* when the Overlook Hotel deputizes its ghosts to convince Jack he needs to constrain his wife and son. The hotel doesn't want anyone meddling in its affairs. His son, Jack is told, has been "a very naughty boy."

Checking in, the first thing I heard, once again, was the sound of laughter echoing through the ornate, expansive lobby of the Cecil. The phlegmatic chuckles traveled along the floor and crescendoed right before the concierge greeted me, eyeball to eyeball.

I was assigned a room on the same floor as the Cecil's second known serial killer, Jack Unterweger.

This is what's known as a happy accident.

DON'T LET THE BEDBUGS BITE

At the very last moment, I suddenly decided to run a bedbug search on the hotel. I had a traumatic experience with bedbugs years earlier, and the fear remained. Bedbugs don't come out of the woodwork until very late at night, just before dawn. You've just entered that precious, nourishing stage of the REM cycle when suddenly you become dimly, unconsciously aware that a cabal of tiny creatures is systematically syphoning blood from your body.

Many landlords and hotel-management teams are awful about

combating the problem because it's expensive and tedious. A building near MacArthur Park where I lived refused to address the situation so I collected bedbugs in a glass jar for evidence in case of a lawsuit. I lost a lot of sleep and mental stability during that time.

Bedbugs are not to be trifled with. In sudden horror that I had forgotten about them, I looked up the Cecil Hotel on the bedbug registry and found multiple entries of people traumatized by bedbugs at the Cecil.

But I wasn't leaving. I would just have to burn my clothes afterward.

I entered my room and immediately looked at the window. Last time I was here, it felt like the hotel was nudging me toward the window. This time, I sensed silence. But calculated silence. I didn't trust the place.

It wants me to stay, I thought, *and if it freaks me out too early, I might leave. This is a game it's played before.*

I was, of course, completely aware of the perverse flow of my logic, of the borderline schizo-affective nature of my paranoia. I'm one of hundreds, perhaps thousands who have come under the insidious spell of the Cecil. I spoke to one karaoke DJ who told me her ex-boyfriend almost lost his mind at the Cecil Hotel. He was convinced a demon infiltrated his mind while staying there and stayed with him for months afterward. This is just one of hundreds of similar stories.

I stripped the sheets of my bed and checked for bloodstains, the telltale mark of bedbug handiwork. No immediate signs, but those critters can burrow deep into the woodwork and floorboards, only to arise in the pre-dawn hours like disciplined farmers.

I learned that hotel maintenance may have eliminated any mattresses with bloodstains. In her investigation of the Cecil Hotel in 2012, Chelsea Damali and her Paranormal Syndicate acquired access to the hotel's basement, where dozens of mattresses lay stacked and sheathed in black plastic.

Evidently, they remove all mattresses from rooms where guests have died. Former assistant manager Tasheyla MacLean interviewed on the show *Haunted Encounters Face to Face*, confirmed this to Chelsea. Employees wrap them in black plastic and store some of them in the basement. A Cecil employee may have glimpsed bedbug bloodstains and assumed they were from a suicide or murder.

In her on-camera interview, MacLean also confirmed something else, something shocking regarding the true death count at the Cecil. Someone has died, she said, in every room at the Cecil Hotel. That's 600 rooms. Even if she's way off, by hundreds even, the implication is clear: the building itself is sheathed in death.

Maybe that's why it feels so claustrophobic.

"They Killed Another Girl"

While I was in Los Angeles, I met with a woman who had lived in the Cecil Hotel. What she told me shaped the way I would proceed with the rest of my investigation, especially after I was able to corroborate some of her claims with other former tenants. Sally wanted to remain anonymous because she feared retribution from the hotel.

Downtown LA changed Sally. In her heart, she was still a nice country girl from rural Maryland, but the necessities of sustenance as a low-income woman in a dangerous area brought out a survival instinct in her that, over time, hardened her demeanor.

Sally doesn't take shit from anyone. When movie crews film in the downtown area, she bulldozes over actors in her power wheelchair, dog in lap. She earned a reputation for this. People would say "here she comes."

She's not as nice with actors, who she considers leeches. "Get out of my way before I hurt your pretty face," she said to a B-lister. "You're a loser with money."

She treats the homeless with more respect, treats them as friends. The homeless in downtown LA are a family and they take care of each other, she told me.

But poverty, drug use, and mental illness can draw out the worst in people, and she saw this firsthand. Before moving to the Cecil, she lived in a Skid Row hotel with her Hispanic husband. Out in the hallway, she said, a white john who had been roughing up a prostitute was being stabbed by a group of six Mexicans. She needed to use the restroom and her husband told them to stop blocking the hall. So they moved down the hall and threw the john out the window.

She saw a man crossing a parking lot get stabbed by a guy, who removed the victim's shoes to see if he had money in them. "I just killed a guy for a penny," he said, laughing.

Sally lived on the 12th floor of the Cecil Hotel for much of the 1980s and all of the 1990s, moving out in 2000. The stories she relayed paint a bleak, hostile scene. The smell of dead bodies from drug overdoses wafting through the hallways; maids turning tricks; blackmail and extortion; rampant drug use. Sally propped her wheelchair against the door at night to delay would-be intruders.

And if they ever did do a proper inspection, they would find a lot of dead bodies, maybe even some in the elevator shaft, she said. As a result, tenants at the Cecil were afraid to walk the halls because dead spirits passed through.

"They need to burn that bitch to the ground and condemn the property," she said of the Cecil.

Then Sally got deadly serious. Cecil employees would use the master key to break into the rooms of young women and rape them, she said. They were told that if they said anything or reported it to the police that they would get kicked out onto the street and would lose their deposit. One woman, Sally's friend, was so terrified of retribution that she would not speak on record about it. "I have no money," she said crying. She was waiting for her Section 8 just to have money for groceries.

The deposit scam was a racket that management kept up for years, she said. Management kicked people out and stole their deposits. Sometimes drugs were planted in their rooms as a pretext. Since these tenants had no money, they had to turn to the streets and try and find a cubby hole to sleep in. Even if they had told the police, it wouldn't have changed anything because she said the police were scared of the Cecil and avoided it at all cost. The Cecil operated outside the bounds of law and order.

Sally said she and others regularly drank on the roof in the '80s and is certain she once saw Richard Ramirez in the elevator.

When she heard about the Elisa Lam case, the first thing she said is: "They killed another girl."

"They don't care about nothing," she said. "That poor child died because they wanted to have sex with her and she probably fought them."

Sally was convinced Elisa was targeted for rape and then killed—a theory she based on her direct experience with hotel employees raping young female tenants and extorting them into silence under threat of eviction. Sally says Elisa's death fits the profile points of sexual predation she saw firsthand. Elisa, she said, probably fought back and must have proved to be too much trouble and too risky to be left alive.

"Her soul is not at rest."

"HIS BEST MURDER"

The second serial killer to live at the Cecil Hotel was Jack Unterweger. In *Entering Hades: The Double Life of a Serial Killer,* author John Leake documented the incredible history of how Unterweger managed to carry out brutal murder sprees on two different continents while becoming an international celebrity.

In 1974, Austrian Jack Unterweger began serving a prison sentence for the murder of an eighteen-year-old girl, who he'd raped and strangled to death with her own bra. While imprisoned he produced a prolific portfolio of works, including a play called *Purgatory,* in which he meditated on the Dantesque idea that he was between Heaven and Hell, neither dead nor alive, but rather undergoing punishment in hope of redemption.

Unterweger also wrote children's stories and in the late 1970s, the ORF (Österreichischer Rundfunk) Austrian state broadcasting company began airing them. He later used this platform to craft a narrative of his childhood—one in which he yearned for his absent mother, and was traumatized by the murder of his aunt, a prostitute who "was killed by her last customer." Unterweger gave televised readings of his work from prison and slowly built a following in Vienna's literary circles, where the idea of a murderer rehabilitating himself through art struck a chord among the nation's intellectuals.

Unterweger's boyish good looks and charm further endeared him to his fans and before long, Unterweger was himself a celebrity. After he served the minimum fifteen years of his sentence, there was a full-fledged campaign to get Unterweger paroled. Literature had cleansed Unterweger's violent instincts, Vienna's intellectuals and political ideologues argued. With the goal of a new resocialization program in the justice system and the dream of a "prisonless society," Jack Unterweger became the poster boy for criminal rehabilitation. Jack Unterweger was not a killer—he was an artist now.

Jack walked out of prison on May 23, 1990 at the age of thirty-nine. Shortly thereafter, Unterweger gave his first reading as a free man. Always one for flair and grandiose style, Unterweger's newfound celebrity curried favor with the nation's rebellious art scene. For a magazine photo spread, he posed in a cobwebbed attic in only blue jeans, his surprisingly muscled and tattooed chest and legs bare. There happened to be a long rope lying about, which Unterweger fashioned into a noose and posed as both the hangman and the executed.

The next year, eerily contemporaneous with the release of the horror film *The Silence of the Lambs,* three prostitutes from Vienna's red-light district were found brutally murdered—and a year later, another was found murdered in the nearby town of Graz. Just as a new kind of serial killer blew up the cinema—the brilliantly sadistic Hannibal Lecter—Vienna received its first real one. It was as though Hannibal had transmogrified from the screen to reality. Terror seized the streets of Vienna.

As the police searched for the killer, Unterweger got involved, writing an article about the murders in which he advocated for the safety of sex workers in the red-light district and criticized the sensationalist angle most reporters took. He accused middle-class readers of "greedy voyeurism" and said that hysteria over the crimes was preventing investigators from finding the murderer, a phenomenon that closely paralleled the Black Dahlia investigation in Los Angeles decades earlier.

"We should be glad there is a red-light district," Unterweger said. "The dead [women] in the Vienna Woods are another argument for why society should do more to provide security for prostitutes."

Unterweger took a keen interest in the murders and planned to report on them extensively. He peppered the police chief with questions, though he couldn't divulge critical details. Jack wanted to know what they knew. What the police could disclose to the public was that there were seven victims, all sex workers, all strangled to death.

What the police couldn't disclose to the public—details that had to be safeguarded because only the killer would know them—were far more disturbing.

The killer's weapon of choice each time was the victim's bra. Because of its elastic bands, a bra is by itself already a sufficient tourniquet by which to strangle someone. But the killer made a cut in a shoulder strap and reconfigured the bands and straps in such a way as to be able to use three ligatures and "tie the nooses at maximum tension." Such complete and total constriction of the carotid arteries, which had the effect of actually compressing the neck by several inches, guaranteed a ferocious death.

Unterweger's interest in violent crimes at the heart of cities—his so-called "underworld stories"—ultimately brought him to Los Angeles. Unterweger was fascinated by the idea of a glamorous, glittering city with a seedy underbelly.

He arrived in Los Angeles, wearing a white suit and a cowboy hat, in 1991 and checked into the Cecil Hotel, the perfect place for him to study and write about the seedy underworld of a great American city. In *Entering Hades,* John Leake writes that "the hotel embodied a motif that ran through all Jack's magazine articles about L.A.—the existence of extreme destitution in the heart of a city known for its wealth."

He'd also heard that one of the country's most notorious serial killers, Richard Ramirez, stayed there during the '80s, which delighted him.

Unterweger had big plans for Los Angeles. He was determined to ingratiate himself into the Hollywood "glitterati" the same way he had taken over the Vienne literary scene. He wanted to interview Charles Bukowski and on at least one occasion walked around Hollywood Park trying to find the famous writer. He wanted to interview Cher; he drove down the Pacific Coast Highway to her home in Malibu but couldn't get past the gate.

Unterweger was certain he would meet a producer interested in developing one of his stories into an American movie.

Unterweger's most pressing professional goal while in Los Angeles was research for his underworld odyssey, "The Dark Side of Los Angeles," for which he wanted to document the nature of crime in the city. In order to do so, he met with a lieutenant at the LAPD and requested a ride-along, presenting himself as a journalist for an Austrian police journal, only half of which was true.

Unterweger's primary research consisted of interviewing as many prostitutes as he could. He started by canvassing the neighborhood around the Cecil Hotel, equipped with a tape recorder and a microphone. And when he returned to his room at night, he conducted additional experiential research. He invited prostitutes to climb the fire escape up to his room on the 15th floor and service him.

He ventured out to the Hollywood strip as well, where a fantastical array of sex workers greeted him.

But what Unterweger didn't know was that the Viennese police had received a tip regarding the murders in Vienna and Graz. And, in fact, before Unterweger had left Vienna, police had put him under surveillance because the method of death in the new Austrian prostitute killings matched the reformed criminal's MO. But they still didn't have enough evidence.

But then a curious thing happened. While the sex worker killings in Austria stopped, a murdered prostitute showed up in Los Angeles. In what must have been an eerie scene, hikers discovered her body in the Malibu hills during the solar eclipse of July 11, 1991. The cause of death for the victim, whose brain matter had been almost entirely consumed by maggots, was asphyxia due to ligature strangulation.

Los Angeles would soon be dealing with its own new string of murders. Less than five years removed from the terrifying reign of the Night Stalker, LAPD detectives were on guard.

Sure enough, two more murders followed, one of them on 7th Avenue only blocks from the Cecil Hotel. In fact, the red, larger-than-life marquee for the Hotel Cecil was visible from the location of the murder, looming in the smoggy, sun-baked air. The victim: twenty-two-year-old Shannon Exley. The murder weapon: Shannon's own bra, tightly garroted in a way detectives had never before seen.

Meanwhile, Unterweger grew sick of the Cecil Hotel. Apparently, even serial killers are turned off by the place. He'd been robbed there and wanted to leave. But not before he stalked, manipulated, and seduced a young receptionist who worked there. She agreed to travel out of the country with him.

By this time, the Viennese police had assembled more hard evidence linking Unterweger to the crimes in Austria. But Unterweger still had strong support in the literary community and among social activists and members of the intelligentsia who believed that police couldn't catch the real killer so they were blaming it on Jack.

The mythology Jack Unterweger created in his apocryphal autobiographical stories while in prison had overshadowed the violent crime of his youth. Many Austrians at the time had an emotional and ideological connection to the idea of criminal rehabilitation, and using his charm and rhetoric, Unterweger manipulated the country by creating an image of innocence. He may be the only serial killer in history to use literature to extend a murder spree.

Jack was on the run, however, and as his true nature became clear to investigators, a stunning realization set in: Unterweger had been reporting on murders he himself committed. And his pathology, later diagnosed as narcissistic personality disorder (a psychiatric illness common to many serial killers), also expressed itself in the way Jack continued to interview detectives while they built a case against him. Jack carefully questioned them to determine what they knew about the crimes and what they knew about him.

Ultimately, Unterweger was arrested, extradited back to Austria, and convicted of eight counts of murder. He knew that this time around, there was no chance of pardon. Only a few hours after his verdict, Unterweger killed himself in his cell in the Graz-Karlau Prison. He fashioned a rope out of his shoelaces and a cord from his tracksuit and made a noose using the same meticulously crafted ligature he'd used to strangle his victims.

A government spokesman later called it "his best murder."

REMOTE VIEWING

As I loitered in the alley, I could almost see Unterweger perched on the fire escape twelve floors above, looking down, his spirit marooned in the Cecil Hotel—his new purgatory.

Psychic Chelsea Damali did a "remote viewing" session for the Lam case and felt that Elisa was running from something that only she could see. A human coerced her into the tank but Chelsea believes the murderer was influenced by dark spirits. Later, when her Paranormal Syndicate conducted their physical investigation of the Cecil Hotel, they studied Unterweger's room on the 15th floor. Chelsea had to leave in a hurry because she felt his sadistic brutality as viscerally as one might feel a bee sting. He's still there, she said. He's in between life and death but probably isn't aware of it. He's still looking for new victims. As is Ramirez, who lived only one floor down.

Remote viewing sessions involve trying to remotely gain information about an event or place using only the mind. Some parapsychologists, like Russell Targ, who ran the legendary Project Stargate (portrayed in the movie *The Men Who Stare at Goats*), believes psychics can tap nonlocal information through quantum entanglement.

Though many people remain skeptical about such psychic abilities, the declassified CIA documents I mentioned earlier show that the U.S. military did, in fact, use remote viewing for psychic espionage during the Cold War, and the Soviets did the same. Other documents describe how law-enforcement agencies around the country regularly employ psychics for remote viewing sessions to help with missing persons and other cases.

Chelsea's statements made me wonder why Elisa was wandering around on the upper floors, which are reserved for longer-stay residents. This is also where Unterweger and Ramirez lived and where many suicides occurred.

What drew Elisa to those floors?

If there's some fragment of those killers still residing in the hotel, traces of predatory pathos entombed in the walls, does it affect the other tenants? Is this why guests who stay in murdered tenant

Goldie Osgood's room continually report feeling like they're being strangled by an invisible assailant? Is this why people's minds
become suddenly infected with suicidal ideation when they enter
rooms where past guests took their own lives?

Did this dark energy affect Elisa? Did it affect the man or men
who may have killed her?

Will it affect me? I thought, walking back into the lobby.

RELAPSE

When I got back to the Cecil, I decided I would have to buck it up
and do some sleuthing. But first . . . a nap.

Naps are always dangerous for me. Sometimes when I wake up, I
feel emotionally raw to the point of terror. This time around, I awoke
with the visceral sensation that someone was watching me. I'd had
an intense dream, but I couldn't immediately recall the details except for colorful textures and edicts of the future. As expected, it
saddled me with dysphoria, rendered me nostalgic for a life I'd never
known, a world that didn't exist.

Then something unexpected and unfortunate happened. I opened
my laptop and saw that there was a new email awaiting me. When
I opened it, my heart stopped. It was from Lauren, my ex. I looked
away before I could see the contents. The only thing I caught was the
subject, which was "Hiiiii."

Something inside my mind broke. Instantly, the untallied weight
of the trauma from our breakup descended upon me. I remembered
the night I found a love letter sent to Lauren by a much older man,
which marked only the beginning of a small cabal of middle-aged
sociopathic predators entering my life.

They ranged in social rank from the homeless anarchist to a university professor. But before I could even start to process this information, Lauren claimed the Professor had raped her. It happened,
she said, after we broke up, while I was driving to Albuquerque.
Perhaps when I was pulling off the freeway to have nervous breakdowns, I was absorbing her trauma from afar.

I had friends cast doubts on the rape, but I believe assault victims
unless given a credible reason not to. And I could tell by the trauma

she was going through that it was real. Though I was angry at her for betraying me, I didn't let my anger stop me from supporting her when she needed it.

Lauren's behavior melted down to the point where I believed there was a very real danger of suicide or fatally self-destructive behavior. The Anarchist, who used to hug me at meetings of the activist group we attended, tried to aggressively control Lauren, using her psychological instability as leverage. He also continued trolling me, inflicting as much damage as possible. In a series of vitriolic Facebook messages, he called me a coward for having to take meds for depression.

I shouldn't have responded, but I did. I had spoken with another young woman affiliated with a website I wrote for who told me the Anarchist aggressively courted her and used her psychological and personal problems to manipulate her. So I responded to his message by informing him he was just as bad as the Professor. Like him, I wrote, you're a predator who grooms and manipulates young women.

His next attack really hurt. Because I had forbade him from entering my apartment, the Anarchist accused me of being responsible for Lauren's sexual assault. If he had been having an affair with Lauren at my apartment on the night of the attack, he argued, the Professor wouldn't have come over and the assault wouldn't have happened. This kind of stuff escalated until I finally blocked him on Facebook.

My attention turned to the Professor, who I fantasized killing. The Professor, an investigation revealed, stood accused of grooming college-aged young women at San Diego State for years and was at the center of multiple sexual harassment complaints being arbitrated by the university. Prior to his tenured job at SDU, the professor taught at the University of Delaware, where other students accused him of sexual harassment. Maybe it was a case of "pass the harasser," which is evidently almost as common in higher education as it is in the Catholic Church.

I looked up his address, planning a confrontation, but ultimately talked myself down from that ledge. This made me feel like a coward, which made me recall the Anarchist calling me that. To this day, the word "coward" makes me withdraw, as though the syntax of the word enforces its very meaning.

I internalized the pain, all of it. The cognitive dissonance of wanting to comfort Lauren, though I was mortally wounded by her actions, fractured me. It brought my brain back to that period at the end of high school when I found out the girl I was in love with—who had sprinkled my first kiss upon me like pixie dust—had been raped. I watched her slowly come apart thereafter, same as Lauren.

In a way, then, my obsession with determining whether a sexual predator was involved in the Lam case could have been my subconscious needing to externalize past pain by bringing rapists to justice.

In the immediate aftermath of Lauren's attack, we still shared an apartment, the Cave of Despair. I watched her become more and more erratic and I saw the Anarchist pursuing her more intently, like a cult leader, hoping to twist and shape her trauma into an artificial love for him. He got one of his friends involved with her, too. Clearly, his infatuation was about control, not love.

Sensing she needed to escape her current environment entirely, I spoke with Lauren's mom, a health-care practitioner, who agreed to drive out and take her back home for therapy. She got her on Celexa, which may have saved her from ruin. Going full circle, the person who used to doubt my need for antidepressants now went on one herself.

I threw my computer on the floor.

I'd made considerable progress on cutting back the drugs and alcohol prior to the trip. After the email, I literally jogged to the nearest liquor store and bought a bottle of whiskey. I swallowed a couple painkillers, puffed on my e-cig, and waddled back down Main Street, oblivious to anything peripheral to the smoggy shimmers of tangerine on the horizon.

As I neared the Cecil Hotel, I stopped and, in my stupor, crouched down to rest. I looked up at the fire escape ladders snaking up the side of the building. I focused on the 14th floor and tried to imagine Elisa climbing out and scaling up to the roof.

I lowered my gaze two floors and imagined Jack Unterweger standing on the fire escape, smoking cigarettes and peering down to the alley below, where he profiled sex workers, surveying their movements, casing up the right victim.

Jack stood there, toying with a bra, adjusting the ligatures for maximum torque so that he could methodically control the pace at which he choked the life out of his next victim. He grinned at me and winked.

I went back inside and sat in the lobby, sinking further into despair, adrift in a universe that felt like nothing more than a cathedral of plunder.

Maybe I should just check out for good, I thought. From the Cecil, from the cathedral at large.

Panic seized me. I had to move, I had to get up. But I didn't know where to go or what to do. There was nothing I could do in the present tense to turn my life around. Maybe this was the demon, feeding off my pain. Or maybe it was the destructive information from the past reverberating in the present.

It's going to be a long night, I thought, taking another pull from the whiskey bottle.

PREDATORS ON THE PAYROLL

There are many accusations of creepy, predatory, and criminal acts by the employees of the Cecil. I recalled several Yelp reviews I read in which guests mentioned this kind of behavior specifically from the security guards. It's relevant to the Elisa Lam case for obvious reasons and after speaking to Sally about her time at the Cecil, it was not something anyone seriously investigating this case could ignore.

After weeding through the most frequent complaints of grime, street noise, bad wi-fi, putrid smells, bugs, bloodstains, and an insufficient continental breakfast, I got to more substantive material buried deep in the review threads of Yelp and Travel Advisor.

One reviewer described his stay as like "a scene out of the *Saw* horror movies." Another said his stay was one of "sleepless terror." I know this feeling exactly.

A complaint I saw frequently pertained to guests feeling like they were defrauded out of the security deposit.

And, of course, during a specific two-week period of time, there were complaints about the water. We know how that ended.

One commenter noted the unusually high number of sex offenders in the area and in the actual hotel. "Apparently, the Cecil can boast an extremely high concentration of child molesters among its guests. City lockdown is just down the road, and its relatively child-free downtown setting makes it an ideal place for said perps to stay."

When I looked into Intelius criminal background records, I found that there were no less than six sex offenders on Main Street and about three in Cecil itself.   ·

After speaking to Sally, who reported that hotel employees have used their master key to enter rooms and sexually assault women, the reviews that interested me the most were the ones describing employee interactions.

Another contact, named Tina, who I was referred to by the bouncer from the Speakeasy, confirmed Sally's accusation. She said that many employees, including maintenance workers, had been sexually abusive to tenants. Her account, I should note, pre-dated maintenance worker Santiago Lopez's employment at the Cecil.

The online reviews document more than a few instances of people feeling creeped out by certain employees.

One man wrote that security guards mean-mugged him as he and his girlfriend entered the hotel and then stared at his girlfriend "disgustingly." He said this behavior continued during the check-in and that two armed guards stood nearby, gazing at his girlfriend and then laughing with each other.

Another wrote a lengthy post in the comment thread underneath John Lordan's "BrainScratch: Elisa Lam's Manipulated Elevator Footage" that I find compelling. In it, a man describes staying there with his girlfriend only weeks before Elisa died. He says one of the security guards essentially stalked them through the lobby, staring compulsively at his girlfriend.

"I did contact someone about this after ms. lams death . . ." he wrote. "I think if they were to find that guy that would be the answer to the mystery."

I heard from a woman named Tanya Danielle, who emailed me

about her experience at the Cecil Hotel in 2006. She was assigned a room with broken locks "on a seemingly deserted upper floor."

> *While exploring the hotel I encountered an employee in the elevator . . . [who] offered to give me a tour of the hotel and the predatory glint in his eye seemed unmistakable . . . I have met my share of creepy guys but this man was different. He just seemed too polished and too sure of himself. I had the sense that he felt he could inflict his will on anybody.*

When I read this, I got chills. We now have a fairly well-established pattern of female tenants feeling unsafe at the hotel because of what they perceived to be predatory employees, employees who sometimes offer to give these guests tours of the hotel.

THE RED SPARROW RETURNS

As I sat down in the lobby of the Cecil, I recalled the weirdest experience we had during the filming of our documentary. Our small crew consisted of only myself, Jared (who, earlier that day, had been chased by a woman with a rake), our cinematographer Jason, and Wilhelmina, the actress we hired to play Elisa in recreated scenes.

Wilhelmina had thus far done an impressive job in the recreation sequences. She took seriously the responsibility of portraying someone who suffered from bipolar disorder. She managed to convey Elisa's quixotic but troubled personality wordlessly, gracefully, adding in nuanced idiosyncrasies of body language that conveyed the intelligent but troubled mind of someone struggling with bouts of depression and hypomania.

For this shoot, Wilhelmina was dressed in Elisa's final iconic outfit, black shorts and a red hoodie. We filmed her in front of the Cecil Hotel. It turned out that the very hour we descended upon Main Street, so too did a paranormal tour whose final stop was the Cecil Hotel. Because of its dark history, it's often featured by tours like Esotouric's Hotel Horrors and Main Street Vice.

As the tour bus ambled by, the DJ guide spoke over a small megaphone audible from the street, and the patrons cast their weary eyes upon the Cecil, the bright amber glow of its lobby extending out to the sidewalk.

". . . . and then in 2013, tragedy and terror struck the hotel once again when twenty-one-year-old Elisa Lam was found by hotel employees in the water tank on the roof. Did she join the long lineage of spirits who have been absorbed by this strange building?"

At that moment, several of the tour patrons spotted a young Chinese-American woman, Wilhelmina, wearing the exact same outfit as Elisa at the very moment the tour guide was talking about the case. Several of them pointed with confused expressions. Others looked at the tour guide, assuming this was a pre-planned stunt. The tour guide, wide-eyed, looked like he had either seen a ghost, shit his pants, or both.

We finished our shots in front of the Cecil and decided to split up. Jared, Wilhelmina, and Jason departed on foot to shoot other exterior footage. I went back into the Cecil. During this trip, we hadn't all booked rooms there, but I wanted to do some sleuthing.

As I waited for the elevator, suddenly I saw Wilhelmina pass in front of the hotel going in the opposite direction I had just seen them headed. And I didn't see Jared and Jason with her.

I left the elevator and went outside. Wilhelmina was at the end of the street, waiting for the walk signal to cross Main.

I called her name but she didn't hear me. I assumed she was walking back to the car to get a jacket or something, but I didn't like the idea of her walking alone at night in that part of downtown.

Wilhelmina crossed the street, and I followed after her. The street noise was particularly loud that night, and she didn't hear me calling her name. When she reached our car, she kept walking and turned right onto Olive Street.

What the hell is she doing?

I texted her. "Hey I'm behind u—where u going??"

About a minute later, she replied, "What? I don't see you—lol. We're headed to get food."

I realized that the woman a block ahead of me was not Wilhelmina.

Whoever she was, she looked very similar from a distance and wore a red hoodie. I remembered the last time I was in front of the

Cecil and saw the woman in red looking up at the hotel. Later, our paths had crossed again at . . .

The woman approached Pershing Square. I stopped and got my e-cig out. *This is too weird,* I thought, as she entered the purple pillars of the Square. I was about to turn back when I saw the woman in red take something out of her pocket. I couldn't tell exactly what it was because I remained a solid forty to fifty yards away. But whatever it was, she tinkered with it and then started making short tossing motions.

Was she feeding the pigeons at night? I recalled the story of Goldie Osgood, the Pigeon Lady, who was brutally murdered at the Cecil.

I turned and started walking back. The *Dark Water* poster was right: Some mysteries are not meant to be solved.

A REVELATION

Back in my room, I did Half-Tortoise like never before, with a desperation. This is a yoga posture that is good for depression because all your blood goes to your brain for a minute. I get a high from it. Then I did some breathing exercises.

I got in bed and pulled the covers up to my chin. The room was dark but for patterns of arterial crimson light that rippled across the ceiling and walls.

The room phone rang, which scared the hell out of me.

"Hello?" I answered. Silence. "Hello?" More silence. "Oh, for the love of God," I said, hanging up.

I laughed. It was so similar to the movie *1408,* in which wise-ass skeptic John Cusack stays at a haunted hotel and ends up losing his mind. At one point, he's so desperate to get out of Room 1408, he climbs out the window and side-steps along the narrow terrace overlooking a long, horrifying fall. That scene stayed with me because I frequently have dreams involving me scaling precarious towers and structures at monumental heights.

I suddenly recalled part of my dream. In it, I had been hurtling through some kind of tunnel or maze. The corridors were cylindrical and seemingly made of something with membranes, and there were trap doors lining the sides. At the end of the dream, desperate to escape the maze, I curved into a trap door, absconding out into a vast nothingness.

Speaking of absconding, I thought, time to get the hell out of this room. I would head back to the 14th floor. Not to Room 1408 but rather Room 1427, where Richard Ramirez stowed the eyeballs of one of his victims.

As I turned onto the 14th floor, I tried but failed to run a quick self-assessment diagnostic. My brain just wasn't working normally. Ever since the email from Lauren, I'd felt a steadily increasing dose of nervous energy intermixing with the depression. It was like the jitters one might get before a performance but compounded with an uncontrollable pulse of hysterics.

Except I wasn't laughing. Or maybe I was but didn't know it. Either way, they say it's good to laugh at yourself, right?

Something was building, actually outpacing the depression, which at first I welcomed if for no other reason than having a sudden source of energy. It was depression with a kick, the sardonic malaise artificially infused with a booster shot of hot agitation. It was new and yet familiar—a more distilled essence of something I'd felt off and on for a decade.

Oh, I get it, I thought, remembering the email from Lauren, *I'm angry.* I slapped my palm against the wall.

Is this the hotel? I thought. I certainly wouldn't be the first person to feel like the Cecil had hijacked his mind. I talked to people who said they didn't believe in anything paranormal but had felt some really weird sensations at the Cecil.

I slapped the wall again and this time I followed it up with a punch to my own palm.

I was used to high highs and low lows. This was the first time I had experienced the two extremes at the same time.

I tried to steady my mind and focus. I recalled another salient review, one that was appropriate to the moment, which described lights turning on and off and the feeling of a demon summoner on the 14th floor. The reviewer said he and his partner checked out early and the receptionist and security guard laughed at them.

As they walked away, the security guard called out, "You guys don't have to leave, the ghosts here are nice!"

I don't know about a demon summoner, but the 14th floor definitely struck fear in me for the mere fact that it was both the floor where Richard Ramirez lived and the floor where Elisa's surveillance video was recorded. There had also been several suicide jumpers who'd plunged from its windows. If the Cecil Hotel was a conscious mind, the 14th floor was a particularly active neural pathway.

The hallways even kind of resembled life-size brain arteries, with industrial pipes festooning the ceiling and walls like veins.

Suddenly, I remembered my dream from earlier when I took a nap. The environment combined with my burgeoning mania triggered images of wandering through a similar structure, though in the oneiric realm of the dream universe the hallways had been cylindrical corridors made of plasma and iridescent vapor. The passages wound through a dense labyrinth of nerves, blood vessels, or neural pathways and along the gaseous walls I saw dendrites, axons, and other glowing neurotransmitters shooting from my peripheral vision and into the vast reaches ahead.

At the time, in the dream, I had been a visitor in Elisa's mind, a reluctant stranger searching for truth and hoping for her blessing. It was a dream borne of anxiety about my intrusion into Elisa's life and fleshed out by my recent viewing of *The Fantastic Voyage,* in which scientists shrink down to the size of molecules to travel through a patient's body.

Presently, in waking life it felt as if I had entered a nether region in between reality and the dreamworld, between life and death. The dream of traveling through Elisa's mind was overlaid upon my journey through the Cecil Hotel. I wasn't hallucinating (I don't think), but summoning an anxious creativity.

In the dream, my speed accelerated through the winding effervescent tunnels that at moments became as colorful and vaporous as nebulas in deep space. The texture of the place was a strange amalgam of organic bodily sinews and interstellar gas and occasionally there was a hint of some underlying digital scramble of programming code.

I recalled an article I read about scientists discovering developmental parallels between brain cells, social networks, and galactic expansion. The title was "Universe Grows Like a Giant Brain."

Panpsychists like physicist Gregory Matloff believe in a universal proto-consciousness. And if there is some base-level sentience to everything in the universe, that would include buildings, wouldn't it? Why not the Cecil Hotel?

Why do I keep returning to this idea that the hotel is alive? I thought. Maybe there was some kind of synergy going on between my mind and the Cecil. Of course, usually a shared hallucination (known as *folie à deux*) is between a person and another person—not a person and a building.

I'm losing it, I thought. *Or it's already long gone.*

But the dream felt so real, the desire for meaning so commanding. I was intoxicated by the idea that I was not a lonely visitor wandering through my own construct of Elisa's brain, but rather surrounded by a living, breathing universe that could make sense of her death—and maybe even my declining mental health, too, while we're at it.

I was also terrified of this, because Elisa's life had ended so horrifically, so tragically. Where was the purpose? Where was the cosmic justice?

As I drew close to Room 1427, my spider senses engaged. I heard rock music playing; and the smell of marijuana wafted into the hallway.

I arrived at the door. *Should I knock?*

I lifted my hand, preparing to rap my knuckles against the door. But before I could, I heard a whooshing sound behind me.

At the end of the hallway, in the cul de sac straight past where someone or something had just turned right, the window to the fire escape was open. A breeze fluttered the white curtains draping the window sill. The corridor suddenly felt contorted, almost bird's eye, as if the vertices were being stretched.

When I turned back to Room 1427, I saw a shadow slip over the eyehole. Someone stood on the other side of the door, staring at the bird's eye view of my face.

I started to back away, sweat streaming down my forehead. That door seemed like the fulcrum of the entire building.

Suddenly, it opened and the shadowy face of a grizzled man appeared.

"Sorry," I said, walking backward. "Wrong door."

He just stared, said nothing. I continued backing up, mesmerized, until the wall interrupted my movement. Wind whipped the white curtain over my face, drawn haphazardly over the window leading to the fire escape.

The man carefully inched out from behind the door and stood in the hallway, staring at me with dilated pupils. I felt like I was in my forgotten dream, *jamais vu* laced with synchronicity, a lucid hallucination.

"Did you see Elisa?" I called out to the man.

He smiled absently and took one step forward. He shrugged and looked over his shoulder, then arched his head back toward me with an almost dramatic grin.

"Aw Christ," I mumbled, light-headed. "I'm—uh—gonna have a smoke."

I had wanted to check out the fire escape as part of my research. I decided there was no time like the present to retrace one of Elisa's possible routes to the roof.

I jumped up into the window sill and edged out onto the fire escape. A warm, sultry night breeze greeted me, carrying with it the sound of traffic below. The foundation of the fire escape felt precarious. I had hoped for something that didn't waver under my feet. Instead I got an obsidian trellis made of what felt like macramé.

I peeked back in to see if the man was still there. He was, but now he was facing away from me with his hands in his pockets. He was either tweaking or a ghost. Or both.

I followed the external fire escape staircase to the tiny ladder affixed to the concrete and leading to the roof. I climbed up a few steps, carefully grasping the side rails. Midway up, I stopped and looked out onto the skyline. Across the street, perched on the terrace of a building parallel to the Cecil, a stone gargoyle overlooked the city.

I wondered how long that beast had been there, how many people it watched fall.

It looked like it was grinning at me. That gargoyle, I realized, was there the night Elisa went to the roof. What did it know? What had it seen?

With one hand on the ladder, I brandished my whiskey and took a long pull; winced, made the "knttt knttt" sound Jack Nicholson patented in *Easy Rider*.

Suddenly, I realized the gargoyle had the face of the winged demon from my dream a year earlier. It was the exact same grin. The dream preconceived it. I stitched together my memory of the rest: I had climbed to the roof of the Cecil—just as I was doing now—and glimpsed Elisa encountering a tall, menacing figure that I now knew to be the same man from inside.

And at the end of the dream . . . I fell.

I stood there, the wind on my face. Should I continue up? I looked down. *What the hell am I doing?* I asked, staring at the gargoyle as I answered, *Drinking whiskey on the ledge of a building during a mixed manic state.*

I climbed back down the fire escape and through the window. The man was gone. The door leading to the staircase to the roof swung shut. He had gone to the roof . . . again, as in the dream.

But none of that mattered now. Back at the elevator, there was a mirror. As I looked at myself, it was suddenly so clear. All those years of inexplicable fluctuations, lapsing from the depths of despair to the heights of imaginative fervor, rising to be "the life of the party" one night only to crash into a bed-ridden mess of despondency for days.

I understood now why the treatment of my mental health had always been incomplete. I understood why my visions of the future, my plans for careers and projects, would change multiple times in one week, sometimes multiple times within an hour. I understood why there was never any telling what my mood might be like on a particular day, how I could watch myself—held hostage in my own body—manifesting a darkness I didn't understand.

Elisa Lam suffered from bipolar disorder type 1—quite likely a severe case of it. This can sometimes be life-threatening and require hospitalization. I'd only recently learned that there is also a bipolar disorder type 2 that is characterized by less-severe manic episodes but still possessing potentially dangerous fluctuations between hypomania and depression.

Bipolar type 2 is notoriously difficult to diagnose. One of the greatest predictors is genetics. It was so clear to me that I almost couldn't believe no one had ever mentioned it before as a possibility. It was the illness that took my aunt Jill's life. *It ran in my family.* Bipolar explained my mood anomalies and erratic depressive patterns. Every symptom checked off against my life.

Did my interest, nay obsession, with Elisa's death then stem, at least partially, from an unconscious need to diagnose myself and understand my own mind? Was Elisa's tragic death the signpost in the wilderness leading me to this awareness? Were the last few years part of one big synchronicity?

I thought back on all my dangerous misadventures, particularly in my twenties, my impulsive decisions and behaviors, my over-the-top drug experimentation and abuse. How many times had I stacked multiple drugs just to feel normal? Just to have the courage to go and get groceries.

I was lucky to be alive.

I'd come to the Cecil for a second time expecting to come face to face with a ghost, or find traces of an epic conspiracy. What I got was my distorted reflection in a mirror.

Congratulations, the Cecil whispered in triplicate. *How proud you must be.*

He, she, it, they—seemed angered by my revelation, incensed that a single epiphanic moment could neutralize its most decorated demons.

You can leave . . . but you'll remain here.

Have fun getting back on meds, coward, the Anarchist enjoined.

I pressed the button to the elevator and waited without responding. You can't argue with chemicals.

PART 3
COVERUP

Reality is shaped by the forces that destroy it.
—D. HARLAN WILSON, *The Kyoto Man*

CHAPTER 19

Revisiting the Cause
of Death

ONE DAY LATE IN MY INVESTIGATION, I sat down and went through the original YouTube video second by second, looking only at the timecode. Even though it's muddled and the numbers are barely discernible, you can still clearly tell where the second-hand digits are ticking (and, right beside it, where the microseconds are rapid-firing), where the minute-hand digits are ticking, and where the hour-hand digits remain still.

At 2:28 of the YouTube video, Elisa disappears off to the left of the screen for the last time. There is stillness as the elevator doors remain open and the timecode continues on.

Then, something peculiar happens, something you can only notice if you're looking at a specific and tiny section of the frame.

At approximately 2:42 the minute hand of the timecode changes. Seven seconds elapse and then, at 2:49, *the minute hand changes again.* The minute hand changes twice in seven seconds.

Then there are several staggered seconds—some kind of glitch in the timecode that makes the seconds tick at an arrhythmic pace. And finally, as the door closes it lurches as though the first fraction of a second of its closing had been removed.

I noticed something else for the first time. When the doors reopen at 3:41, the hallway wall is bright red. Previously, it was a muted, greyish maroon. There are three possible explanations for this (in order of likeliness, from least likely to most likely): one, the timecode cut to the next day when the daylight illuminated the wall, exposing the vibrant red color; two, the timecode cut to a few minutes later, when an open doorway from a tenant's room admitted light onto the wall, exposing the red color; and three, the elevator had traveled to another floor.

There is a tragic irony here. Only seventy-one seconds after Elisa walks out of frame, the elevator doors finally close and the elevator visits another floor.

My mind returned to the timecode cut, though. This was the north star, the mother lode. Did this cut represent the moment that someone had entered the frame in pursuit of Elisa? Had this person(s), or someone they knew, edited the tape in order to remove video evidence of Elisa's assailant? As someone with experience with video editing, I can tell you it would be the perfect place for it because there was no movement in the frame, which means that one could cut out several seconds without there being an obvious jump of movement.

However, this lack of movement could also be the result of the surveillance camera being motion-activated. There are other short sequences with little to no motion that do not trigger such a jump, true, but a recent article I read regarding the controversial and tragic case of Kendrick Johnson—who was found stuffed inside a vertical school gym mat, a circumstance police later determined to be a tragic accident—explained how convoluted and tricky timecode analysis can be. The family's lawyers argued the school's surveillance footage contained anomalies but police disagreed.

The Elisa surveillance definitely has suspicious cuts. Whether there's an innocent explanation will require digital forensics experts getting involved. But this was just the beginning of a whole new phase.

A Shift in Perspective

For many months, if not years, I suspected that some conspiracy theorists and websleuths were using the sensationalized specter of homicide and paranormal activity to ignore the reality of mental illness. The idea that someone could have a manic, psychotic, or "mixed" episode and die as a result was and is incomprehensible to some people. In the absence of any hard evidence of foul play, I'd found it troubling that people refused to consider the power of mental illness as a cause of death.

In the coming months, however, new evidence finally began to surface, a string of shocking allegations and discoveries that punched some major holes in the LAPD narrative of Elisa's death. And with this shift, I began to suspect something far more insidious than "blaming ghosts": people using mental illness to conceal a botched investigation and/or evidence of manslaughter. Had the LAPD used Elisa's bipolar disorder in order to close the case and cover for sloppy police work? Had they (knowingly or unknowingly) released a doctored surveillance tape to stigmatize Elisa and lay the groundwork for their explanation?

To try and answer these questions, I went all in on the case. I quit my jobs and emptied my bank account. Because I can think of few worse miscarriages of justice than being murdered and having your killer get away because you had a psychiatric illness.

First, there remained anomalies associated with the autopsy report. Why had it taken so long to release? Why did they scratch through "undetermined" and write "accidental" at the last minute? Why didn't they include the results of the rape kit? Did they even conduct a rape kit? What about the fingernail kit to determine if there was any foreign DNA?

The question of the rape kit becomes especially important when one notes that Elisa had suffered a perianal hematoma. The autopsy says that "the anus is edematous and shows pooling of blood in the subcutaneous tissues surrounding the orifice." One medical explanation for this is that it is non-traumatic and resulting from gas expulsion during decomposition. However, two independent coroners implied that this kind of bruising could be the result of sexual abuse or trauma. At the very least, this would be cause for the LAPD to process the rape kit. Yet they didn't.

Most critically, of course, what was the cause of death? As we previously discussed, the autopsy released by coroner Yulai Wang and inspected by Associate Deputy Medical Examiner Jason P. Tovar stated that Elisa's death was an accident caused by drowning with bipolar disorder listed as a relevant complication.

However, in what would be the first of several large cracks to appear in the police narrative, I soon learned there is sufficient reason to doubt the LA coroner's cause of death.

Coroner Trouble

In her book *The Skeleton Crew,* author Deborah Halber described coroners as a paranoid bunch, overworked and suspicious of larger organizations they fear may fire or dismantle their offices. Usually rising through the ranks of former cops, police chiefs, and death investigators, Halber notes, modern coroners are under a lot of heat.

A recent study shows that coroners, who are elected to their position, report fewer suicides (11 percent for women and 6 percent for men) than medical examiners, who are appointed. "Coroners would . . . be worried about antagonizing local community stakeholders who might bad-mouth them."

A *Washington Post* article entitled "It's Time to Abolish the Coroner" contained several stunning statements regarding corruption in California's sheriff-coroner system of death investigations. In all but three counties in California—San Diego, San Francisco, and Ventura—autopsies are controlled by someone working for the sheriff's department. California is therefore one of only three states in the country that allows an elected officer to overrule professional forensic pathologists as to the cause of death in suspicious cases.

"A coroner's determination about cause of death could determine whether or how much a life insurance company had to pay out," the article states. "It could swing the outcome of a lawsuit in a factory death or negligence case. A bribed coroner could also help a rich or powerful family avoid public embarrassment when a relative committed suicide."

The article's focus is on California, where in anywhere between forty-one and fifty of the state's fifty-eight counties ". . . once a death is determined to be accidental or natural, there is no investigation."

The sheriff-coroner system becomes especially problematic when a death is officer-related, such as when a deputy is under investigation for excessive force or homicide. For a sheriff—who is elected, not appointed—the conflict of interest is obvious. This was underscored in two cases in San Joaquin County, where a sheriff-coroner overruled the conclusion of the medical examiner, reclassifying the cause of death from homicide to accident. The medical examiner, Dr. Bennet Omalu, also stated that the suppression of evidence in death investigations is "routine."

In the aforementioned *Washington Post* article, another section stood out to me: "Sometimes, a sheriff or prosecutor may not want to deal with another unsolved murder and might pressure a coroner to rule an obvious homicide to be an accident, a suicide or a natural death."

This idea that local power brokers can use their influence to shape or alter the findings of a coroner or medical examiner disturbs forensic pathologist Dr. Judy Melinek. She authored a study for the National Association of Medical Examiners (NAME) that issued a shocking conclusion: "43 percent of forensic pathologists who worked in a coroner system reported that the coroner had changed the cause on a death certificate in a way that conflicted with the autopsy findings."

The county of Los Angeles contains a separate department for the coroner-medical examiner team that is ostensibly shielded from the influence of the LAPD and the District Attorney's Office. However, in the Elisa Lam case, one of the big questions is why the medical examiner changed his conclusion from "undetermined" to "accident" right before the release of the autopsy. It's literally scratched out in pen.

There appeared to be no bruising anywhere on her body. No one choked her; no one struck her. But does this necessarily rule out foul play?

Then there is the issue of the toxicology report. There was no alcohol (besides the tiny amount which is naturally produced during decomposition) or illicit drugs in her system. But no tests for date rape drugs or exotic substances were conducted.

The autopsy lists the components of a rape kit test (swabs for Oral, External, Vaginal, Cervical, and Rectal) but does not confirm whether it was processed or, if it was, what the results were. How a rape kit was not used in a case in which a young woman was found naked on a roof, concealed in a tank, is difficult to comprehend, particularly when you consider that the autopsy noted pooling of blood from her anus.

As mentioned above, the medical explanation of this offered by some is that after death a corpse produces gases that can expand, build pressure, and finally cause the rectum to prolapse. But several independent coroners questioned this. Wouldn't it be helpful to have a rape kit confirming that this was indeed a postmortem biological process and not trauma from a sexual assault?

The same goes for the fingernail evidence kit. Along with rape kits, fingernail kits are hugely valuable pieces of evidence in sexual-assault cases because it can preserve forensic biological evidence from a perpetrator. Yet, once again, there is no indication in the autopsy as to whether a fingernail kit was processed and, if it was, what the results were.

This in a case where the autopsy took almost six months to be released.

THE DEPUTY CORONER SPEAKS

I managed to get phone time with former Coroner Supervising Investigator Fred Corral, who was part of the team that processed Elisa's autopsy. Mr. Corral struck me as a decent, honest man. He said he was interested in writing a book about his time working on death investigations.

I actually spoke with Mr. Corral twice. The first time he said that tests for date rape drugs were not conducted on Elisa. Further, he said, such tests usually count as supplemental information for which the family is charged. Basically, the coroner's department tests for about five major drugs and after that, the family must pay for additional tests.

During the second call, Mr. Corral said the Lam family was not convinced that Elisa's death was an accident. This may not sound surprising but remember that in the civil trial, the Lam family attorneys explicitly stated that Elisa's death was the result of mental illness and not homicide. They made a special point of saying this and critics of the conspiratorial interpretation, like Paul Brevik, hailed this as confirmation of an accidental death.

But it turns out, the Lam family attorney's statement was likely more about legal strategy. Since it was a civil case in which they were explicitly trying to prove that Elisa's death was a preventable accident for which the Cecil Hotel was responsible, their lawyers pretty much *had* to take homicide off the table in their arguments. Because if a killer was responsible for her death, that exonerated the hotel of blame.

So hearing that the Lam family was indeed very suspicious of foul play came as important news to me. And Mr. Corral would be the one to know how adamant this belief was. Families challenging the results of the autopsy, he said, is very common and is one of the parts of the job that can be difficult for coroners. It's not easy explaining to a bereaved, devastated family that no one is to blame for their loved one's death, that there will be no justice.

Apparently, the coroner department had many exchanges with the Lam family, who wanted to know who found Elisa's body and how that person knew the body was there. Both reasonable questions.

The detectives, Mr. Corral said, at one point considered that maybe Elisa was knocked unconscious and dragged into the water tank. They considered that maybe she was strangled. But when the autopsy turned up no signs of bruising, nor any evidence of physical trauma indicative of a struggle, they dropped suspicions of foul play.

What Corral said next surprised me.

Apparently, he asked one of the detectives, "What do you think happened?"

The detective (he didn't specify which one) said that he thought Elisa may have gone to the roof to go swimming and that an employee granted her access.

This is a mind-boggling statement on several levels.

For one, it's a confirmation that the detectives had reason to believe an employee at the Cecil Hotel was on the roof or at the entrance to the roof with Elisa at some point during the night she died (something Robin the websleuth had theorized). Two, it's hard to imagine that this employee would have encouraged a guest to go swimming in the water cistern. In fact, it's absolutely absurd (unless, of course, this employee was lying to her with the intention of harming her).

In addition to its criminal implications, the disclosure contradicts deposition statements made by General Manager Amy Price, Chief Engineer Pedro Tovar, and maintenance worker Santiago Lopez, all of whom stated under oath that the alarm at the entrance to the roof was not deactivated. The alarm would have had to be deactivated for an employee to let Elisa onto the roof. If deactivation was unnecessary, that means the door alarm wasn't working properly, which also contradicts employee statements.

This was the first, but not the last time I would find evidence of possible perjury in those depositions.

Perhaps most important, though, if an employee knowingly led Elisa to the roof or granted her access, it makes the timeline of the discovery of her body exponentially more suspicious. It means that for the entire time Elisa was missing—nineteen days—whoever had been with her on the roof, or whoever had granted her access, remained silent about their knowledge of her whereabouts.

If Elisa's body had been found sooner, it's far more likely that her cause of death would have been easier to determine. The duration of time she was submerged in water greatly limited blood quantitation for tests, eliminated forensic clues, and may have allowed certain under-the-radar drugs to disappear from her organs and blood.

Naturally, one can presume the person would have known he would appear suspicious by admitting he was with Elisa on the roof and remained quiet to avoid being a suspect. The person may have also been protecting their employment status, as allowing a tenant on the roof was surely a violation of staff rules. At best, this supposed person—who knew Elisa had been on the roof and did not tell the police while she was missing—is responsible for greatly damaging the investigation; at worst, this person may have been involved in her death.

Finally, I asked Fred about the rape kit. Why wasn't it processed?

He paused. "It was," he said.

"Oh . . . hmmm, let's see here." I pretended to look through the autopsy, but already knew there were no results.

I told him this and he said there should have been a supplemental document with test results. There is, of course, no publicly available supplemental document with test results. I filed a records request with the LAPD asking for such a document and was told none existed.

Later, I spoke with the Chief of Coroner's Investigations, Brian Elias, who furnished another surprise. He said that the Coroner's Department gathered the evidence for a rape kit but the LAPD did not process it.

I thanked Mr. Corral profusely. After all, he was literally the only person directly associated with the case who had been willing to answer questions about it over the phone. I gave him my email and told him to send me a draft of his writing if he would like an editor.

A couple of months after I spoke with Corral, a leaked Coroner's Department memo instructed employees to not speak with journalists until the department had crafted their talking points on specific cases.

I was already skeptical about the autopsy, but then I started reading analysis from independent coroners, who were far from certain that foul play could be ruled out in Elisa's case.

And then we interviewed a forensics expert on camera and everything changed.

SHOCKING NEW ANALYSIS

Dr. John Hiserodt is the owner and director of Path Lab Services, a Garden Grove-based medical reference lab that receives and processes blood tests ordered by clients, most of whom are doctors. The results of such blood tests dictate about 80 percent of the doctors' subsequent decision-making. So accuracy is the lifeblood of Hiserodt's professional reputation and business.

Dr. Hiserodt is a board-certified pathologist and physician, a forensic pathologist by training. He was formerly a deputy coroner in Pittsburgh, then provided medical consulting training and conducted autopsies in the private sector as an independent contractor. Between his work with the coroner's office in Pittsburgh and his time doing independent autopsy work in California, Dr. Hiserodt estimates he has worked over 5,000 cases in his career.

He graciously agreed to an on-camera interview about the case, with which he was familiar.

Right off the bat, Hiserodt questioned the cause of death. The LAPD coroner's department concluded that Elisa drowned. But how did they deduce that?

"In a drowning case," Hiserodt said, "most victims have voluminous fluid in their lungs. They aspirate the water, they breathe the water, and that's how you die; the lungs are heavy, they're boggy, and full of water. In the Elisa Lam case, there was no water in the lungs.

"It's a bit unusual," he continued, "but in about 15 percent of cases, there are dry drownings, in which the person begins to aspirate the water, but the larynx spasms and closes tightly—and when that happens, no water can get [in], nothing can get in. It's not really a drowning, it's asphyxial death. It's not literally drowning because there's no water."

So Elisa's death was a dry drowning? I wondered.

"But in most cases of either wet or dry drownings, the person swallows the water, they're doing everything they can to get air and so the stomach usually has a lot of water in it. In this case, there was no water in the stomach either. No water in lungs, no water in stomach."

Jared and I looked at each other in disbelief.

"There are additional soft findings that are commonly present," Hiserodt continued, "that can also help. One is the presence of hemorrhage in the middle ear, in the mastoid air cells. The mastoid bones are the two bones that come down behind the ears; when you look at the mastoid air cells in a drowning case, there's usually hemorrhage present. In this case, neither the middle ear—the pitrust temple bone—nor the mastoid bones were examined. I don't know why they were not examined, but they weren't."

Finally, he said, there's another finding that can help determine drowning and that's the sphenoid sinuses.

"In drownings," Hiserodt explained, "the pressure of trying to breathe in water usually means you will find water in the intricate cavities behind the nose. You can dissect them and find the fluid. That wasn't looked at either."

In the absence of the two primary indicators of drowning, water in the lungs or stomach, you would have expected these additional factors to be looked at, Hiserodt said.

Sensing we were shocked, Hiserodt paused and shrugged his shoulders. "It's not really a drowning until you see some objective evidence supporting that conclusion."

"How could they have concluded it was a drowning with no evidence for it?" I asked.

Hiserodt seemed reluctant to be too vicious in his critique or to promote any conspiratorial motives to the coroner.

"It seems that basically because there was no evidence of traumatic injury and she was found in a water tank, and this was enough for him to conclude she drowned."

Hiserodt wasn't done. There were more anomalies. He noted the fact that Elisa was found floating face-up and said this, too, was problematic.

"Typically when a person drowns in a body of water, they are found face-down. They float up because of gases produced in the body which inflate it like an innertube. When you die underwater your body tends to go into a natural fetal position—your arms and legs go down and act as a rudder, or a keel, that turns your body downward. It is unusual in a body of quiet water—with no currents or interfering animals—for her to have been face-up."

Dr. Hiserodt expressed concern over Elisa being naked in the tank with the clothes in there with her.

"Is it possible she took them off to have less weight as she floated there?" I asked.

"That is very unusual in drownings. You are under tremendous pharmacological stress from your catecholamines [hormones]. Your adrenal glands are just releasing norepinephrine, you're struggling like crazy, you're panicking to get that breath of air. You're not stopping to unbutton your blouse or take your sandals off at that moment in time—you're trying to get out of the tank."

On the issue of Elisa struggling in the water, there was more that didn't make sense to him.

"In a drowning, the first phase is panic. You do everything and anything to grab hold of things, scratching objects around her [for example, the sides of the cistern]. It's unusual that her fingernails were not damaged in any way."

Jared asked him about the drugs in her system. There was no evidence of a date-rape drug, but they also didn't test for any.

"Not all labs test for all drugs," he replied, echoing Mr. Corral. "When an autopsy says no drugs were found it means 'no drugs that they tested for were found.' It doesn't mean 'no drugs are in the blood.' It is not possible to conclude that she was not under the influence of certain drugs."

"Based on the information available, what do you think the cause of death is?" I asked.

Hiserodt flipped through the documents, frustrated, then sat quietly for a few moments.

"Honestly, the possibility is higher that she would have been thrown in the tank," he replied. "It's true, no traumatic injuries were found . . . but there are other ways you can kill someone, quietly, and then dispose of the body in a tank of water and move on with your life.

"One that comes to mind is a simple pillow on the face," he continued. "So if you have an individual with nefarious ideas about her who was able to get her alone in a room . . . it's possible, even likely, that several days passed [before she was put in the water tank]. Possibly someone was stalking her, got her into a room, put a pillow over her face, caused an asphyxial death, put her in the tank and left."

This would explain why there are no signs of drowning. Elisa was already dead when she was put into the water tank.

I sighed and ran my hands through my hair. I asked about the apparent rectal injury noted in the autopsy.

"Yeah, there appears to have been pooling of blood around the anus . . ." Hiserodt took a long pause. "That bothers me a little bit. We can't know for sure, but this could be trauma from anal sex."

"If they had conducted a rape kit, we might know the answer to this," I said.

Hiserodt nodded.

His answers truly shocked me. Besides a small accumulation of fluid in her pleural cavities, there is literally zero forensic evidence that Elisa drowned. In fact, the evidence points to Elisa having deceased before entering the water tank, which completely eviscerates the police narrative.

The LAPD Coroner's Department spokesman, Ed Winter, did not respond to my query about the independent analysis of the autopsy. I was particularly hoping to speak to Yulai Wang, the forensic pathologist and Chief Medical Examiner who signed off on the Lam autopsy. However, Wang may be too busy defending himself against a civil lawsuit in which he's accused of *falsifying an autopsy*. The cause of death in this case was inexplicably changed from an accident to a homicide in the autopsy report.

As we assess the problematic aspects of the Lam autopsy and try to determine why Wang might have changed Elisa's cause of death from "undetermined" to "accidental," it's important to keep in mind that he is literally being sued for allegedly falsifying an autopsy.

Wang did not reply to my phone calls. The press spokeswoman for the Coroner's Department answered a couple of my basic questions about the division of the Coroner's and Sheriff's departments, but when I asked her about the rape kit, I heard nothing back.

BACKLOGGED

Sadly, the fact that the rape kit was not processed is not terribly surprising. The backlog of untested rape kits has been well documented in recent years, with a 2014 study putting the estimate at 400,000 nationwide. In a 2018 *Los Angeles Times* article entitled "The unconscionable backlog of unprocessed rape kits in California," the Joyful Heart Foundation conservatively estimated that statewide, California has 13,000 unprocessed sexual-assault evidence kits.

There's such a brutal irony in that DNA testing has such a high success rate and yet is so rarely used on the cases in which it would be best utilized: sexual assaults, which often leave behind a variety of biological evidence. The failure to process rape kits is certainly one factor in why under 5 percent of rapists ever see the inside of a prison cell for their crime. In fact, only 30 rapists out of a 1,000 ever even face trial. Only 70 more are even reported.

By the time the FBI developed its criminal forensic database in the mid-1990s, police departments around the country were already backlogged. The continued bottlenecking has a lot to do with money. Local law-enforcement agencies cover the cost of rape kits for victims. They run between $500 and $1,500. This ends up producing a triage system where police will usually only process kits in cases they think they can solve.

CHAPTER 20
Whoever Chases Monsters

As I MENTIONED AT THE BEGINNING of this book, from February 3 to February 12, 2013—almost the exact timeframe of the first two weeks of the investigation of Elisa's death—an unprecedented event transpired in Los Angeles. Former police officer and naval reservist Christopher Dorner waged "asymmetric and unconventional warfare" on the LAPD in retaliation for being fired nearly five years earlier.

Dorner posted an infamous eighteen-page "manifesto" to Facebook, in which he provided lurid details of LAPD corruption, racism, and criminal activity. The accusations painted a picture of a police department in which excessive force, institutional racism and sexism, and cover-ups are common. He claimed the South Bureau divisions had white officers who had joined the force "with the sole intent to victimize minorities . . ." He said that one of the officers caught on videotape beating Rodney King was not only still employed but had risen in the ranks to be a commanding officer.

There were officers, he said, who "will let you bleed out just so they can brag to other officers that they had a 187 [code for homicide] caper the other day and can't wait to accrue the overtime in future court subpoenas." Dorner recalled officers taking photos of dead bodies and playing a game with officers from other divisions in which they competed for who had "the most graphic dead body of the night."

The manifesto also detailed Dorner's militaristic strategy for how he planned to murder dozens of cops, which he described as "a necessary evil." He referred to himself as a jihadist who did not fear death and who could not be stopped.

After Dorner shot and killed a newly engaged couple, authorities called his rampage "domestic terrorism." They called on the press to stop tweeting because broadcasting their moves might hinder Dorner's arrest.

By the time police cornered Dorner in a cabin in Big Bear, the manhunt was already one of the biggest headlines in national news. During the standoff, Dorner opened fire on two officers, killing one. What happened next depends on whether you want to believe the reports of the LAPD, who are adamant that a cabin fire started unintentionally due to military tear gas cartridges. Dorner, who was barricaded inside, reportedly shot himself before his body was incinerated.

The Dorner manhunt is highly relevant to the Lam case for two reasons: One, it used a tremendous amount of resources and almost assuredly distracted all LAPD personnel, diverting attention away from other cases, including Elisa's; and two, Dorner's manifesto corroborates—and is corroborated by—already existing information related to LAPD corruption.

The more I looked into past claims, the more connections I began to see with the anomalies presented in this case. An unsettling pattern emerged.

The Rampart Scandal

The Rampart area reported roughly 150 murders a year occurring within a densely packed neighborhood. The LAPD CRASH (Community Resources Against Street Hoodlums) unit that policed gang activity there operated almost as an occupying army. They viewed themselves as different kinds of cops who could bend the rules.

Their slogan was: "We intimidate those who intimidate others." They awarded each other plaques for taking down a gang member, black for dead, red for injured.

The revelations of the Rampart scandal, which Matt Lait and Scott

Glover of the *Los Angeles Times* began publishing in 1999, exposed nothing short of a crime syndicate operating within the ranks of the LAPD.

The whistleblower who blew the lid off was former officer Rafael Perez. Prosecutors charged him with stealing an eight-pound bag of cocaine from an evidence room.

Amid Perez's cooperation with feds, he helped corroborate a number of cases showing police corruption. This included LAPD officers serving as private paid security and confidantes to Death Row Records. Specifically, off-duty cops took large payments from Shug Knight to conceal their activities. This fueled the conspiracy theory that LAPD officers were involved in both the Tupac and Biggie assassinations.

Perez and his lawyer negotiated a proffer agreement, what's sometimes known as a "Queen for a day" immunity deal: Perez would sing like a bird and in exchange the government would agree not to prosecute him.

Perez had a guilty conscience. Ghosts from his past plagued his dreams. And what he began to tell federal agents shocked them and rattled the LAPD to its core. Perez didn't just discuss the crimes he was involved in; he implicated a disturbingly large percentage of the LAPD in a criminal conspiracy that had operated just under the surface for years.

The disclosures started with a haunting story about how he and his partner, Nino Durden, had shot and paralyzed a young, unarmed black man, Philip Ovando, during a stakeout. They had planted a .22 caliber rifle next to his bleeding body, which Perez said was common practice. In fact, CRASH officers regularly carried spare firearms specifically to be used if a suspect needed to be framed. If any of this sounds familiar it's because it's almost exactly what Chris Dorner reported in his "manifesto."

Based on their false testimony, the innocent man Perez and Durden had brutally paralyzed received twenty-three years in prison while they received commendations.

But within a week of his confession, a judge issued a writ of habeas corpus, releasing Ovando from prison. He ultimately settled with the LAPD for $15 million dollars, the largest settlement in city history.

Perez wasn't done, though. LAPD officers and detectives within the CRASH division, and in other departments, he said, regularly stole drugs and cash from evidence lockers; they planted evidence on gang members; they conspired to shakedown drug dealers; they tortured suspects during interrogations, sometimes killing them; and they tampered with the crime scenes and doctored evidence to conceal and cover up their activity. The CRASH unit began to look more like a "criminal gang in uniform," just as corrupt and violent as the very gangs they were tasked with policing.

Plaintive lawyers used Perez's testimony to overturn over 100 cases. At least seventy cops were dismissed and charged in the Rampart scandal, including one who was arrested at the hospital where his wife was giving birth. Perez insisted as much as 90 percent of the CRASH division engaged in the misconduct he described.

Meanwhile, during this period of time, LAPD supervisors overlooked the criminal activity, allowing prosecutors to score major convictions in court based on doctored evidence and perjured testimony. The Rampart scandal showed the extent to which the entire criminal justice system was mired in corruption.

Before he was sentenced for the drug-related charges, Perez stood before the judge and gave a tearful statement:

"In the Rampart CRASH unit . . . I succumbed to the seductress of power . . . Whoever chases monsters," he concluded, "should see to it that in the process he does not become a monster himself."

But ultimately the Rampart scandal, an unprecedented police cover-up of corruption, was itself covered up and resulted in very little actual reform or "house cleaning" within the LAPD or the D.A.'s office.

Understanding the endemic corruption of the LAPD and, specifically, the CRASH division at the turn of the millennium may seem off-topic but there is actually an important connection. And it goes beyond the credible supposition that such corruption still goes on within the ranks.

The CRASH division is where Detective Wallace Tennelle got his chops. One of the lead detectives on the Elisa Lam case earned his mettle on the force as a CRASH detective in the late 1980s, during its heyday. As we began to assess various claims of criminal conspiracy and/or gross negligence within the ranks of the LAPD, the historical foundation of the lead detective's police work in the Elisa Lam case must be considered.

"DARK ALLIANCE": CIA AND LAPD DRUG TRAFFICKING

Over a decade before the Rampart scandal, another major expose revealed corruption in the LAPD. This scandal is not only considered one of the biggest in Los Angeles history, it involves the CIA, FBI, and DoJ and may be one of the most nefarious conspiracies in modern U.S. history. The CIA drug-trafficking scandal, exposed in 1995 after intrepid reporter Gary Webb published one of the first major pieces of online investigative journalism. He developed his work into a book called *Dark Alliance: The CIA, the Contras, and the Crack Cocaine Explosion.*

Webb exposed a criminal cartel of Contra rebels in Nicaragua who ran a massive crack cocaine trafficking ring with the protection and cooperation of the CIA and the LAPD. Again, the CRASH division (Tennelle's initial home as a detective) played a major role in policing what was considered the "most active rock cocaine area on earth." Ultimately, the LAPD was forced to "quietly disband . . ." its thirty-two-member anti-crack task force in South Central Los Angeles. Prior to that they had found thirty one-gallon garbage cans of cocaine.

Webb's reporting suggested that the epidemic of crack cocaine in black communities was facilitated by the very agency using drug gangs as a pretext for violent policing against young black men. His book was a bombshell, evoking outrage and shock across the country. The CIA and the *Washington Post* worked hand in hand to not only destroy Webb but to cast doubt on his report. To this day, it is still the subject of considerable controversy, and mainstream media outlets still seek to discredit Webb.

In 2004, the LAPD reported that Webb took his own life. The

coroner stated that he died from two self-inflicted gunshot wounds to the head. That's right, two.

RECENT CORRUPTION

In September 2014, federal agents announced that the "Fashion District" in downtown Los Angeles had been operating as the "epicenter" of an international money-laundering operation undertaken by drug cartels. "Operation Fashion Police" seized over 100 million in cash and pinpointed what they described as a "black market peso exchange" run by the Sinaloa drug cartel.

Business Insider described the operation as a way "to buy legitimate goods with dirty cash and then resell those goods to turn what appeared to be a legal profit—all while avoiding Colombia's tariffs on imports."

The twist here is that about the same time as this operation was exposed, the FBI also used a sting operation to bust and arrest a Los Angeles County sheriff's deputy Kenneth Collins and three other law-enforcement officers for being involved with an international drug cartel. Collins is charged with accepting bribes in exchange for sheltering drug traders. According to the FBI, Collins admitted to an undercover cop that he and his men would provide security for the cartel and assault people if necessary.

A 2014 *Los Angeles Times* investigation discovered that the LAPD systematically underreported and misclassified violent crimes. According to Capt. Lillian Carranza, high-ranking officers actively misled the public about the number of aggravated assaults in 2016, underreporting them by 10 percent and misclassifying approximately 1,200 violent crimes. The LAPD as a whole, she said, "engaged in a highly complex and elaborate cover up in an attempt to hide the fact that command officers had been providing false crime figures to the public attempting to convince the public that crime was not significantly increasing."

So in addition to the drug connections, a new picture begins to emerge regarding the context of the Lam investigation. You have a department that is undertaking a massive coverup to conceal violent crimes while simultaneously exhausting its resources on the biggest manhunt in city history, which took a major toll on the morale and psychology of the department. This was going down the exact week Elisa disappeared.

I sent a tweet to Detective Greg Stearns requesting to ask him a few questions about a case. He said, "What case?" I wrote, "Elisa Lam." He replied: "I'm not interested in discussing it."

Another Twitter user saw this comment and replied to him, "Yea well thousands of others are interested."

I emailed Detective Tim Marcia about the overlap with the Chris Dorner manhunt.

"You're correct—Dorner jumped off the first evening RHD assumed responsibility for the Lam case," Marcia wrote. "Based on our initial assessment surrounding Elisa's disappearance, we classified the investigation as a 'critical missing.' Per RHD protocols, a critical missing is a high priority investigation and personnel resources will remain dedicated to the case. The Dorner case consumed a majority of RHD's personnel; however, Detective Tennelle, Stearns, Gable and myself remained on the Lam case."

He said he had an opinion on the Lam case but that out of respect he would have to check with Stearns before he spoke.

I know what that meant. And sure enough, a couple weeks later, he replied, "I hit up Greg again and he has a blanket 'no talk' policy pertaining to the Lam case. That makes it difficult for me to participate. However, if you're willing to write out your questions, I'll try to respond to those that I can . . ."

I sent him a short list of peripheral questions that did not tread into critical case questions. But when I pressed send, my email bounced. I looked up the error code and it appears highly likely Marcia blacklisted me. Perhaps he received a follow-up directive from Stearns to not talk to me at all. I emailed Marcia from another account, in case the bounce was a server error. He did not respond.

Later in my investigation, I reached out once again to Detective Greg Stearns. This time, I wrote that I had received troubling information and that I would like the LAPD to answer some questions.

He blocked me.

CHAPTER 21

Inside Job

IN 2016, JOHN LORDAN LEFT Los Angeles and moved to Minnesota to devote himself full-time to BrainScratch. There wasn't a particular event that made John want to put all of his heart and soul into pursuing criminal justice through YouTube. He told me it was "just an understanding that I came to and saw reinforced time and time again throughout my life. While most people don't want to harm others, they also don't want to necessarily HELP others. I think a lot of people decide they don't want to see the dark."

John decided to devote himself full-time to criminal justice via his YouTube channel.

He found his dream in Minnesota, where the cost of living was cheaper and all he needed was an Internet connection. By this point, John had created hundreds of videos (over half a dozen devoted to the Lam case) and he felt he was in a groove. His channel subscriber list topped 50,000 and he was regularly adding another 2,000 each month.

But though the Lam case had, in large part, launched the popularity of BrainScratch, John felt a searing emotional pain from it. He had seen firsthand how the story unsettled people.

"As humans," John said, "when we hear a story like this we want a reason, a lesson, that we can glean from this."

The case left John with a "pit of emptiness in [his] stomach and a broken heart."

No shortage of producers had reached out to him for potential documentaries on the subject. Among them, Robert Kiviat, the producer of the infamous "Alien Autopsy" video, which is widely viewed as a fake, hit John up to produce a documentary about the Lam case. Kiviat even called me trying to poach information.

Though John had released what he called his "final word on the Elisa Lam case," he was still more than happy to revisit the investigation with us.

THE SUSPICIOUS TIMING OF A CORPORATE MERGER

Jared and I were in Los Angeles to film some interviews and sequences of our documentary. We'd flown in several people: our cinematographer, Jason; Joni, the paranormal investigator; Wilhelmina, the actress we hired to play Elisa in re-creations; and, finally, John "BrainScratch."

The problem was that the Cecil Hotel was closed to the public. They were renovating and the only people who could get in were long-term residents, who'd been issued special key fobs to access the lobby.

So we arranged a meeting between John and two other websleuths, Frank and Genevieve, the ones I met at Contact in the Desert. They were fans of "BrainScratch," and the group of us shared a warm reception and the theories immediately began to pour out.

One central question we kept returning to is whether Elisa died in the water tank or was placed there after her death. John articulated some of his thoughts around a relatively new theory, one for which I would subsequently find circumstantial evidence. The theory, whose origin he credited to his co-investigator, revolved around whether anyone might have been directed to delay the revelation of Elisa's death.

Could there be two different crimes or events to this story? The first being whatever caused Elisa to die; the second being a subsequent cover-up of her death ordered by people who manage the interests and assets of the Cecil Hotel. This theory supposes that Elisa's death may not have been immediately reported to the police by hotel management and employees but was instead reported to the top executive officers of the Cecil Hotel corporation.

But we need to back up and take a closer look at the Cecil Hotel prior to and during this time period. Earlier we discussed some of the frenetic corporate rearranging that went on at the executive level of the hotel during the twenty-first century. In 2008, just before the economic bubble popped from the Great Recession, business developer Fred Cordova was brought on to help broker a deal to sell the hotel. At the time, downtown Los Angeles was undergoing a renaissance of sorts, with developers trying to rebrand the downtown area as a "hip yuppy destination" where business owners could turn a profit off the new gentrified population.

In order to do this, they needed professionals to be able to live in the area (avoiding a commute in LA's horrific traffic is a huge incentive), so developers wanted to terraform buildings in the area into hotels with residential living quarters. As money poured in, the LAPD helped shepherd the homeless population out of the higher-priced neighborhoods, like Main Street and 5th Avenue, displacing them to the Skid Row area, which swelled to become the largest concentration of homeless people in the country.

Cordova eventually joined a group of buyers to take over the Cecil Hotel himself for $26.5 million. Part of his plan was to flip rooms and make the property appealing to tourists. To avoid rent-control violations, he attempted to exploit a loophole in a "citywide moratorium that prevents turning low-income housing into market-rate residences" by creating a new hotel that basically shared the same address as the Cecil. This is how Stay On Main was born, as what was likely Cordova's backdoor attempt to price out lower-income residents.

When he took over, Cordova sent a personal letter to the City Council explaining why he wanted to revamp the hotel from residential to a commercial property and why he felt he should be able to skirt the City Ordinance.

"When we took over the Cecil it was in crisis," Cordova wrote. "The previous operators turned a blind eye to what was going on inside with their guests. Drug dealers would check in and set up shop and customers would come in, rent a room and spend the next several days getting high. Police reports reflected an average of *more than a death a month,* and in some months *as many as six,* from overdoses and drug-related matters. Since we 'cleaned' up the hotel, incidents of such have practically disappeared. Many lives have been saved! The Cecil is no longer a *safe haven for criminals to prey on the less fortunate* in our society." [italics mine]

In two sentences, Cordova publicly confirmed that the hotel was a playground for predators and criminals.

In one "BrainScratch" video, John Lordan noted that even before Cordova left the Cecil corporate partnership in 2012 because of the financial challenges—compounded many times over by the Great Recession, which saw a massive capital divestment from the area— you already start to see an incentive for the hotel to actively reshape the narrative of their role in the downtown area.

"For me," John stated, "that ties directly into what happened to Elisa. Would someone have a vested interest to steer that perception?"

Shortly after 2008, with the Great Recession in full swing, Herb Chase took over and Cordova dropped out. As lawsuits piled up and the flow of money tightened, Chase nixed plans for renovations.

Interestingly, Chase intended to turn the Cecil into a full homeless housing facility. But there may have been an ulterior motive to this plan that was far from altruistic. Chase may well have been banking on using his plan for new homeless services at the Cecil to cash in on enormous federal and state subsidies.

It could have been the "right idea at the wrong time," Lordan noted, and the City Council ultimately rejected his plan, after which the Cecil Hotel/Stay On Main hybrid experienced an "identity crisis . . . caught between two ideas of what it could be." A haven for the disenfranchised or a beacon of gentrification and development.

This is where things get really interesting.

Chase's next plan was to partner with one of the largest real estate firms in the world, CBRE Group. Chase was in negotiations with CBRE in early 2013. John Lordan and his co-investigator turned up a press release from February 20, 2013, entitled "Multi Housing Capital Advisors Team Joins CBRE." The memo announced that a "team of seven executives [which] formed the nucleus of Multi

Housing Capital Advisors [MHCA] . . . founded with Herb Chase and Peter Sherman" would become part of the CBRE network. This anointed the Cecil Hotel, which was owned and operated by Chase and the MHCA board, as a new asset of the CBRE.

One day after Elisa's body was finally found—after weeks of a bungling investigation that saw two different teams of officers and a K-9 unit failing to turn up a corpse that was right under their noses— the Cecil's owners finalized and announced a multi-million-dollar deal with one of the largest real-estate firms in the world.

John questioned the significance of this memo in his video:

"Is there some potential that [Chase] did not want the news of an international traveler being killed or even just found dead on a property managed by [a newly recruited member of the CBRE]? To figure this out, we need to start looking at the flow of information around the discovery of her body. Did they call the LAPD immediately? Or did they call their managing partners first? Did the management company have a different idea about how to handle it? You have someone [Pedro Tovar] who has been with the company for thirty years, pretty much his whole life—how hard would it have been for management to convince him that we can't have this getting out."

Shortly after the merger, I later discovered, Tovar ascended to the corporate board of the hotel.

John and his co-investigator considered the possibility that there are two sets of circumstances constituting criminality or gross negligence here. "Elisa might have been killed under one set of circumstances . . . and then her body was hidden because of another set of circumstances."

So let's imagine, John suggested to Frank, Genevieve, and me, that Elisa was killed (or, perhaps, simply died from an accident) somewhere in the hotel. Employees and security guards first consulted management, who then consulted with their corporate overlords, who said that the body should be temporarily concealed.

Known as the "body dump" theory, this line of thinking imagines that Elisa may not have initially been in the water tank when the police searched the roof. This would explain why the K-9 unit missed her scent completely. It would also explain why, as Dr. Hiserodt stated, there is no forensic evidence in the autopsy to support drowning and that it is just as likely, if not more so, that Elisa died before she was inside the water tank.

Within that narrow timeframe in February 2013, there may have been an acute financial incentive for delaying the discovery of Elisa's body. I would soon receive additional information suggesting the Cecil Hotel corporate team has enjoyed an abnormally cozy relationship with the LAPD.

The Informant

In early October 2018, I met with a former LAPD consultant who had inside information regarding the Lam case. This person, who because of the sensitivity of the subject matter spoke to me on the condition of anonymity, worked as a professional legal consultant. Let's call her Mary Jane.

I'd been going back and forth with Mary Jane for over a year and was eager to hear what she had to say. In the two hours leading up to the meeting, scheduled to take place at a seafood restaurant in San Diego, everything that could have gone wrong did. Car problems, cell phone problems, bank problems. By the time I arrived at the restaurant, I was drenched in sweat and talking to myself.

Mary Jane ordered the halibut and told me her story. She had worked for several years as an independent contractor for the LAPD. They hired her as a consultant, and she assisted with multiple drug-related cases.

Her first case with the LAPD was in 2011. Everything was normal for a while. She helped detectives with specialized analysis, questioning, and trying to locate the chain of custody in drug cases. In several cases, her assistance was crucial in securing prosecutions.

But Mary Jane began to notice something odd. In many of these cases, the LAPD was refraining from prosecution. She would follow up with them and ask, "Do you need me to testify?" In several instances she was told they weren't prosecuting even though she knew there was enough evidence.

Now, if you're like me and you think the Drug War is a crime against humanity, you might not mind this passivity. But the real reason for not prosecuting, it turned out, was corruption.

Mary worked with an LAPD officer who ultimately had a guilty conscience and left the LAPD. This man told her that the LAPD regularly takes a 20 percent cut of drug deals from individuals and cartels. They basically give arrested drug dealers and cartel members a chance to buy their way out of prosecution and get cuts off both the profit and product. Additionally, Mary Jane was told, some of these officers are regularly involved in money laundering.

MJ didn't see money laundering firsthand but she did see clear evidence of corruption. She also saw evidence of systematic racism in the department.

"If they have a black suspect, they assume he's guilty," she said.

At a certain point, MJ stopped asking questions because she didn't want the answers.

"Crime," she told me, "is an opportunity to make money for the LAPD."

Putting criminals in jail is not their goal. There's no money in that. They are part of the "chain of drug trafficking" that works with cartels. This sounds incredible, but when you consider the recent FBI bust showing that Southern California law-enforcement agents received money from cartels in exchange for shielding them—not to mention past scandals—it fits the pattern.

One of MJ's contacts also told her that there is a Motel 6 somewhere in Los Angeles that is used for the LAPD to leverage a prostitution ring.

"There are good cops," MJ said, taking a bite of halibut, "but they refuse to rat the bad ones out. This was shocking to me. The big picture is that they are completely corrupted."

When she heard about the Elisa Lam case, MJ immediately thought the LAPD was involved in some way. When she began to ask questions, they became extremely hostile. Records that should have been made public were concealed. They have an obligation to release these, she said, and the fact that they didn't led her to believe the case was dirty. If the case was clean, why were they being so secretive? The public deserves transparency.

Then we got to the core of her information.

MJ knew a high-level private investigator (PI) who worked for an association. The LAPD contracted two lower-level PIs to work on the Lam case specifically. These PIs eventually told MJ's contact that the surveillance video was heavily edited and that they think an officer was involved. He also said the hotel was involved in buying out the LAPD to drop the case.

I was eating a chowder and almost spit some of it out in shock. Some of it dribbled down my cheek and Mary passed me a napkin, shaking her head. At first, I thought she was just disgusted with the way I eat, but then I realized she was angry about what she was telling me (or maybe it was a little of both).

MJ said that during the time of the Lam investigation, she received information strongly suggesting an abnormal relationship between the Cecil Hotel corporate executives and the LAPD. This included private dinners, activity, behavior, and relationships that are "beyond the scope of a normal investigation." Normally, a meeting such as this—between the owners of a hotel where a crime may have taken place and police detectives—would be supervised and surveilled in an office or precinct.

Based on her experience working with the LAPD and the information reported to her, MJ is convinced there were, and possibly still are, financial improprieties between the Cecil Hotel and the LAPD. This may explain why the hotel has been shielded from criminal investigations and prosecution for so long.

MJ's contact told her he and the other PIs couldn't disclose more info because it would jeopardize their careers and maybe even their lives—a stunning statement in and of itself.

"Good God," I said, realizing the implications of these accusations. If even a fraction of this information were true—and I have no reason to believe it isn't all true—it reveals nothing less than a criminal conspiracy to obstruct justice. Full stop, MJ's source suggests the LAPD was bribed to throw a murder investigation.

To be clear, her source believes foul play was involved in Elisa's death, but neither he nor the other PIs can talk about what they know. No one was expecting the case to become an international true-crime sensation. What would have normally been swept under the rug and easily managed suddenly became far more complicated.

This is an important point to consider, I believe. At the time of the investigation, there's absolutely no reason why the LAPD would have imagined that the Lam case would explode to become one of the most viral true-crime stories of the decade. Their usual business got a wrench thrown in it and they were forced to clam up.

While I was excited to receive the information, it only raised more questions.

For example, if the PIs believed foul play was involved, what evidence pointed toward that conclusion and why was that not enough to make an arrest? Did the detectives also suspect foul play, or just the PI's? Is it possible that the LAPD suspected foul play but could not prove it? What elements of the surveillance video were edited and who did the editing? If someone at the hotel edited the tape, how could the police not have known this? If they did know, why did they release doctored footage to the public?

I practically begged my informant to answer these questions and more. She smiled and shook her head. "I don't know. They wouldn't tell me . . . they *can't* tell me."

I can understand why they are reluctant to disclose more and go on record. The reality is, given the fate of previous corruption claims, it's more likely than not that their efforts would have no effect. For decades the LAPD has managed to weather extraordinarily well-corroborated corruption scandals with virtually no punishment or meaningful reform. With draconian measures taken by both government, law-enforcement agencies, and corporate powers, the incentives to be a public whistleblower are lower than ever.

One faces a stark existential question: Is it worth having your life ruined to speak a truth that may have no impact?

The next day I met with one of my secret weapons, John Carman, a former Secret Service agent turned private investigator. John had interrogated John Hinckley Jr., the attempted assassin of President Reagan.

We met in a Barnes & Noble parking lot. I hadn't been sleeping well, felt like crap, and was probably pretty crabby. I was also sweating profusely. Neither of these characteristics seemed to bother John at all.

When I told him the full story, John stated directly that we had enough evidence now to petition the LAPD to reopen the case. I was skeptical. If there was a cover-up of a crime, it seemed almost certain to me that the cover-up would continue. And if there was evidence of a cover-up, I reasoned, why wouldn't the next crime be a cover-up of the cover-up?

John, a veteran of corruption cases, believed that LAPD officers would go to jail over this case. It went far beyond gross negligence at this point, he said, this is now a criminal conspiracy. And the answer was to write a letter to the California State Attorney General.

Oh Christ, I thought. My bad mood was kicking in now, fueled by a fresh cortisol infusion of stress and fear.

CHAPTER 22

A Missing Element and a Bombshell

IN THE MIDST OF THE FLURRY of new developments, my depression worsened. My mood fluctuations became more erratic and debilitating. Some days I sprang out of bed in the morning like a tree monkey; other days, I remained there until bedtime.

It took a month to get an appointment with my psychiatrist. By the time I went in, I had read just about every contemporary article on bipolar and mood disorders I could find online and was reasonably certain I was on the "spectrum." After all, my aunt had it and genetic predisposition is one of the strongest indicators when it comes to bipolar.

I realized that this wasn't new and that, in fact, the antidepressants I had taken for a decade and a half, though helpful for one end of the spectrum, had likely masked many of the most telling symptoms of hypomania.

I also realized that for many many years I had unknowingly channeled hypomanic episodes into social experiences and creative projects. The nights at parties, when I suddenly became an extroverted savant working the room like a celebrity diva; the nights I burned the midnight oil writing stories or editing video until the sun peeked through my blinds. These were all flip-sides of a crushing depression that sometimes rendered me incapacitated, barely able to feed myself.

Your manic side writes checks that your depressive side can't cash. Promises, projects . . . purpose. You wake up in the morning checking for yourself like you'd check for your keys. You survey your previous night's activities like you might scan your bank account records, asking: who is this stranger impersonating me all over town? Who is this scoundrel writing bad checks?

"I'm pretty sure I have bipolar disorder," I said to my doctor, as I sat down in his office.

"Very likely, yes," he replied.

"Oh. You knew?"

"I suspected it, yes."

Why didn't you say anything then, you river toad?

I told him about the mood fluctuations, hypomanic episodes, and depression. I told him I was still a bit skeptical that I had full-blown mania.

"No two people will have exactly the same symptoms of bipolar disorder. It camouflages itself uniquely into different people's personalities and behavior. Manic episodes, especially hypomanic episodes, are fairly easy to identify, though."

"I didn't know there's a difference between hypomanic and manic."

"Manic is more severe. Manic usually ends up with someone in a hospital. Hypomanic is often reported as enjoyable for people. But it's usually followed by a depressive episode."

The doc explained to me that many scientists now view bipolar affective disorder as involving a huge spectrum with at least five different types—not just two. Because so many different symptoms cross-pollinate and affect each other, the bipolar spectrum can include borderline personality disorder, neurotic depression, certain affective disorders, cyclothymic disorder, "mixed states," ADHD, and even substance abuse.

And this isn't just a chemical balance, Andrew Solomon and many contemporary medical professionals argue. Depression can be an effect of both "socio-emotional pollution" and triggering life events. Mental pathology, writes Stephen Hinshaw in *The Mark of Shame,* is the intersection between personal and social.

Combined, a psychosocial trigger can actually affect the structure of the brain. New medical research, Solomon writes, shows that depression changes the structure and biochemistry of the brain. This creates a vexing situation in which the "syndrome and symptom blur together" and it is difficult to discern "when depression triggers life events, and when life events trigger depression."

Ultimately, he says, it becomes "impossible to see the line between one's own theatricality and the reality of madness."

I experienced this cross-pollination firsthand and the ambiguity doesn't make it any more tolerable. No matter the origin of a depressive spell, once it hits it can be incapacitating and unbearable. In her legendary book *An Unquiet Mind,* author Kay Jamison describes her struggles with bipolar disorder (though she insists on calling it by its original designation, "manic-depression").

She describes her preoccupation with death and the sense that her reality was permanently shattered. Jamison's condition became so dire she attempted suicide, which is statistically very common for people with bipolar disorder. During her suicide attempt, she left a note that read ". . . my body is uninhabitable . . . In the mirror I see a creature I don't know but must live and share my mind with."

After this, she drew up an agreement with her psychiatrist and family, granting them the authority to hospitalize and give her ECT treatments if she lapsed into a severe depression. The contract allowed them to apply these measures against her will.

Ultimately, Jamison forced herself to go on lithium. "The choice . . ." she writes, "was between madness and sanity, and life and death. My manias were occurring more frequently and, increasingly, were becoming 'mixed' in nature (that is, my predominately euphoric manias, those I thought of as my 'white manias,' were becoming more and more overlaid with agitated depressions); my depressions were getting worse and far more suicidal."

Some of Jamison's delusions featured all the world's plants slowly decaying and screaming as they died. Her descriptions of her mixed states are particularly interesting and relevant, given that earlier I posed the question as to whether Elisa experienced a "mixed state" on the night she disappeared.

I experienced a moderate mixed state at the Cecil Hotel and that was enough for me to understand its horrifying potential. Simply said, the combination of severe depression and delusional mania is a noxious, potent condition.

Yet, despite the ubiquity of mental illnesses like depression, which is slowly rising to be one of the most common and destructive diseases on earth, those who live with these diseases still find themselves shunned by society or, at the very least, relegated to the fringes of social groups, unable to represent themselves in their totality for fear of stigmatization.

How could this be? Why did Elisa write about feeling so socially alienated as a "professional depressed person"? Why did Elisa feel so certain that her closest friends not only were unable to understand her illness but that they distanced themselves from her? Is there some psychological principle that may explain why peers are so likely to treat friends with mental disorders differently than friends with physical illnesses?

Terror management theory (TMT), which Hinshaw describes, is a fairly recent idea that draws upon evolutionary psychology to argue that most human social behavior is undertaken because of a deep existential anxiety over mortality. Primal fears cause people to react, sometimes unconsciously, by stigmatizing outgroups that challenge their social status.

Hinshaw describes how the anxiety over death creates a need among "social perceivers" to consolidate stability by discriminating against outgroups seen as threatening to the social order.

TMT may hold that mental disorders remind "neuro-normative" people not only of their own "tenuous" grasp on mental health—and life itself—but the tightly controlled reality that bestows them with social prestige.

Hinshaw argues that one day elite social classes will try to use biotechnology to remove the genes of bipolar disorder and other mental illnesses from the human bloodline entirely. Whether the eradication of pathology at the cost of psychological homogenization is a good or bad thing he does not say.

"It can be dangerous for those with severe bipolar to take SSRIs, but they seem to have helped you in the past," the doctor said. "Or we can try something new and I can write you a prescription for a medicine that specifically treats bipolar. Since depression seems to be a far greater problem for you than mania, Lamictal could be a fit. It targets depression more than mania."

The drug sounded familiar to me. Then I realized why. This was one of the meds Elisa took.

I was tired, demoralized, and exasperated all at once. Depression and mood swings had ground me down to a pulp.

"Do it," I said.

Big Pharma took me back into its arms like Darth Sidious.

ANOTHER BOMBSHELL

The mystery of Santiago Lopez and his discovery of the body had persisted since the beginning. Firstly, there is the question of whether the lid was open or closed. This to me is one of the most important issues. The claim has been—and, in fact, he went under oath to declare it—that the lid to the water cistern was open.

The reason this is important is because if Elisa got in the water tank herself, it makes much more sense that the lid would remain open. If the lid (which is actually more of a removable hatch) was closed on top of her, it's indicative of foul play. How would she have closed a heavy metal lid over herself as she was climbing into a hole that provided no footrests? Simply said, it's just about physically impossible given the conditions.

To try and get a better understanding of the lid situation, I reached out to a Wisconsin chief of police, Andrew Smith, who in 2013 was an LAPD officer and was one of the first officers on the scene at the Cecil Hotel. I emailed a number of questions, but the one that stood out to me was his response to whether the lid was closed.

"The tank was completely closed," Smith said in an email.

This was after Santiago discovered the body, after he said the lid was open. If the lid was initially closed, Santiago likely perjured himself in the court deposition. It's difficult to imagine he discovered the body with the removable hatch lid open and then closed it while waiting for police to arrive. More important, in my analysis, if the lid was indeed closed when he discovered the body, it makes foul play close to certain, though I'm not asserting that Santiago was directly involved in this activity.

John Lordan, however, has questioned whether maybe the entire discovery story was manufactured.

For years, I had tried to get in contact with Santiago to answer these questions. I called the hotel and asked for him. I stayed at the hotel and physically searched for him.

Finally, I tapped another one of my secret weapons, my friend Lou Colagiovanni, a Las Vegas-based journalist and political blogger with an aggressive gonzo style. I met him through the alternative media channels that opened up to me when I started writing for the *Anti-Media*.

Lou is an old school muckraker and shit disturber updated for the Internet age. He is probably best known for being one of the journalists that broke the Anthony Weiner "sexting" scandal, which precipitated the congressman's political demise.

I tasked Lou with helping me locate Santiago Lopez. Lou wasn't able to find Lopez (no one has been able to), but he did contact one of his half-brothers, Domigue Lopez, who confided something interesting.

Something mind-blowing.

At some point after the discovery of Elisa's body and presumably after Lopez gave his deposition statement, *someone* gave Lopez a large sum of money for the express purpose of moving him out of Los Angeles and back to Mexico. Domigue said this move took place very quickly, so quickly that he didn't know what had happened until Santiago reappeared and told him that he'd been paid a large sum of cash to relocate his family.

Lou tried to get more information from Santiago's half-brother but he stopped talking, probably realizing he had said too much, and the trail went cold.

I told John Carman about the information and he recommended a Mexico private investigator, Jose Baldomer, who I conscripted into the effort. Jose, a PI who specializes in Mexico-based cases, has not been able to locate Santiago. As of right now, Santiago Lopez is essentially off the grid. The Cecil employee who discovered Elisa's body, possibly perjured himself, and allegedly received a large payment to relocate out of the country, is missing in action.

THE MYSTERY OF THE MISSING LITHIUM

Let's take a brief moment to consider that the universe is missing an enormous amount of lithium. Cosmologists figured this out after studying cosmic microwave radiation, primordial light nuclei, and measurements from the first ten to twenty seconds after the Big Bang.

I recalled this fact one day after finding a lithium quartz crystal in a rock shop. The fist-sized, silvery-gold chunk was bulbous and mesmerizing. Imagining that the element was forged in the furnace of an exploding star, I became obsessed with it.

Then I remembered the article my San Diego doctor had slipped into my hand, which discussed evidence that small amounts of lithium may be beneficial for everyone. From the Big Bang to that moment in Southern California to the present, as I held a lithium stone in my hand, I suddenly became convinced that lithium is what my mind had been missing this whole time. The mystery of the strange synergy between my depression and mood disorder became crystal clear—my brain needed lithium, a cosmic element forged by the primordial explosion that created all of time and matter.

Lithium is not some concoction birthed by scientists in a lab. It's a naturally occurring unstable light metal, first discovered by humans in 1800 on a sparkling island near Sweden. When it was first applied as a psychiatric treatment, its potential was immediately seen as medicine that could discreetly treat neural networks and reduce severe mania.

Lithium became so popular in the 1940s that people were using it as a substitute for table salt. It was briefly an ingredient in the drink 7Up. But, unsurprisingly, such feckless overuse caused sickness and several deaths, leading to it being banned by the FDA in 1949. Though it has made a resurgence in recent decades, lithium presented a weak profit motive. Author Lauren Slater writes: "Perhaps better than any other drug, lithium reveals the extent to which psychiatry is tightly tied to capitalistic corporate interests."

The recent resurgence of lithium can be attributed to studies showing that in places where lithium is found in tap water, such as 27 counties in Texas and several areas in Japan, suicide rates decrease. This was described in the article my doctor gave me as well as in Slater's book.

I told my doctor I wanted to give lithium a shot. He was receptive but said I would have to get regular blood tests, as lithium can cause permanent thyroid and kidney damage.

Interestingly, this may be why Elisa was not prescribed lithium. Though I have no information on whether her doctor ever ran tests on her thyroid, her autopsy noted that her thyroid had anterior hemorrhage/erythema, leading some to speculate Elisa had an underlying thyroid condition, which is common in women but underdiagnosed. It is also worth noting that thyroid conditions frequently cause depression.

I became convinced that lithium was the answer to all my problems, that my years of depression, anxiety, mood disorders, and ADD were the result of not being properly medicated. That I had stumbled upon a cosmology article about the mysterious missing lithium in the universe on the same day as I accidentally retrieved the old article about lithium in tap water and then discovered a lithium crystal registered as yet another bewitching synchronicity, a signpost in the wilderness.

When the lithium kicked in, it draped me in a velvety calmness. It curbed some of my anxiety, evened my temperament, mellowed my mood.

But there was one problem, and it was a big one: Lithium did nothing for my depression. I know that for people who do not experience these chronic disorders, the distinction between depression and anxiety may seem specious, but it's like describing the difference between a broken bone and a deep cut. Qualitatively different ilks of pain.

Depression without anxiety is like starving to death in the woods without a massive bear nearby.

The honeymoon with lithium lasted a few more weeks before I broke down and told my doctor that I would have to get back on an

SSRI. I cycled through two or three that did not help. This included a reunion with Prozac, which I had taken for years in my twenties. Now it seemed to have very little effect, which terrified me.

I remembered the story of the great author David Foster Wallace, who went off his antidepressant Nardil, an MAOI, and then when he got back on it, the drug no longer worked for him. Months later, he hung himself in his garage.

As these thoughts circulated in my head, I began to panic in the Portland rain. I had gone through a half dozen prescriptions, on top of the dozen or so I had already experimented with over the course of my entire adult life. Was I treatment-resistant?

The mystery of my psychiatric illness competed tooth and claw with the Lam case itself. And they felt connected somehow.

Later that day, I spoke with the LAPD's chief psychologist, who told me that Stearns and Tennelle never contacted him or his staff regarding bipolar disorder. This struck me as almost unbelievable. This means that as the LAPD detectives ruled out foul play by way of *not* running a rape kit and assuming Elisa's death was an accident resulting from her bipolar disorder, they did not once consult with their in-house team of psychiatric professionals about said illness.

Their interest in bipolar disorder, it seems, was only as a convenient explanation that helped them close the case.

ENDGAME

By autumn of 2018, things were escalating much quicker than I had anticipated. I had to start thinking about my endgame for this book. The manuscript was due at the first of the year. It had once seemed inconceivable to me that there would be even a glimmer of hope for solving this case. There was simply too much deception and silence, too little information, too few of the principal players willing to speak (at all, much less on the record).

But the landscape had begun to change. The new information coming to me from several sources suggested a coverup. There's a saying I like that goes something like this: When people show you who they are, believe them.

I decided to apply that to the two powerful entities in control of this investigation: the Cecil Hotel and the LAPD. The first, the Cecil Hotel, has a history of employees sexually assaulting tenants; the second, the LAPD, has a history of corruption and covering up crimes. Why should be it be surprising then that these are the two voices saying, "Nothing to see here" in a case in which a predatory crime against a young woman appears to have been covered up?

But I was running out of time and resources. Our Kickstarter money for the documentary had long been spent on filming, and I was dipping significantly into my own funds, money originally invested in cryptocurrency, to hire investigators and consultants. Our supporters remained understanding about the shifting timeline and the reality that it costs a lot of money to make a documentary, especially one that requires an investigation like this.

I decided to take one final trip to downtown LA. I didn't have a specific plan, just a vague feeling that something would happen.

I was in a better headspace from a new antidepressant, Viibryd, which is expensive as hell but has virtually no side effects, and the lithium, which managed the mood swings. While I still had damage, my systems were pushing forward. I was like a used car with a check engine light on and in need of a tire alignment—but still pushing toward the destination. With the synchronicities still at play, it felt like the stars were aligning, that there was a mystery ready to be revealed and by tinkering with the right gear of the clockwork, I could crack open the truth. But maybe that was the serotonin speaking.

When I landed at the Burbank airport, I got a rental car, loaded up as much synthwave music as I could find, and got to work.

First, I got a drink with the filmmaker Ama McDonald, who was stuck in post-production hell on a documentary about the Cecil Hotel. The last third of his film is about the Lam case. Ama claimed to have interviewed several residents there, and, based on their testimony, he believed Elisa was killed.

One of those interviewed was Alvin Taylor, a long-time Cecil tenant who drew the suspicions of websleuths from early on because he appeared briefly in a CNN segment on the case—and he is a registered sex offender, a fact I verified with an Intelius background check.

I wondered if Ama might use that sex offender status to make Alvin seem more suspicious than he really was. Almost a year earlier, Ama passed along Alvin's phone number to me but with a caveat: "He won't answer. After I interviewed him, he stopped returning my calls and now he won't answer the phone for anyone."

This matched up with an experience Jared had outside the Cecil. He saw Alvin using his special fob to enter and politely asked him for an interview. Alvin said no, and when Jared asked why, he responded, simply, "Trust."

I told Ama that together our projects could help reopen the case. He seemed doubtful about this, which surprised me.

Then, our contrasting visions came to light. I had just briefly outlined some of my research on the LAPD and some of my evidence regarding a cover-up. Abruptly, Ama remarked that he felt like I was going way off topic. It stunned me that he didn't view police corruption as relevant to the case.

Overall, our conversation was pleasant and interesting. Ama is a devoted filmmaker, and I respect him.

But something didn't square: He didn't think we could get the case reopened, yet he believed he had evidence of foul play; at the same time, he didn't think there was a police cover-up. If he truly had evidence that cracked the case, I thought, the only reason it would be impossible to get the investigation reopened is police negligence.

The Cecil Hotel was closed for renovations. In fact, as I write these words, it's still closed. But a dozen or so full-time residents still lived inside. I watched them from the cafe next door using their special keycards to enter the building. I decided to delay another direct approach to the hotel. I would work in concentric sweeps around the Main Street area, canvassing the neighborhoods.

It was my third time doing this, but I didn't start until around 2015. I should have started in 2013. The early bird gets the worm.

I had one untapped lead, a man named Henry who used to live in the Cecil. I got his phone number from one of our contacts, and when I called him, he was receptive. Like many Cecil residents, he had a plethora of stories from the inside—paranormal activity, drug busts, gang-related activity, missing persons—but at this point, I felt I had covered enough of that. I needed direct clues from Elisa's final evening.

The information I really wanted was the name of someone who currently lived there. Henry had moved out a few years before the Lam case.

"I know one guy who still lives there," he said. "His name is Dred. At least that's what I call 'em."

He gave me Dred's number.

The canvassing was a bust. Lots of people had heard of the case, of course, but no one knew anything or had even the slightest semblance of a lead. I talked to security guards, street cops, store owners, hotel concierges, local residents, transients, etc. I must have talked to a hundred people.

I took a break and called Dred. No answer, so I left a message.

Then, on a lark, I walked to the alley behind the Cecil and looked at the graffiti etched on the back of the hotel. There was a lot of it. I scanned for anything that resembled the graffiti seen on the roof, or any names. Nothing to write home about.

I left the alley and hove right on Main to approach the front of the Cecil, under the gaze of several external surveillance cameras. As expected, the door didn't open. I cupped my hands around my eyes and peered through the glass into the lobby. The beams of the setting sun made it difficult to see, and I couldn't detect any movement. The front desk appeared unmanned.

What an eerie thought, that this giant, haunted 600-room hotel should be closed and empty but for a dozen tenants residing in the upper floors—with seemingly no management in operation.

Suddenly, a dark shape appeared at the back extremity of the lobby floor where the elevators are stationed. Through the glare of the sun on the glass, I identified the outline of a figure, a silhouette in motion, that gradually grew bigger. It walked toward me. As the figure reached the halfway point, I could distinguish a security guard uniform.

It reminded me of a scene in *Eyes Wide Shut* when Tom Cruise's character waits at the gate of the mansion where the secret society held their masked orgy; a surveillance camera spots him and then a black limousine slowly snakes a windy path around from the mansion to reach the gate. A stern, older man in a suit exits the limo, walks up to the gate, and hands Cruise a letter through the bars. Then he turns around and gets back in the limo, which retraces its path in reverse.

The letter reads: "Please cease all inquiries, which are completely useless. Consider this your final warning."

The security guard arrived at the door and stared at me through the glass. He didn't seem happy. This was the same guy who accosted me on the 14th floor and berated me in the alley when our drone operator, Ryan Washburn, tried to deploy Falcor (his drone).

"We're closed," he said, his voice muffled through the glass.

He started walking away from the door.

"Did you work here in 2013?" I called out.

He kept walking and his shape disappeared in the darkness. At least Tom Cruise got a letter.

The day's frustration continued, but I wasn't done yet. And I was about to find a juicy worm.

WHEN WEBSLEUTHING TURNS PATHOLOGICAL

One of the aspects of this case that has fascinated me the most is the extent to which it has burrowed into both popular culture and fringe conspiracy circles. The case has become a fixture in the public imagination, a part of the zeitgeist, and is deeply personal for some people.

One result of this was the preponderance of online witch hunts. Earlier, I discussed how the musician Morbid found himself targeted by websleuths who accused him of killing Elisa. At first, Morbid seemed to have found the attention mildly amusing and he ran with it, playing along with what he thought would be a short-lived Internet curiosity. But more users flagged his videos and soon YouTube terminated his channel. He lost ten years' worth of original works, much of which had not been backed up.

In addition to losing the content from his channel, he also lost the revenue he earned by monetizing his account with AdSense. This was one of his primary sources of income. Then Google terminated Pablo's email account and he lost more important files of his.

When I spoke to Morbid, it was clear that the events had significantly damaged his life.

What happened to Morbid was not an isolated incident. Earlier, I also relayed the story of how Dillon Kroe's name surfaced in connection with the case. Apparently, Kroe painted a portrait of Elisa that raised some eyebrows. Some websleuths accused him of being involved with Elisa's death, especially after he took the portrait offline. When I started a conversation with him, he abruptly broke it off with what sounded like legal talk.

I hadn't really intended on speaking with Dillon again until one day, a websleuth I had been in contact with emailed me an IMDB link for the 2016 film about Richard Ramirez, *Nightstalker*. The link directed me to the trivia section of the film, where there were five facts listed. One of them was the following:

"The drawings that are seen hanging in Richard Ramirez's cell in the film were actual drawings done by Ramirez, that were originally sent to his personal acquaintance: Dillon Kroe."

I couldn't believe it. Was this another weird link between Dillon Kroe and the Cecil Hotel? Was Dillon really a "personal acquaintance" with one of the most brutal serial killers of all time? The same guy who painted a portrait of Elisa and liked her posts?

Now I had to reach out to him again. This time, he opened up.

"Downtown LA is a second home to me. I love all that trash," he said.

I told him that his name has surfaced in the forums.

As far as the social media and painting, he said, "Anyone can follow Elisa Lam. She doesn't follow me back. Quite a few people have done art of her. It's because I have a dark art persona. If I was a yuppy guy, no one would care."

Then he told me the real reason he couldn't talk about the case earlier. He had worked with Ama McDonald on his documentary and didn't want to "leak" anything.

Ama. My competitor rises again. Always one step ahead of me.

"No one and I mean no one knows more detail about Elisa and the Cecil than him."

"Great, yeah. He's cool," I muttered.

Then Kroe told me how he knew Ramirez.

"I used to live in Whittier, grew up there. And Ramirez killed a few people there. During his killing spree, someone tried to break into our home. My mom saw a tall skinny man in black run away. Two weeks later the news broke of the murder he committed about five blocks away. It's always haunted me that it was him. I initially wrote him to ask if it was. But the prison system blacked out any questions pertaining to his crimes in the letters. I could only talk about miscellaneous stuff, like his paintings."

And so he became art pen pals with a serial killer.

"So many serial killers start painting in prison," I noted, recalling the works of John Wayne Gacy, Keith Jesperson, Henry Lee Lucas, and many others.

"Honestly, he sucked. He traced everything."

As I have documented earlier, the videos made by one websleuth, Wilhelm Werner Winther, feature graphic rape speculation complete with images of men having sex with a bound body. Winther documents specific narrative sequences of the men who he believes raped and killed Elisa, how long it took, and what they did with the body afterward.

A member of the Elisa Lam Facebook group, Caitlin Ellisa, posted one of his videos on July 31, 2018.

"Look at this video and this entire youtuber. What the actual hell?" She posted above it. "One video says he was her online boyfriend and she whined too much about feminism."

Caitlin is an amateur sleuth and became immersed in the Lam case in 2017, determined to help solve it. She believes her intuition gives her an important perspective on true crime cases. In my conversations with her, she stated that her intuition, "as well as many symbolic connections in the videos on [Winther's] page," leads her to believe that he was somehow involved in what happened to her.

"He seems sick but he also says there were 4 men on the roof, yet only names 3. So he is the 4th?" she wrote to me.

And so one websleuth began hunting another.

The more I watched Winther's baffling videos, the more it struck me that in several instances he claimed to have pictures and video of Elisa from the night she died. He outlines incredibly specific details from the night of her death, details that only someone there could know. In other videos he purported to show footage of her body in the water tank. However, in the text accompanying the pictures he frequently lapsed into bizarre tangents that feel unhinged.

Caitlin believed this fit the profile of someone with a disturbed, pathological mind with sadistic impulses. We discussed it over Facebook, wondering if the police knew about him or would be interested in his videos.

Caitlin, convinced that Winther was involved, amiably demanded that I watch all the videos and get back to her with my opinion. I didn't believe Winther was involved in Elisa's death, but it gave me chills to think about someone making videos about their victim for years afterward. There was something extra perverse about it, like a murderer who keeps an article of clothing from his victim so he can recall their scent. Except in the Internet age, he makes video memorials.

To clear things up, I wanted to confront Winther again about the situation. Knowing I was walking into a minefield, I messaged him again on Facebook,

He interrogated me over my last name, demanding to know if I was Swedish. We were off to a good start.

"Did you ever meet Elisa?" I wrote, recalling our first chat when he claimed Elisa visited him in Norway.

"A gentleman doesn't tell."

"That's an odd thing to say. As in, you were involved with her?"

"Right."

"Seems like she would have mentioned something about that in her blogs."

"Not at all—the blogs are, pretty much, cover up. She's not depressed or confused. She wasn't bipolar in any way."

"How do you know that?"

"If you ever have studied at a university, you'll know that 50 percent of the girls appears to be suicidal and crazy. Have you ever been at a party with drunk students . . . ?? Well, Elisa is certainly more sane and smarter than the average, female student. Take a look at the Skulls & Bones in the USA . . . madness. But of course; later they'll become President of the United States!"

"What does that have to do with Elisa?"

"You're governed by MADMEN, pseudoswede."

"Yes, aren't we all?"

At this point, I readied to discontinue the conversation. He had displayed more than enough misogyny and delusional aggression. Then he said something that made me think he had some level of self-reflection.

"Internet is flowing over with psychopaths and maladjusted people. I think weak individuals need to put a negative label on others in order to compensate for their inferiority complexes." Then he abruptly switched lanes. "You probably should know that the case involves a cooperation between the Mexican mafia and Cosa Nostra. At least a couple of head officers and security guards at the hotel were a part."

"The Mexican mafia was involved with Elisa's death?"

"Yes. She discovered the drug trafficking—they left the key in the basement door, and Elisa saw 'em. They stood beside the secret tunnel used for transporting money, drugs and people into the hotel. But one night they forgot the key in the lock . . . and Elisa was there. I've been attacked for looking into it."

"Well, that sounds dangerous," I said, recalling the numerous rumors I'd heard of gang and cartel activity being facilitated through the Cecil—and, of course, the cartel money laundering operation running out of the Fashion District only blocks from the Cecil. Who knows, maybe Winther was on to something.

"You can't be afraid of killing or being killed in this game; carry a gun, and learn how to use it."

After this he got belligerent again and blocked me.

I was about at my wit's end with online conspiracists and was about to swear off the forums completely when I saw a comment by some-one claiming to have made contact with the parents. He spoke guard-edly and seemed like he had done his research. I messaged him and asked if he would speak to me on the phone. He gave me his number.

"So you spoke to the parents?" I asked. "You would be the first."

"I know. It's been a long journey, but I felt they needed to know the truth. That their daughter was murdered."

"Why do you think she was murdered?"

"I took a different approach to this, Jake. I went back to the source, the primary piece of evidence: the surveillance tape."

Ok, you've got my attention, I thought. The surveillance tape has timecode cuts and definitely seems to have been doctored.

"And what in the surveillance tape shows conclusively that she was killed?"

"The killers are right there, Jake."

I paused. "You mean in the hallway?"

"No, in the elevator with Elisa. You have to train your eyes to see them and to understand what's going on."

Oh God no, I thought. It's him. It's Mark. I had forgotten his name and now I was once again talking to the man who believed Elisa was already dead in the elevator tape and was being controlled like a puppet by a cabal of satanists.

"Oh, we've spoken before," I said, weakly.

"Yes, yes, and I told you they use these belts and straps that you can only see with a special web tool . . ."

I honestly wish I were making this up. I took the phone away from my ear while he finished his monologue, but there was still one thing I wanted to know.

"Did you really talk to her parents?" I was praying he had made that up. The thought that he had contacted Elisa's parents with such a conspiracy theory made me ill. This was exactly the kind of thing that made websleuths look like bad faith actors, deluded provoca-teurs who can't be trusted.

"I was able to speak with their spokeswoman," he said. "She said the family is at peace with the investigation and does not wish to pursue it any further."

Thank God he didn't directly get through to them.

I politely ended our call, but Mark continued texting me for days. He kept telling me he was going to send screenshots proving what he was saying. He practically begged me to believe him.

Finally, a few days later he sent the screenshots and I cast my eyes upon incoherent scrambles of pixelated shapes he had zoomed in on. Mark could see patterns in the digital static and he knew just how to interpret them. In the chaos he saw killers and demons and, with the raw dynamics of evil laid bare, this world made sense to him.

One of the stills was just a close up of the pixels of Elisa's eyes, which were just smeared dabs of pure black. This was Doppelgänger Elisa, apparently.

At its core, the issue comes down to the perception of patterns. Conspiracy theories, synchronicity, and paranormal activity may be a primal psychological impulse to find order in chaos. The human brain is hardwired to find meaningful structure in the natural world because for most of human history, our survival depended on identifying patterns in the surrounding environment and storing the memory of beneficial patterns for future use.

One team of scientists argues that conspiracy theories are the remnant of an evolutionary defense mechanism that in modern times essentially amounts to a mental disorder they call "illusory pattern perception." Conspiracy theorists, they suggest, subconsciously need to find connections. A similar study in 2008 claimed that people who feel they have no control or agency over their lives are more likely to experience "illusory pattern perception." The experiment found a correlation between people who found patterns and meaning in random images, such as static on the TV.

Another study found that people who feel ostracized or excluded are also more likely to believe in conspiracy theories and supernatural stories.

A series of 2015 studies, published in *Social Psychological and Personality Science,* concluded that there is a strong correlation between conspiracy theories, narcissism, and low self-esteem. Such pathologies, they argue, may fuel a strong belief in ideas that the conspiracy theorist perceives as being the lonely truth that only he or she can understand; the conspiracy theorist subsequently personalizes a deep psychological need to feel morally or intellectually superior to the larger social class from which they may subconsciously feel they have been excluded.

As a conspiracy-theory buff myself, I had always viewed them as harmless, an alternative, experimental way of analyzing the construction of reality. But in the Elisa Lam case, the conspiracy theories were not harmless. They stigmatized the victim and significantly hindered efforts to get new information from the LAPD.

That mental illness, not killers or demons, may be to blame (whether exclusively or not) induces deep anxiety in people and causes them to search for, and manufacture, answers. Because what if the great mystery in this tragedy is the unknown depths of the mind itself? What if the most popular true-crime case of the century was crimeless? Then we're hunting a whole new type of killer.

Two weeks later, Mark texted me again: "Hello again. I'm no longer interested in being involved with this endeavor. I was contacted by a police officer and verbally assaulted and I feel threatened because of it. I have no right to risk the safety of my wife and my grandson, so for their sake I'm forced to withdraw from helping the families."

He'd mentioned he was working on other cases. My guess was that he probably contacted the families of victims, feeding them his outlandish analysis. I imagine a detective learned of this and came down hard on him. Or maybe he directly contacted a detective with his "evidence."

Either way, this is the exact opposite of what websleuths should be doing, according to Websleuths owner, Tricia Griffith, who attempts to block websleuths from contacting victims' families and the police.

One thing was for sure: I was done with the forums.

MORE STUNNING CLAIMS

Annoyed by everything, I decided to get a drink at Cole's, a restaurant around the corner from the Cecil that dates back to the 1920s.

While awaiting their signature French Dip sandwich, I received a call back from Dred. He was affable and direct. No bullshit. After I explained to him what I was doing and how he could be of help, it didn't take long for Dred to open up. Most of the Cecil residents I've spoken to are apprehensive, some of them outright paranoid. And, from the sound of it, for good reason. But Dred was different.

"So you currently live at the Cecil?"

"No, not anymore."

"Oh, okay. I guess I misunderstood Henry about that."

"No, they evicted me, man. Over some bullshit, and then they kept my deposit."

"I keep hearing about that." Multiple tenants told me about the eviction racket. When I looked up the hotel on a court database, I found about a half-dozen civil lawsuits brought against them by former tenants regarding eviction disputes.

"But I was at the Cecil for years."

"Were you there in 2013? During the Elisa Lam case?"

"Oh yeah, I was there. Pretty crazy stuff, man. They lied to us," Dred said with a laugh.

"Who lied?"

"The hotel. They didn't want to admit that a body had been found up there, in the water we'd been brushing our damn teeth with."

This matched up with what another hotel guest told me. This woman stayed at the Cecil the week Elisa died and claims that she was one of the first guests to report the water problem to management. She said that during the initial discovery of the body, the hotel deceived residents and lied to them every step of the way, even after police found the body.

The bartender deposited my plate of food before me. Weak from hunger, I took a bite.

"Do you think the hotel management knew more about what happened to Elisa?" I asked, chewing.

"Oh definitely," he said. "I think one of them was involved."

I choked a little on the French Dip. Somehow, I always receive surprising information while eating.

"Involved . . . like involved with her death?"

"Yeah. I think a couple of them were up there on the roof with her."

"Why do you think that?"

Dred explained that while living at the Cecil, he heard a lot of rumors, rumblings, from other tenants. Some said that an employee let her on the roof; others said that a tenant, a "sketchy" guy who is the son of a convicted sex offender (I'm assuming this is a reference to Aidan, supposedly the son of Alvin Taylor—websleuths in the forums were suspicious of them both) followed her.

After eating I went to the bathroom and saw a shiny placard above the urinal that read: "Charles Bukowski pissed here."

I wonder if Unterweger saw this, I thought. The serial murderer had wanted so badly to meet Bukowski.

On my way out, I stopped and took a puff from my e-cig next to the bored-looking bouncer. Earlier, I mentioned my two experiences with bouncers, how the second one produced shocking information. This was that second experience.

On a lark, I asked him if he had heard about the case.

"The thing at the Cecil . . . the girl on the roof? Ah man. Her friends were here looking for her."

"Her friends . . . from Canada?"

"I don't know who they were, but they were going around everywhere asking questions."

These so-called friends could have easily been websleuths using the "friend" appellation in order to get info, but it was still interesting.

"You hear any rumors about what happened?"

"All I know is what one of 'em told me."

"One of who?"

"A cop."

"A cop talked to you about the case?"

"He was off-duty. Cops blather all the time. They come in to get drinks and, on their way out, they strike it up with me."

"So what did he tell you?"

"Not much, but he did say they found a few of the lady's things in a dumpster over in Skid Row."

"Some of Elisa's things??"

"Yeah."

I was shocked.

And this is why I like bouncers: They protect us from drunk assholes, of course; but more important (for me, at least), the nature of their job makes them valuable nodes in the information transfer pipeline. They are in a unique position to sponge up stray comments from people, including cops, who are unwinding with a few drinks.

I pressed him on it because I wanted to be sure the information hadn't pertained to a different case. It's easy in everyday jumbled conversations to get your wires crossed and have details from one story jump ship into another. But he insisted emphatically that the cop was talking about the Lam case.

If true, his claim almost single-handedly proves some kind of foul play. Someone disposed of evidence that connected them to Elisa's death. There's no other credible explanation for why her belongings would be in a dumpster in Skid Row.

I went to Skid Row. I knew it was ill-advised but there was still daylight and I couldn't help myself. I didn't intend to check the dumpsters, of course, but rather to canvas the people nearby. Anyone who lived on the street in eyesight of the dumpster might have information.

But it didn't take long for the reality of the situation to make itself clear. Skid Row comprises roughly fifty-four blocks, stretching over four miles. That's a lot of dumpsters. I did some canvassing but realized pretty quickly that it was like looking for a needle in a haystack, at best.

As I walked back through the soiled streets of Skid Row, a great sadness came over me. Of the estimated 48,000 homeless people living in Los Angeles, around 4,000 homeless dwell in Skid Row. At least one third of them are severely mentally ill. Many of them have spent their lives being cycled by the state through hospitals, prisons, and ultimately the streets. They are casualties of both the chaos of nature and the sadistic zero-sum game that is human civilization.

With a slight tweak in my life's conditions, that could be me. It could be any of us. We like to think our place in this crisp reality is fixed, but it isn't. Someday we will all lose everything. Some of us get started early.

CHAPTER 23
What Happened to Elisa Lam?

HER SHADOW PRECEDES HER down a silent corridor. It passes over each of the tenant doors, stretched at the vertices like a phantom being sucked into a black hole. All she can hear is the sound of her own breathing. It reminds her she's alive—and alone.

Always alone, even in company.

As she turns a corner, her shadow darts around the path and reconstitutes as a wall-sized entity looming over her. She stops and stands before it in stillness. But the shadow convulses ever so slightly, like it's catching its breath after a long journey. Or seething in anger.

She lifts her hand and makes a wave gesture, the kind you might assert against the wind outside the window of a moving car. Now it's the shadow that remains still.

She hears a sound behind her, a whispering in triplicate, and she turns her head to look. But there is nothing.

My new "friends" are having some fun, she thinks.

NEW ANOMALIES AND OLD QUESTIONS

Having gathered critical new evidence, I began to recalibrate my analysis of the case and my working narrative of what happened to Elisa. This necessitated revisiting old questions and wrestling with them once more. What took place on the 14th floor before and after Elisa was recorded in the elevator? How, when, and why did she get on the roof, was she alone and, if not, who accompanied her? When did Elisa die, was she still alive when she entered the water tank, and did she do so on her own? These are the grand questions, questions that remain unanswered by the LAPD.

In December 2018, I finally sat down to write my letter to the California Attorney General, requesting that the Elisa Lam case be reopened. I was out of resources and money to continue the investigation on my own. In fact, I'd sunk so much of my own money into the endeavor, I had to once again move back in with my parents in the snowy mountains.

Meanwhile, strange synchronicities and anomalies persisted. I would spend a couple hours researching and writing about the psycho-social aspect of depression only to go for a drive and hear the song *Psychosocial* by Slipknot immediately come on the radio. I would write the phrase "letter of the law" only to hear it instantly echoed on the television in the most random of contexts. Late at night, I wrote the scene in which I saw a woman in a red hoodie feeding pigeons at night; at the exact moment I wrote the word "pigeons," I looked up and one of my mother's antique pigeon sculptures sat staring at me from the corner of the deck as a strong gust of wind animated the surrounding wind chimes.

After spending two hours writing the scenes involving the mirror on the 14th floor, the mirror in my bedroom collapsed. One of the wall fixtures had broken. Two weeks passed, during which we did not speak about the mirror at all. Then the very night I resumed work on the mirror sections, my mother brought it up, mentioning the mirror at the exact moment I was writing the word "mirror"; when I looked up, I saw myself in the living room mirror.

This kind of stuff had been happening over and over, nearly every day, for two years running. It got to the point where my rational side stopped making excuses for it. I don't know what synchronicity is. It may be a legitimately meaningful narrative of archetypes supporting an as-yet unknown cosmic convergence of mind and matter; or it could be an evolutionary defense mechanism, a pattern-recognition utility that serves as a way for humans to acquire meaning in the chaotic information around us.

Then, Dred—the former Cecil tenant who was convinced of foul play involving, or at least covered up by, hotel management—disappeared, his cell-phone service cut off. The same thing went for Henry, another former tenant who had referred me to Dred. The most practical explanation was that these two men hadn't paid their phone bills and had their service discontinued. But I couldn't help but be suspicious given that other former tenants told me they were terrified of retribution by the hotel if they told their stories on the record.

The prohibitive nature of inquiring into the case is definitely real though and it goes beyond detectives refusing to talk. One websleuth wrote that she messaged one of her legal friends, whom she regularly consults with on various investigations, about the Lam case. This person had always been very forthright and kind, but she responded that the websleuth should not pursue the case any further.

I did not expect the level of secrecy I encountered with this investigation. I went into it assuming that, over time, I would be able to earn enough trust from the LAPD and certain executives at the Cecil Hotel to eventually extract statements clarifying certain anomalies. If there's nothing to hide, I reasoned, it's in their interest to set the record straight. An innocent corporation or agency that is accused of corruption or negligence should have no problem briefly discussing core elements of a high-exposure case to dispel damaging rumors and conspiracy theories.

I was wrong. The secrecy worsened; they doubled-down. Detective Stearns literally has a "policy" of refusing to discuss the case at all. There was a chokehold on all three major nodes of information: the family, the police, and the hotel. The silence was so widespread, so total, it felt orchestrated.

Even Elisa's roommates at the Cecil Hotel have not spoken on the record. It's as if they don't even exist. We have every reason to believe they do, as GM Amy Price confirmed the women initially shared a room with Elisa on the 5th floor before requesting that she be relocated due to strange behavior. It drives me nuts that there's no information on them—not one interview. We don't even know their names.

These women could be enormously helpful in figuring out what happened. They would likely be able to characterize Elisa's behavior

to help determine if she was experiencing a manic or psychotic episode and, if so, the degree of severity.

Paul Brevik, a websleuth whose YouTube channel Lepprocommunist at one point contained several videos of his analysis of the
case, told me that he spoke with a Cecil Hotel employee who said
Elisa's behavior included running around while maniacally laughing. This sounds like an extreme version of some of the behavior
Elisa admits to in her blogs, when she talks about getting the attention of strangers in a strange, purposefully flamboyant manner.
Brevik, who believes Elisa's death was an accident and is a critic
of homicide theories, took the statement as more confirmation that
Elisa was experiencing severe psychiatric illness the night she died,
which for him rules out foul play.

Elisa's roommates might know if she was spending time with any
of the tenants or employees (perhaps one of the full-time tenants on
the 14th floor, for instance, or a security guard), or if she felt threatened by anyone during her stay. These women could fill in a lot of
blanks but they have been completely scrubbed from the case. They
are veritable ghosts, fictional characters. It is a total mystery to me
why during the early days of the investigation—when police were
asking the public for help and assuredly interviewed the women (one
would certainly hope)—reporters did not receive enough information to know the importance of the roommates as witnesses and get
them on public record.

They are great examples of the deep-seeded, unnatural silence
that surrounds one of the most talked-about cases of the century.

There may be some legitimate reason for such silence. But given
the level of hysteria that already surrounded the case, I don't see the
logical purpose of not answering a few basic questions to put public concerns to rest. This is exactly how the government deals with
corruption scandals, and silence only makes the populace more dis-
trustful while breeding conspiracy theories that persist for decades.

I understand why the family would not want to speak, which is
why I only made one meek attempt at contacting them. As I noted
earlier, they were persistently pestered by journalists and websleuths
for years. One particularly conspiratorial websleuth told me a spokes-

woman for the family emailed him that Elisa's parents had sold the family restaurant in Vancouver and moved back to Hong Kong while Elisa's sister remains in Vancouver. According to this websleuth, the family is at peace with the conclusion of the investigation and does not want to be involved with efforts to reopen the case, although they do not mind if others do.

While I don't view this source as particularly credible, I visited the restaurant in Vancouver and spoke with the management in person; they confirmed that the Lam family sold the business a couple years ago. As for the rest of it, who knows? Though it is difficult to get a case reopened without the cooperation of the victim's family, they are more than justified in remaining silent if doing so helps with their emotional health and managing the trauma. They experienced every parent's worst nightmare and then witnessed that nightmare turn into a public spectacle.

I don't expect them to read this book, but my hope is to reverse the narrative and turn a gruesome public spectacle into a call to action. This is a two-part mission, which I will explain shortly.

THE EVIDENCE

On the eve of 2019, while most of the world stayed up all night partying, I stayed up all night writing. I had already been granted a generous three-month extension. Now my manuscript was due. It was time to play my hand.

In summarizing the findings from my research, I knew I lacked hard evidence. I didn't have a murder weapon, a confession, or even a suspect (at least no one I was willing to accuse on record), but I had a small mountain of circumstantial evidence at the top of which lay an eagle's nest of damning new revelations.

I broke this summary down into sections, starting with some of the circumstantial anomalies and building toward the strongest evidence.

The police investigation was flawed or negligent at best, corrupt at worst.

The LAPD did not process a rape kit even though the coroner's department collected evidence for it and noted anal bleeding in their autopsy. Likely distracted by the Dorner manhunt, the LAPD searched the roof (the "crime scene") twice—with a K-9 unit—without finding Elisa's body, causing the loss of critical forensic evidence, such as blood, DNA, and drug remnants. The LAPD either failed to find, or neglected to disclose, any trace evidence (DNA) that could help reconstruct Elisa's movements on the roof. The LAPD didn't consult with their own department's psychology department about the nature of bipolar disorder and Elisa's behavior in the surveillance tape.

The Cecil Hotel has a long history of systemic criminal activity, some of it perpetrated by employees or management.

The hotel has a history of unsolved murders, unexplained deaths, and sexual assaults, the latter of which is corroborated by three former hotel residents who claim employees sexually assaulted female tenants. Multiple guests and tenants allege predatory employees and exploitive, criminal business practices (such as withholding rental deposits under threat of arrest for drug possession). Three employees, including the general manager, chief engineer, and maintenance worker, may have perjured themselves in depositions regarding access to the roof and whether the lid to the water tank was open—two critical aspects of the case. The corporate executives finalized a major financial partnership, worth tens of millions of dollars, during the week Elisa's body was finally found, which, according to some researchers, constitutes a motive for delaying the discovery of the body.

The autopsy contains a number of anomalies and critical flaws in methodology and analysis that may disqualify its conclusions.

Several independent coroners have noted major inconsistencies and flaws with regard to the cause of death. One prominent forensics expert says the autopsy does not establish that Elisa drowned and that it's just as likely, if not more so, that Elisa was already dead when she entered the tank. There is a possible injury suggestive of a traumatic sexual attack that was not ruled out with a rape kit. The victim wasn't tested for GHB (or any date rape drug) intoxication. The Coroner's Department took an unusual amount of time to declare the cause of death and crossed out and changed its conclusion. Only a few years after the chief medical examiner released the Lam autopsy, he was sued in court and charged with falsifying an autopsy and misclassifying a decedent's cause of death.

Some of the case's most important mysteries and questions have not been explained or answered.

The surveillance tape of Elisa Lam from inside the hotel contains multiple anomalies, including missing time, spliced frames, and timecode cuts and errors that indicate it may have been doctored. Another surveillance tape of Elisa with two unknown men has not been made public or explained. Still other surveillance, which should have been available from cameras on the 14th floor staircase, was not released or disclosed. The civil case seems to have been thrown out prematurely by a judge who was accused by a credible witness (an associate attorney) of being a serial sexual harasser and misogynist. A former LAPD officer, who was part of the original search of the roof, says the lid to the tank that held Elisa's body was completely shut when first responders arrived, a claim that contradicts testimony given to police by the hotel employee who discovered Elisa's body.

There are multiple new bombshell allegations that need to be fully investigated.

A new witness claims an off-duty cop told him investigators found Elisa's belongings in a Skid Row dumpster. A family member of the hotel employee who discovered Elisa's body alleges "someone" paid this employee a large sum of money to move his family out of the country soon after testifying in a deposition in which he may have perjured himself. A police informant, who worked closely with the LAPD for years, claims independent investigators that worked on the case privately concluded (1) the surveillance tape was doctored, (2) foul play was likely, and (3) that there may have been be a financial quid pro quo between the Cecil Hotel and the LAPD. A statement by a deputy coroner who worked on the autopsy says that one of the main detectives believed an employee was either with Elisa on the roof or gave her access to the roof (claims that could have been verified by the 14th-floor cameras).

I am not making allegations of criminality against any specific individuals associated with the LAPD or the Cecil Hotel. However, I am reporting here new evidence, allegations, and disclosures from a wide array of sources that implicitly identify both as being in some way involved with (potentially) criminal negligence or conspiracy.

When you add all of it up besides the voluminous cases of major corruption within the LAPD as well as the allegations of predatory behavior and sexual assaults committed by Cecil Hotel employees, even the most diehard of skeptics should smell the sulphur of a smoking gun. We have a more than reasonable justification for the commission of an independent legal body to audit the LAPD's case files and launch a new investigation of Elisa's death.

REVISITING OCCAM'S RAZOR

You've heard it a thousand times if you've heard it once: The simplest explanation—that which requires the least amount of assumptions—is the most likely explanation. Some have captured its essence with pithy maxims like, "When you hear hoofbeats, think of horses not zebras."

Unfortunately, there are those who would repeat this while inside a zebra enclosure.

Occam's Razor has long been a weaponized philosophical concept. This abductive heurism is a favorite among government and law enforcement officials when deflecting accusations of wrongdoing or corruption. Over time, it has accumulated significant and, some would argue, misguided utility.

Many philosophers and scientists say that when you look at the nature of reality—cosmology, biological evolution, and even developmental psychology—Occam's Razor rarely applies. Some of the shocking discoveries made by physicists in the field of quantum mechanics, for example, discoveries that exposed our universe to be wildly bizarre and inscrutable at the most fundamental level, fly in the face of Occam's Razor.

In the medical profession, some physicians argue that the Occam's Razor mentality frequently causes misdiagnoses. Doctors may become overly reductionist and look for a single cause to explain multiple symptoms. In response, a counterargument to Occam's Razor, its rarely cited philosophical nemesis and inverted doppelgänger, Hickam's Dictum, states that a multitude of symptoms should not necessarily be distilled down and explained by one common ailment. Expanded to a larger context, Hickam's Dictum suggests that the answer to an enigma is more likely to be a complex and pluralistic web of causes.

In the Lam case, I ask you, which is more practical, which is more reasonable: that the young woman seen on surveillance looking terrified, and thereafter found dead and naked in a water tank, died as the result of a skinny-dipping accident in a tall, difficult-to-access metal cistern on a near pitch-black, difficult-to-access roof, or that she was the victim of some kind of foul play in an area and hotel rife with sexual predators?

Hickam's Dictum could apply to the Elisa Lam case very specifically, in that there may have been a complex situation, like involuntary manslaughter, that unfolded. Maybe there was no single cause of her death, but rather a constellation of interacting factors.

As the years ticked by, I spent countless nights, logged countless hours, pondering what actually happened that night on the roof of the Cecil. Despite my discoveries, the absence of hard answers began to drive me nuts—as if I needed any help in that department.

This sense of frenzied urgency to excavate the truth was compounded by Kickstarter supporters complaining that our documentary was taking too long. Let me remind you, I felt compelled to argue (in my head), that it's been well over half a century since the President of the United States had half his head blown off on live television and we still don't know the full truth of what happened.

Thus far, I've tried to refrain as much as possible from indulging in uncorroborated conjecture. For the purpose of transparency, it's now time to depart ever so slightly from that framework and occupy a space where analysis and narrative co-exist.

It's certainly possible that Elisa's death really was an accident with no foul play involved. She may have, during an intense mixed episode of mania and depression, removed her clothes and climbed into the tank on her own. Or she may have climbed in with suicidal intent.

It is possible either of these actions could have been the result of
Elisa taking a med like Ambien, a sleep aid that has been known
to facilitate people accidentally or purposely killing themselves—
sometimes in their sleep. This includes cases of drowning. Elisa
mentions in her blog at one point that she was out of sleep meds,
indicating she was not opposed to taking them. Ambien can cause
unusual sleepwalking-type behavior, even psychosis, and also has
a very short half-life, meaning it would have likely been out of her
system for the autopsy.

When I first started writing this book, I deferred more to the reality of mental illness and believed that to be the more likely cause for
her being discovered in the water tank (by a factor of something like
60 to 40).

However, based on the evidence I've uncovered, I now believe it
is more likely that Elisa was not alone on the roof and that something unexpected happened involving other people; furthermore,
it's more likely Elisa was not alive when she entered the water tank.
Which means, someone (or, likely, *more than one person*) placed
her there.

This conclusion is based on Dr. Hiserodt's forensic analysis of the
autopsy, the multiple reports of sexual predators employed by the
Cecil, and a series of allegations and disclosures reported to me: that
some of Elisa's belongings were found in a dumpster; that private
investigators looking into the case concluded foul play was involved;
and that the man who discovered Elisa's body was paid to leave the
country shortly after the police investigation.

Based on this evidence, I am convinced that something criminal was and is being covered up. As important as the mental illness
narrative is to this story—and to me, personally—no one is served
when law enforcement agents scapegoat victims' mental illnesses
to evade hard questions or due diligence in a criminal investigation.

So then, what the hell happened? Much to my dismay, I don't
know. My hope is that this book will help reignite a discussion over
the case that forces the LAPD to disclose more evidence.

In the meantime, I've constructed what I call my "walking narrative," a supposition with legs. It's a blend of hypothesis and evidence; creative non-fiction applied to the scientific method: what is the most likely scenario?

When I take what we know to be true regarding the history of the Cecil Hotel and the 14th floor, Elisa's accelerated bipolar disorder (which, at the time, she was not managing with either of her prescribed mood stabilizers) and potential for mania, apply the new disclosures and then let "the extremes inform the mean," I arrive at my walking narrative—the aggregate of analysis and narrative.

While my "walking narrative" certainly shouldn't be taken for gospel truth, it's based on meticulous attention to detail with regard to Elisa's behavior (the nature of her bipolar disorder and what I believe may have been a "mixed episode"), the history of the Cecil Hotel (both mythic and material), and the new evidence turned up in my investigation.

THE LAST NIGHT

Something eclipses the point of light shooting from the eyehole of the door. The tenant inside must be watching her as she shuffles down the 14th floor and then banks right into the elevator. She doesn't know where she wants to go, so she presses multiple buttons, an entire column of them.

Let the Cecil decide my destination, Elisa thinks and steps back to wait. But the doors don't close, and as she stands there, she hears the sound again.

It comes from outside the elevator, roughly halfway down the hall. Masculine voices whispering over each other. This time there is an additional layer to it: giggling. Someone laughing at her.

Those assholes are messing with me, she thinks. *Should have never told them where I'm staying.*

She inches forward and then pokes her head out of the elevator for a lightning quick examination of the hallway. The upper floors house long-term residents, she remembers the concierge telling her when she checked in. Some occupants never leave.

The elevator doors still haven't closed. If the lurkers move down the hall and pass the elevator, they will see her. Elisa backs against the wall, takes a sidestep, and positions herself in the corner.

Even more than the sense of being followed now is the sense of being watched. She catches a peripheral glimpse of a ceiling camera catercornering her and remembers the wall of surveillance screens behind the front desk—and to the left of the screens, a security guard. As the receptionist checked her in, the security guard checked her out.

The guy who moved her to a new room earlier that day, the guy who said he could show her the roof later. What a smooth operator.

He can see me now. ANYONE can see me.

She emerges from the corner of the elevator, starts to look out, says *to hell with it* and hops right out into the hallway. *Alright, assholes, here I am.*

No one to the right, no one to the left. *This was all in my head,* she realizes. *No one's following me, no one gives a damn about me.*

She does a little square walk, left, back, forward, left again, and comes to a stop to the left of the elevator whose doors, apparently, will remain open until the end of time.

There's something royally wrong with this hotel, she thinks. *It's not just the elevator doors, it's not just the shitty wi-fi, bad breakfast waffles and unscrupulous people—there's a darkness here that is aware, a faceless presence with eyes in every room, sentries posted in the minds of every guest.* She recalls some of the stories her ex-roommates told her (before they kicked her out!) about the history of the Cecil. Murders, suicides, serial killers, reports of creepy paranormal stuff. She looked it up herself online in the lobby—where the security guard watched her from afar—and was shocked. *Of all the places I could have stayed*, she thought.

She'd dreamt strange things while there. Bodies falling, blood-stained pigeons lifting into flight, broken people suffering in small, sultry rooms; dismembered victims pieced back together and going about their days, unaware of their own murders; still, black water parted by a lifeless face that surfaces and opens its eyes.

In one dream, she was online working on her blogs as someone observed her, scribbling notes like a scientist conducting an experiment, a journalist transcribing an interviewee's thoughts.

One night Elisa had a dream within a dream in which she met a spirit friend who fluttered in and out of shadows, intermittently illuminated by beams of moonlight. In the language of the dream, this friend was an ancient myth taking human form. She said as a human she'd lived at the Cecil and warned Elisa that all who die there, remain.

It keeps us, she whispered. She also warned her: *It will come for you.* She woke up still dreaming and, sure enough, found herself being pursued by the spirit of a man with intense black eyes. But he was only the temporary greeting face on a much larger, amorphous entity, a decentralized sentience evading the charters of time and space, a veil of countless writhing souls cocooned within its folds. Captive there she saw her spirit friend, who started to smile but was pulled under and beyond into the depths.

She woke up saying, "What the hell?"

Her most recent dream image was, again, a body falling, this time in ultra slow motion, so slow that it was almost geological time; the person's descent from the Cecil was decelerated such that they experienced in perpetuity that final act of despair.

When she woke she was compelled to go to the window of her room, as if there was something there that needed to be done. It felt like the sentience had probed her dreams while she slept, its tendrils infiltrating her mind and inserting thoughts and images. As usual she had jumped on Tumblr to get her day started and Elisa, who'd recently taken an interest in synchronicity, immediately saw a digital illustration of a shadowy figure falling from a building. Though it stunned and disturbed her, she reblogged it.

Presently, on the wall across from her, a face stares at Elisa. Naturally, she isn't expecting to see a face, much less her own, and she gasps. The Elisa in the mirror doesn't gasp, though, she laughs. It is a wide-eyed, manic laugh that frightens her.

Isn't it considered healthy to laugh at yourself? She asks, certain she hadn't been laughing. Who is this imposter?

The hotel is playing mind games with her, she thinks. Or is it her own mind sabotaging itself . . . again? Alone in a strange land, an even stranger building, her intensifying battle with bipolar was manifesting unusually intense dreams, thoughts, and fears.

Going off her meds may not have been wise, she realizes. She'd wanted to experience herself again without a pharmaceutical filter, but now she is under siege, rattled by the feeling that something is watching her sleep, watching and shaping the contents of her mind. Is the surveillance here so comprehensive that it even monitors your dreams?

To her right she hears it again. A whispering, a triumvirate of hushed voices hatching some plan. Is it coming from inside one of the rooms maybe? It's muffled, but so close, as if she could reach out and touch it.

Presently, on the wall across from her, a face stares at Elisa. Naturally, she isn't expecting to see a face, much less her own, and she gasps. The Elisa in the mirror doesn't gasp, though, she laughs. It is a wide-eyed, manic laugh that frightens her.

Isn't it considered healthy to laugh at yourself? She asks, certain she wasn't laughing. Who is this imposter?

As far as the voices, it has to be her new "friends." She went to lunch with them, then when they returned to the lobby, they handed off the leftovers and asked her what room she was in. She made up a number, but then while she was waiting for the elevator, she saw them laughing with the security guard and staring at her.

These weren't healthy gazes. Too many guys must have grown up under the impression that there's something noble about one-sided "love at first sight." Because of those stupid rom-coms that make the male protagonist a Romeo simply because he's attracted to a woman he's never even met. In reality, it's creepy. And when there's three of them doing it, it's, well, creepier.

It has to be them out there, lurking.

Meanwhile, the doors still haven't closed. Maybe they are manipulating the elevator, using another button panel to prevent the doors from closing.

She reenters the elevator and presses more buttons. *I'll throw them off,* she thinks, her patience waning before a machine, a day, a life that no longer makes sense.

Meanwhile, the sense of being watched persists, grows stronger by the second. It's not just the creepers in the hall, who seem to remain just out of view, or the feeling that the hotel has a mind of its own.

The voyeurism has a vastness she can't explain. At first, she thinks it is an affectation, a mixture of the paranoia of being followed with the despair of sensing that her mood disorder will never relent. But now she's picking up something even weirder: the sense of a collective gaze, something disembodied, *eyes without faces.*

Yet she hasn't seen anyone in the hall.

She can only hear them. The whispers return but now it's different. They're discussing her. Analyzing her every movement, commenting on her every mannerism, dissecting her every thought. It's like she's a rat in a maze and a million scientists are debating whether she can find the cheese.

She's the star of a secret reality TV show.

Smile, you're on TV. She waves her hand in the open doorway to the elevator, a horizontal version of the "wax on, wax off" motion from *Karate Kid.*

Maybe the elevator doors are motion-activated, she thinks, like grocery store entrances.

The doors don't close, though. Because of course they don't. That's her luck today.

This day—this whole trip—has been a sequence of absurdities. She counts them off with the fingers of her left hand, grasping dramatically at each digit: First, she loses her phone in San Diego; then her roommates completely betray her; and now, the elevator seems to be sabotaging her right when she's reasonably sure some creepers are following her.

Thank God I'm checking out of this place in the morning. Never to return.

To her left, she sees an open window, the fire escape. It occurs to her that she could use this to bypass the elevator and evade her followers. Two birds, one stone.

She walks away from her position in front of the elevator and climbs into the window sill. The white curtains snap against her face. She breathes in the air of the city, hears the street traffic below; without her glasses, it's a neon smudge. She looks up and realizes she can reach the roof.

Her adventurous side beckons her, recalling the dreams and the image of the falling body, but she thinks better of it and retreats into the hallway.

Suddenly, she can see things clearly. Not objects but the contours of her life. She can handle this thing. She has an illness, yes, (doesn't everyone?) but she believes in herself. Though she cannot control everything, she can control some things. And that is what deserves her attention.

Her illness is a problem, a barrier, a huge pain in the ass—but it is not her destiny. She is far more than the sum of her suffering.

She smiles.

Then a gruff, familiar voice calls to her. "Miss Lam . . ."

The security guard, who earlier that day had escorted her to a new room, passes by the elevator.

"What are you doing?" It's not a question but an accusation, delivered with a grin.

"Just looking around," she says.

"You still wanna check out the roof? I've got the key," he says, patting his pocket.

"What, uh, what's up there?"

"There's a great view of the downtown. There will be a few of us up there." He can sense her reluctance. "It's your last night, come on. It's worth it, I promise."

She thinks of the creepers. They were talking to him, laughing with him, but he's the *security guard*. Surely, he's the safest person she can be with here.

"Okay," she says, and follows him up a narrow staircase.

The security guard uses a fob attached to his keychain to activate access to the door, which swings open and admits a breeze and view of the black sky. He holds the door open for Elisa and waits for her.

As she steps through the threshold, a chill seizes her as she remembers that "a few of us" will be up there.

THE CASE FOR MANSLAUGHTER

It's hard to present the narrative past this without analysis because there are too many contingencies and possibilities. The disclosure that LAPD detectives believed an employee let her on the roof combined with multiple accounts of tenants regularly drinking beer on the roof lead me to believe Elisa was not alone up there. So what happened?

Did Elisa die, as Robin the websleuth believes, during a sexual assault attempt by a tenant or employee (he specifies security guard)? If so, what was the cause of death? This is something I had trouble getting around for a while because the autopsy does not describe any evidence of an assault. No blunt force trauma, no bruises, etc.

The autopsy does, however, note anal bleeding, which, as I've mentioned several times, has been explained by some coroners as resulting from decomposition gas. So it's possible Elisa was raped and then put in the water tank alive.

It's also worth considering whether Elisa was drugged. Since the autopsy did not test for date rape drugs and since the rape kit was not processed, we can only speculate on the rape theory. But if Elisa was drugged while on the roof or before, it's possible she was given too much and died from overdose.

Or perhaps Elisa died elsewhere in the hotel and never even stepped foot on the roof that night. This would tie into John Lordan's "body dump" theory, which posits that Elisa died, or was killed (perhaps asphyxiated by a pillow, a method of homicide mentioned by Dr. Hiserodt), and then was later hidden in the water tank. This scenario would also explain why Elisa's lungs and stomach contained no water—as she didn't drown, she was already dead when placed in the tank.

Her placement in the tank brings us to a new and important discussion that I believe is critical to understanding what may have happened. Over the years, I've seen an oft-repeated myth that it would be impossible or extremely difficult to carry Elisa's body up to the tank. It's time to debunk this belief.

If you look at the roof, you'll notice that next to and overlooking the water tanks there is a small utility room. On the far side of this room, there is an easily accessible staircase that ascends with a commodious gradient from the rooftop surface to the midway point of the utility room. At the midpoint, there is a door and to the right of it, a vertical ladder that scales the wall a short distance to the roof of the utility room.

If two people positioned themselves at the pole ends of a body, they could very easily carry it up the first staircase. Once they reached the door, the first person could climb the ladder and position himself over the roof. The second person would only have to lift the body a few feet in order to get the body at a height whereby the first person could grab hold from above and pull her to the roof.

Once on the roof of the utility room, they simply had to carry the body to the other side, where the tops of the tanks rested only a few feet down, and repeat an easier version of their previous collaboration to get the body on the top of the water tank. Elisa, either already dead or unconscious, could have been lowered into the water tank without receiving any nicks or bruises.

Having established that it is completely possible for Elisa's body to have been placed in the tank, here are three additional scenarios that are among the most likely to me (listed in order of least likely to mostly likely):

1. Elisa was being harassed and pursued by someone or multiple persons in the hotel and hid in the water tank. She removed her clothes to stay afloat longer. It's also possible that her pursuers forced her into the tank at gunpoint.

2. Elisa died inside a room of the hotel after either homicide or some kind of accident (a date rape drug like Rohypnol, which the autopsy did not test for, already has a high risk of overdose and may have interacted with her medications to slow

down her central nervous system). The perpetrators subsequently concealed her body in the tank. This would likely have been accomplished late at night, perhaps with the help of employees. Critics of foul play often question why employees would have concealed the body in the hotel's drinking water. My reply is that people who kill other people at their place of work—or assist in the coverup—are unlikely to be strenuously deliberating on water contamination. Even assuming they are thinking strategically at all, there are dozens of other logistical concerns they would likely prioritize over that issue—for example, ensuring they are not seen in the surveillance tape.

3. After being coerced or convinced to join someone on the roof, Elisa died as the result of either a malicious action, involuntary manslaughter, or criminally negligent manslaughter. Basically, Elisa was the victim of some kind of predatory scheme, but her death was unintentional. The people responsible for her being there did not help her and instead concealed her body.

Scenarios 2 and 3 explain again why Dr. Hiserodt says the autopsy failed to show evidence of drowning, as she was already dead when placed into the tank. Scenarios 2 and 3 also tie back into the "body dump" conspiracy, that employees informed high-ranking Cecil Hotel corporate officers that a young woman died in the hotel under suspicious circumstances and were told to conceal the body until their multi-million-dollar deal was finalized.

Because there were no clear signs of violence, I am less inclined to think Elisa's death was a premeditated murder. But the distinction is so muddy that even law-enforcement agencies do not have statistics on whether the majority of murders are premeditated (predatory) or impulsive. A one of a kind 2013 study suggests that while predatory murderers are more likely to have an emotional or psychotic disorder, impulsive killers are more likely to have a cognitive or intellectual impairment.

Having said this, and considering both Dr. Hiserodt's analysis of the autopsy and the fact that the medical examiner who signed off on it has since been sued for falsifying a cause of death, I don't think we can say for sure whether Elisa was assaulted or not.

Based on my analysis of the severity of her bipolar disorder and the fact that she had discontinued two of her meds, it is not inconceivable that her death was a total accident or even a suicide. But based on my overall analysis, I believe Elisa's death was most likely a case of involuntary manslaughter followed by a cover-up.

Involuntary manslaughter or negligent homicide would not even necessarily contradict all of the police narrative. Her death was still an accident—though with criminal malice involved—with bipolar disorder as a contributing factor. And it would explain why no charges were filed, as such a crime would be extremely difficult to prosecute in those circumstances. Loath to bring a flimsy case to prosecutors, the police may have just tossed it aside and used the mental illness narrative as an easy out (remember that the LAPD was systematically underreporting violent crimes during this time period).

This is a point that should be emphasized. Remember that now-retired supervising coroner Corral confirmed that at one point in the investigation, the LAPD detectives considered multiple theories of foul play. It is quite possible that they simply could not gather enough evidence or find a perpetrator and defaulted to the "accidental death" theory when the autopsy allowed for it. Lawyer and professor Seth Abramson wrote on Twitter that it is "absolutely routine in criminal investigations" for police and prosecutors to have "an enormous amount of evidence someone committed a crime but be just short of sufficient evidence to bring a criminal charge."

As the truism goes: absence of evidence is not evidence of absence. Though there is voluminous evidence of a coverup—or, at best, a botched investigation—at this point, we're still missing a big piece of the puzzle. The fact that the LA Coroner's office took so long to release the autopsy may underscore that the investigators were reluctant to deem Elisa's death "accidental" but could not figure out what happened and lacked forensic evidence. Needless to say, there are many, many serious crimes that go uncharged and unprosecuted simply because the evidence available does not meet the threshold of proving guilt beyond a reasonable doubt.

For her sake, I hope that whatever took Elisa's life happened quickly and painlessly. One of the scenarios that keeps me up at night is the thought that Elisa could have been in the tank for hours, desperately treading to stay afloat, before she died.

While I cannot at this time—with my current resources—determine what happened to Elisa Lam, the content of my investigation contradicts several key points of the police narrative and mandates action. Unfortunately, asking the LAPD for answers, much less to reopen the case, will accomplish nothing. Little has changed from the days of the Rampart scandal, and any expectations of accountability or transparency are fictive.

It's time for the California Attorney General to get involved.

We're left again with the ultimate question of what drew Elisa to the roof that night? The demon, the killer, or the mind—which of them stalked and manipulated her, which of them called to her from the roof, from the dark waters of the cistern, and whispered to her such an incomprehensible fate? Maybe it's aspects of all three. Perhaps the homicidal, the psychiatric, and the paranormal narratives co-evolved. The demon, the killer, and the mind spoke as one. Let us always consider that there may be multiple truths weaving in and out of our subjective experiences of reality, simultaneously composing and unraveling the larger tapestry whose totality we will never see—and which may not exist at all.

ANOTHER KIND OF JUSTICE

Justice for Elisa, however, goes beyond reopening the case and establishing whether Elisa's death involved foul play. Delivering justice posthumously to this young woman involves another component that has far-reaching social utility. This has to do with counteracting the stigmatization of Elisa's psychiatric problems, humanizing her, and leveraging her case to help people better understand mental illness.

If you go to Elisa's blogs and read the comments left under the posts, you will be shocked at the psychological spectrum of how this case has touched people. You can find thousands more in YouTube comment sections. Of course, you will also find people speculating about satanic cults, so it's a mixed bag.

Elisa's case carries with it the potential to create new online communities of solidarity for people suffering depression, bipolar disorder, and other forms of mental illness. In fact, it's already happening. The rising tide of awareness about mental illness in our society can be seen most prominently on social media, where Facebook groups allow people to share their symptoms and receive emotional support. Sometimes it's as simple as a post that reads: "Today my depression is almost unbearable" or "I can't go on any longer." The comments underneath rapidly fill up with support.

This is one of the great assets of the Internet. People who in the past would have been stranded alone in their isolation and suffering can reach out to others and receive help almost instantaneously.

Even within informal forums, such as the comment threads underneath YouTube videos, you can find a burgeoning movement of mental illness awareness. A friend of mine with bipolar disorder uses Facebook to post his new comic book, called "Nirvana and Bipolar Man," in which he documents adventures with mania and depression.

This momentum is important and long overdue because people with mental illness, or the non-neuronormative community, have typically had a weak advocacy movement. One reason for this is that our illnesses can sabotage cognition, emotions, and personality, making alliances and activism difficult to sustain.

Another reason—and, in my opinion, the more significant one— is the strong stigmatization that persists in our culture about mental illness. Many people still view psychiatric disorder as a spiritual or psychological deficiency. Many people still suggest, some more explicitly than others, that an illness like chronic severe depression is a personal construct that can be fixed with simple attitude adjustments or lifestyle changes. Both views lay the fault of the suffering at the hands of the sufferer. For those who understand the complex, almost infinitely varied, underlying causes, such viewpoints often sound just as absurd and arbitrary as claiming someone with congenital heart disease is responsible for their ailment, or that they don't need to take meds for it because they can control their heart disease with positive energy.

Battling stigmatization is at the forefront of the new advocacy movement. Whether she knew it or not, Elisa Lam was definitely an activist on the frontlines of this war, publicly chronicling her battle with depression and bipolar disorder. While many authors have written books about their struggle with mental illness, including celebrities like Carrie Fisher, who was an incredible advocate for bipolar disorder, you rarely see someone publicly describing to the world online in real-time their battles. Elisa deserves tremendous credit for this.

I've read online comments about how Elisa faced extra stigma from her family's cultural heritage. While she does not explicitly say this in her blogs, she certainly experienced enormous guilt for worrying her family and using financial resources for therapy. There is well-documented research showing that Asian families are less likely to acknowledge and seek help for mental health issues. Andrew Solomon, who has exhaustively studied mental illness all around the world, states: "Many East Asians avoid the subject [of depression and mental illness] to the point of abject denial."

In working on the documentary, Genevieve and Wilhelmina, both Chinese-American, confirmed that the cultural stigma over mental illness is real and significant. Further, they said, many Asian communities are far more likely to look at the Elisa Lam case and attribute supernatural or paranormal causes. Jared and I saw this firsthand when a Chinese production company asked us if we would be able to change our documentary to be more like a horror film that focuses on the paranormal angle.

Of course, the stigma of psychiatric disorders is not unique to any one demographic and is, moreover, rampant in all societies. Fittingly, a Canadian company also asked us if we could change our film to focus more on the paranormal. For many people around the world, the secret agonies of the mind are more terrifying than any ghost, so terrifying that many families simply do not discuss them.

Mental illness surfaced in my investigation in many ways and not just with regard to my own struggle with it. One of our investigators learned in 2018 that her niece had died from suicide. When I told some of my interview subjects about this angle of the book, many of them opened up with their own struggles. One woman, a psychic who stayed in the Cecil during the week Elisa disappeared, discussed her experience with Borderline Personality Disorder, an illness sometimes classified on the bipolar spectrum. Clyde Lewis told me about how when he was growing up, mental illness greatly impacted someone close to him.

In addition to online communities, local, in-person communities can be powerful, too. Clyde and his producer, Ron, host a monthly get-together called the Ground Zero Lounge. Clyde hosts a Q&A session, where fans of his show can ask him questions face-to-face. In attending these, what surprised me is that the larger discussions didn't always revolve around conspiracy and paranormal issues. Many times, attendees shared their experiences with mental health, managing pain without opioids (such as using Kratom and medical marijuana), and a variety of other civic concerns.

In an age in which so much of our discourse is mediated by the Internet, in-person meet-ups like this are important in reaffirming the power of people to take care of each other in their communities.

THE PATHOLOGY ENGINE

One of the sub-narratives threading through this book is the conflict between truth and delusion. It's a conflict that must be confronted anytime one is on a quest to unravel a mystery or determine the nature of reality.

Delusions factor into our story almost every step of the way. Delusional thoughts are a hallmark of many mental illnesses; they are also a hallmark of many conspiracy theories, particularly some of the more extreme ones that have surfaced in forums regarding the Elisa Lam case.

In terms of diagnostic criteria, delusions are one of several distinguishing characteristic features of a psychotic disorder—the other four being hallucinations, disorganized speech, and disorganized or catatonic behavior.

In *Suspicious Minds,* Rob Brotherton notes how delusions "adapt to culture and morph with history," shaping themselves to align with the cultural environment and "harmonize with the worldview of the period."

The most common delusional themes include: persecutory delusion (which is the most common type), the belief that one is being followed, sabotaged or maligned; delusion of reference, the belief that random objects or events carry special personal meaning (could include some instances of synchronicity); grandiose delusions, the belief that one is especially powerful, important, or chosen by God; nihilistic delusions, belief in certain catastrophe; somatic delusions; thought insertion or deletion; delusions of control; jealous delusions; delusions of guilt or sin; erotomania; etc.

Delusions, we must remember, aren't necessarily based on false beliefs. Government and corporate surveillance revealed this century to be just as ubiquitous, expansive, and sinister—if not more so—as past conspiracy theories portended, proves that for decades tens of thousands of people weren't really delusional, though the intensity of their paranoia may still qualify as pathological.

Most people view the idea of mind control as a delusional conspiracy theory. But the fact is that clandestine government programs led by the CIA experimented with mind control for decades and are likely still doing so. MKULTRA is an established historical reality. As president, Bill Clinton made an address to the nation on broadcast television to apologize to its victims, who were previously maligned as delusional.

In the Cecil Hotel, myself and several others may have experienced the "thought insertion" delusion, when we believed that the Cecil Hotel was telling us to go to the windowsill and consider jumping. I'm still not sure if this was a delusion or not. Maybe there's a hive mind situation in which one person's delusions bleed into another's, or maybe all human truth is inherently a hybridization of delusion and reality.

Brotherton discusses the age-old delusions associated with "the influencing machine," which are marked by an overwhelming fear of technological control. Sometimes this delusion merges with other delusions—for example, when someone is convinced that a machine is inserting thoughts into their heads. These delusions continue to evolve with culture and society, changing and adapting to integrate new technologies.

While the biological origins of delusions are still nebulous, some scientists endorse the idea of "useful delusions," or delusions as an evolutionary adaptation.

Edward Hagen, a professor of anthropology at WVU, suggests that delusions may have evolved as an unconscious tool to protect social relations and prevent isolation. His hypothesis suggests that our ancestors realized the necessity of deception in establishing and protecting social relationships; their unconscious minds may have developed delusions to make those deceptions convincing. In other words, they needed to believe their own lies and strong delusional conviction helped make the sale.

Applied to the Lam case, it begs the question: Was Elisa experiencing paranoid delusions in the hotel as an unconscious response to real or imagined predators?

The Elisa Lam case intersects with delusions in a way that may have still larger sociological meaning. With regard to the many casual observers and websleuths obsessed with the Elisa Lam case, I believe the surveillance tape triggered a primal reaction in people, a profound anxiety over the nature of identity in the Internet/surveillance/data-mining age.

In *Suspicious Minds,* Brotherton discusses the *Truman Show* delusion, a real pathological illness that arose in the decades after the 1998 release of the movie *The Truman Show*. People who suffer this delusion fear that their lives are staged reality shows. Sociologists say instances of this delusion, and various persecutory variations of it, have increased in frequency since September 11, 2001, which marked the rise of the surveillance state and the "panopticon" society.

The Truman Show delusion—a manifestation of the age-old "influencing machine"—signals the merger of two colossal social shifts:

loss of privacy and near-constant self-representation online. It's not just Big Brother watching you now, Brotherton notes, your entire social circle and overlapping circles of pseudo-friends-of-friends are watching you, too. Modern paranoia now constitutes not just the "fear . . . of being watched, but of being watched by an indefinitely large number of unknown others." This flips the panopticon into what sociologist Thomas Mathius calls a "synopticon" society, in which the many monitor the few.

Based on her own writings on the subject, I believe that it is partially this fear and anxiety, this tension between privacy and online self-representation, that worsened Elisa's hypomanic delusions. Her case—the most commonly noted feature of which involves a viral YouTube video of her final moments that has been viewed by tens of millions of people—is the tragic epitome of the "synopticon" society. Like rubberneckers at the scene of an accident, people are transfixed by this video, and there may be elements of both terror management theory—in which social groups stigmatize individuals exhibiting unusual behavior—and "synopticon" culture fueling this transfixion.

Eerily, Elisa seemed almost unconsciously aware that this would happen. In her post about Psycho #5, she speculates about whether millions of people will someday Google her name.

In our search for truth and meaning, the Internet has turned into a feedback loop where we try to manifest reality—because if we can make our delusions real, maybe we're not delusional. The pathology engine weds together truth and delusion, data and disinformation, into a product of identity. Is the Internet—with its druglike dopamine infusions of conspiracy theories, spirituality, narcissism, and consumerism—accelerating mental illness?

ESCAPING THE RABBIT HOLE

As I get my depression and bipolar disorder under control (sorry, no cinematic happy ending here—the struggle goes on), one of my battles is reconciling my own conspiracy theories and distrust of establishment control and "consensus reality," not letting my belief that we live in a polluted mental environment, one that probably played a large role in my depression in the first place, cause me to eschew treatment.

Many conspiracy theories these days revolve around antidepressants themselves, particularly SSRIs, which are viewed as some mind-control tactic by the Illuminati. There's an entire online campaign, voiced by thousands of conspiracy theorists, that SSRIs do more harm than good and are actually to blame for many suicides and school shootings. Such conspiracy theories, usually repeated by people who know virtually nothing about mental illness or psychopharmacology, represent a mortal danger to people with mental illness, as patients who may otherwise get the help they need decide they will be socially shunned if they take a medication, or that they will lose their soul.

One websleuth interested in the case messaged our Kickstarter forum to claim that the real story behind this case is the psychiatric angle: that SSRIs cause suicide and violence and are what probably killed Elisa. I responded that while I agree that the psychiatric angle is important, I take the polar opposite angle, which is that psych meds are a symptom, not a cause. People are taking psych meds because they feel awful and are looking for relief. The major effects and side effects of the psych meds mix and interact with patients' natural thought impulses and sometimes that is going to create an emotionally activated person with deep-rooted psychological issues who suddenly has the fortitude and clarity to commit acts that he thinks will make him feel better.

Either way, mental illness is too complex and dangerous for this kind of reductionism and speculation.

I will say that in retrospect, I wish I hadn't started taking SSRIs at such a young age. New research suggests that once a young, developing brain carves out certain neural pathways, it is extremely difficult to create natural psychological defense mechanisms. Many adults are simply stuck taking SSRIs for a lifetime. But a great number of people benefit from these drugs and others. People who previously couldn't get out of bed are now enjoying their lives.

If I hadn't started taking antidepressants when I did, I may not have eradicated the stigma that comes with taking them. Many adults, steeled against the idea of change, won't start taking psychiatric meds even though doing so might dramatically improve their lives and the lives of friends and family members they interact with.

There's a spiritual stigma to this, a sense that these meds stifle your soul and that you can control your mood through sheer will power. Human consciousness may very well play a large role in establishing reality. Synchronicity may be more than coincidence. But that doesn't necessarily mean depression and mental illness are fictions that any given individual can freely edit out of their minds.

For one of his shows entitled "Quantumplation," Clyde Lewis interviewed author Paul Levy, who wrote the book *Quantum Revelation: A Radical Synthesis of Science and Spirituality*.

They discussed the anomalies of quantum mechanics, retroactive precognition, synchronicity, and thought-forms. Levy argues that the quantum realm is the key to unlocking a revolution in consciousness he believes will alter human existence for the better. When I listened to this show, I was struck by Levy's story of how he arrived at certain epiphanies after experiencing a kind of mental breakdown that his doctors told him was symptomatic of bipolar disorder. Even though he was demonstrating life-threateningly manic behavior, Levy rejected treatment and medication, threw his meds out—as well as his eyeglasses—convinced that both his psychiatric and vision problems were the result of him ascending to a higher consciousness.

This made me think of people I've known who have attempted suicide but remain adamantly against taking medication for psychiatric illness. It makes me think of how every time there is a celebrity suicide—from Robin Williams to Anthony Bourdain to Chris Cornell—invariably there are conspiracy theorists who, without a shred of evidence, claim it was an Illuminati assassination.

An alarming number of people would rather believe the most improbable of theories than simply accept that severe depression and mental illness are a reality. Our world is so full of heartbreaking atrocities and the personal experience of existing here is so overwhelmingly traumatic at times that it is tempting to believe that intention alone can act as a remedy.

The synchronicities seemingly guiding me through the last few years—and all my weird research on new metaphysical and philosophical ideas—made me want to believe so desperately that consciousness alone can hack and redirect the energy of the cosmos. It made me want to believe there was some universal significance to Elisa's tragic death. Perhaps by reading the signs around me, by realigning and attuning, I could harness my depression. Maybe it really is just a social disease, I thought, my brain's own unique reaction to this twisted cathedral. Maybe the brain is like a radio that receives consciousness—and with practice and disciplined intentionality, one can learn to control the frequency dial.

Maybe. But over the years, I've learned the hard way that the idea that I can control my mind, that I can override the currents of my own neurochemistry—so inextricably encoded by genetics and social contagion—is probably misguided. But I don't think self-actualization and psychiatric medication are mutually exclusive. In fact, for millions of people, they may be interconnected. In a sense, meds (combined with therapy, exercise, and healthy living) offer a way to hack your own genetic destiny and reprogram hereditary and psychosocial trauma out of your life.

While researching another case, the tragic death of Tiffany Jenks in Portland, Oregon, I spoke at length with the victim's boyfriend, John. John believed that although Tiffany's murderers had been apprehended, that a larger conspiracy was at play. John and I broached the idea of making a documentary about her case. But when I looked at the details, I saw parallels to some of the more extreme conspiracies surrounding the Elisa Lam case.

John had developed a website (currently defunct) on which he argued that Tiffany, who was seeing a psychiatrist for severe depression and bipolar disorder, was the victim of a mind control experiment being conducted by the Illuminati. Once again, we see a case in which mental illness and a tragic death served as a base for extraordinary conspiracy theories. He posted transcripts of Tiffany's psychiatry sessions, which he believed showed that the psychiatrist was using something called neuro-linguistic programming to manipulate Tiffany. While NLP is a real phenomenon with an interesting backstory, I wasn't seeing the connections John did and decided not to pursue the project.

I felt bad for him and suspected that the death of his partner triggered some trauma of his own replete with telltale signs of PTSD that may have triggered or worsened latent pathologies. He told me that the Jenks family didn't want anything to do with his investigation and I can only speculate that his conspiracy theories exacerbated their trauma.

This brings me to another central point that is based on my interactions with certain websleuths while working on the Lam case. While the Internet birthed websleuths, making possible a future of revolutionizing criminal investigations, I fear that the pathology engine may end up spoiling our endeavors. More specifically, I fear that unchecked delusions and irresponsible conspiracy theories could sabotage the websleuth and "citizen journalist" movement before it fulfills its promise.

The Future of Websleuths

As an advocate for criminal justice reform and transparency, I believe the Lam case demonstrates the intertwined promise and peril involved in crowdsourcing and "democratizing" criminal investigations. My journey on the case introduced me to disciplined and resourceful websleuths like John Lordan and others, who utilized the Internet responsibly to raise important questions about anomalies in the case.

But I also experienced firsthand the danger involved when rogue researchers—possessed by the zeal of vigilante justice and too often guided by extreme, possibly delusional beliefs—launch holy wars without deference to due process or logic. I found people attempting to contact the Lam family with "evidence" of a satanic conspiracy; I found people using YouTube to disseminate graphic, disturbing videos about Elisa's death that made extreme claims without providing sources or corroboration. I saw it in the irresponsible, borderline libelous witch hunts of people based on flimsy sketches that don't even qualify as circumstantial evidence.

These examples cut against the philosophy of Tricia Griffith,

owner of *Websleuths,* who established a system of information vet-
ting specifically calibrated to prevent renegade researchers from
contacting law enforcement and victims' families. Nothing good
comes from pestering detectives with shoddy evidence; and harass-
ing victims' family members, who are dealing with indescribable
trauma and pain, is simply unacceptable.

Sloppy journalism mixed with uncorroborated conspiracy theories risks the very future of the websleuth movement. This is why
Griffith's system creates a funnel of analysis that ensures the "evidence" is iron-clad.

In her book *The Skeleton Crew,* Deborah Halber discusses a war
going on in the websleuth community between the mavericks and
the trust builders. The mavericks practice rogue sleuthing and feel
entitled to contact law enforcement and the families of victims without submitting to a hierarchical order. The trust builders practice
restraint and try to forge relationships with law enforcement. There
may be room for a reasonable spectrum that includes both.

As I outlined earlier, there are documented cases of websleuths
providing critical evidence to law-enforcement agencies. Sometimes
this evidence assists in opening new avenues of inquiry for detectives; sometimes websleuths straight-up solve cold cases. Griffith
told me that she's seen websleuths do in a few days what police detectives couldn't do in twenty years.

I asked her what she sees in store for the future of websleuths.

"You're going to see organized groups who work with police
hand in hand, all volunteer," she said. "I see the old guard going
down. Not all police departments but the corrupt ones, they'll be
replaced . . ." And with regard to cover-ups, she said all we can do
is shine a light and hope the Justice Department steps in. "Law enforcement will have to understand that the days of covering things
up behind a black curtain are over. There's too much of a bright light
on what you're doing."

It's impossible to overstate the importance of this issue. With
the rise of hacktivist collectives and decentralized, encrypted file-
sharing networks that facilitate and protect whistleblowers, we're in

a new age of transparency. But the old forces of tyranny are on top of this movement. The Empire always strikes back.

In recent years, the government has outsourced censorship to the private sector, working with "gatekeeper" tech companies like Facebook, Twitter, Google (YouTube), and others to algorithmically suppress information and ban pages that challenge authority. I saw this firsthand when Facebook banned *The Anti-Media, The Free Thought Project* and dozens of anti-establishment and police-watchdog pages.

This is a plot twist that even George Orwell couldn't have anticipated: an alliance between the State and the private sector to control the flow of information. And the Internet is the battleground.

This relates to criminal justice in several ways. It's a direct affront to transparency and it portends a very real scenario whereby law-enforcement agencies could take punitive measures against web-sleuths who they claim are spreading disinformation. The "chilling effect" of lawsuits against journalists has intensified in recent years and I expect it to get much worse before it gets better.

Transparency should be a two-way street but instead there's a double standard. We live in a surveillance grid in which the federal government, law-enforcement agencies, and corporations claim to have the legal right to track our every movement, read our private messages, and harvest and sell our meta-data. Yet when private citizens and advocacy groups request transparency from police, feds, and executives, they receive draconian evasion. While we have a select few legal levers at our disposal, such as Freedom of Information Act Requests (FOIAs), which John Greenwald of the Black Vault has turned into a veritable art form, the law is not on our side.

This is where I stand with the Lam case. I've uncovered credible evidence of a cover-up, yet the LAPD refuses to answer the most basic of questions. When I spoke with her on the phone, Griffith speculated that maybe the detectives talked to the perpetrator and let him walk and now don't want to discuss it.

They claim their silence is to protect the privacy of Elisa and her family. But if that was the case, they wouldn't have published a surveillance video of Elisa on YouTube that accomplished nothing except to stigmatize her and cause millions of people to question her mental stability.

The Dark Tower

In 2017, the Los Angeles City Council voted to approve the Cecil Hotel for landmark status. Citing its status in the Historic Core of downtown LA and its representation "of the early 20th Century lodging industry in the U.S.," the Council effectively voted to preserve the Cecil as a historic-cultural monument.

I almost lost my lunch when I heard this news. And I'll never forget one woman's reaction to it. Sally, the former Cecil tenant who reported to me sexual assaults by employees there, is alone now but for her dog. Her late second husband was an abusive alcoholic, consuming a half gallon of Black Velvet (or more if he could find it) every day. When he finally went to the doctor he had late-stage cirrhosis of the liver and was discolored from gangrene. It was before the age of medically assisted death, so Sally watched her love rot away for two weeks before finally passing.

"Maybe he never really cared about me," she mused, sitting resolute in her wheelchair.

Sally needs a hip replacement and requires her power wheelchair to get around, but other than that she's doing pretty well. She has a rare blood disorder that should have killed her 30 years ago, but she lives on. And she's free from the seven tumors she once hosted, which she says she beat only with the use of medical cannabis.

Sally curses the evil and human suffering that lived inside the Cecil Hotel for almost a century. No amount of renovation will save it. One of her dreams was to see the building razed to the ground. Instead, the Cecil has received a great honor and endures as a symbol of Los Angeles.

The landmark status could mean that Simon Baron Development, the firm overseeing renovations (yet another corporate partner that entered the picture this century), can request financial subsidies from the city under the Mills Act, which could allow the hotel to receive lower property taxes and other subsidies for up to ten years.

While a landmark status title is usually requested in order to pre-serve a monument, the Cecil Hotel has massive renovations planned. Matt Baron of Simon Baron Development says that while the exterior of the hotel will remain untouched, the inside will be "completely gutted." SBD plans to spend $100 million to add 301 micro-units to the boutique hotel. According to Ollie, the company designing the units, these additions will make the Cecil Hotel "the largest coliving community on the West Coast."

I have a vision of the Cecil Hotel still standing in a thousand years, still whispering mortal invitations to guests and logging un-explained deaths. Being as how the building and most of the sur-rounding metropolis was established by Spanish settlers only after systematic exploitation—forced labor and enslavement of the native Tongva peoples of the San Gabriel Valley—maybe the place really is cursed and doomed to echo its past horrors forever.

Despite the reality that gentrification and the criminalization of homelessness has largely failed to improve downtown LA, corporate owners remain determined to cash in. It's a seemingly never-ending cycle of hubristic American pioneers generating new wealth from old exploited assets. An unstoppable force meets an immovable ob-ject, industrialism versus social decay; intrepid entrepreneurs un-afraid to challenge the reality of a cursed building and a tragically disenfranchised populace. It's an eternal battle between demons and venture capitalists. Maybe they're one and the same.

An initial concern is that the landmark status could make future investigation into the hotel's past more difficult. But my biggest worry, a thought that keeps me up at night, relates to one of the changes SBD has planned for the building. My jaw dropped when I read it.

It turns out that renovations to the Cecil Hotel will include the addition of a rooftop pool and bar. That's right, in the near future, people will be drinking and swimming within eyesight of the water cisterns where Elisa's body was found. What could go wrong?

My interest in the Lam case started as an idle curiosity that snow-balled into an obsession. The case ultimately revealed to me that I am on the bipolar spectrum, a diagnosis my doctor confirmed and that should help me in seeking more comprehensive treatment plans in the future.

Another unanticipated effect of writing this book was that it dredged up suppressed feelings about my aunt's suicide. Jill died when I was in my mid-twenties, and we hadn't been close since I was a teenager. Revisiting her life in a new context triggered memories from my childhood—of the riotous cackle of her and my mother joyously and hysterically laughing in the kitchen during Thanksgivings, the hours they would spend on the phone reminiscing over their tumultuous childhoods—mixed with the deep pain of my mother's loss.

And, of course, I have to contend with the mystery of the illness that ultimately took Jill's will to live, the mystery of its tentacled history in my family and, of course, the foreboding reality that I inherited some permutation of it.

I had never cried over Jill's death until writing this book. My mother told me how most of their family didn't believe Jill when she spoke of her illness. She also disclosed to me one of the lines from Jill's suicide letter, which hit me hard.

"I don't belong anywhere," she'd written.

I understood this feeling acutely, as do many others. I've been lucky enough that despite my problems, my relationship with my family has not only remained intact, it has grown. My relationship with my mother, father, and sister are among my greatest sources of strength.

Jill was not so lucky. By the end, she had almost completely alienated herself from her family, including her own son. Elisa seems to have maintained loving relationships with her family, though she struggled with her friends and peers.

Perhaps more than any other mental illness, bipolar disorder is notorious for dividing families and friends. This highlights the importance of destigmatization, education, and treatment—so that not only can the person suffering a mental illness get the medications and therapy they need, but their family and friends can establish through-lines of trust and support.

We may never know the full story of what happened to Elisa. But

I'm not going to stop searching for the truth. Now that I know there is a cover-up—now that I know where to dig—I will retool and keep pushing for transparency, even if it takes me another decade. In the meantime, let's give Elisa her humanity back and recognize her for the great writer and fighter that she was. Maybe she can bring out the fighter in us at a time when, collectively, we must change our ways.

While we can't alter what happened to Elisa, we can make a good-faith effort to prevent it from happening to someone else. It starts with transparency. Then we must remove the stigma from mental illness and push it onto injustice itself, so that corruption, coverups, and unconscionable crimes are not accepted.

We must fight against injustice even when it doesn't appear to directly affect us. Because what happened to Elisa—both before, during, and after her death—can happen to any of us. And, ultimately, her fate is ours, too.

ACKNOWLEDGMENTS

This book wasn't just a true-crime exploration; it became a journey of self-discovery that humbled me to my core. Nothing happens in a vacuum, though, even acts as solitary as websleuthing and writing.

First off, I must reiterate the extent to which the love and support of my mother, father, and sister have centered and lifted me time and time again. To the Anderson clan—Cindy, Steve, Jesse, Ryan, and Sage—I commit nothing less than my heart and soul. With this particular project, I give special acknowledgment to my mother for revisiting painful memories of her sister (my late aunt Jill), in service of helping me shed light on the reality of mental illness and how it affects familial relationships.

I am deeply indebted to my buddy Jared Salas, who has been instrumental in shaping our documentary about the case but, more important, has remained a true friend during absurd times. He is representative of a small but loyal gaggle of friends, spread across the country, who have nurtured the development of my heart and mind over the last couple of decades. You know who you are.

On this note of friendship, I cast a special thanks to Elisa's friend Joe Elwell, who was critical in constructing a humanizing portrait of Elisa. I am also appreciative of Elisa's other colleagues at the PNE and her friends who chose to speak off the record. Many of these people have been traumatized by their loss and the sensationalism that catapulted this case into Internet infamy. I admire their loyalty to Elisa's memory.

John Lordan, whose tireless and principled devotion to not only this case but hundreds of others—as well as the websleuth movement and the ideals of democratized criminal justice itself—has been a huge inspiration for me. Other admirable researchers, investigators, and websleuths whom I was privileged to meet and work with on this case include Frank Argueta, Genevieve Federhen, John Carman, Lou Colagiovanni, Joni Mayan, Natalie Davis, Chelsea Damali, Robin and many others. John Carman and Lou Colagiovanni get special thanks for going down the rabbit hole of the cover-up narrative. I have a feeling we've only seen the tip of the iceberg, and I'm relieved to have them as tunneling partners.

It was a great honor for me to not only meet my favorite radio host (and one of the great philosophy minds of our time), Clyde Lewis, but to be a guest on his show and mind-meld about synchronicity and thought-forms. The zeitgeist is way more interesting with Clyde's vision. His producer, Ron Patton, has also been enormously helpful and uplifting.

One of the great challenges of this case has been getting people to speak on the record about some of the unpleasant details and for this reason, I am very thankful for Fred Corral and Dr. John Hiserodt.

Another challenge has been finding Cecil Hotel tenants willing to speak about their experiences there. Sally helped me expose the true extent of suffering and calamity that has gone on there, and her stories will resonate with me for the rest of my life.

One of the great shaping influences in my life has been my journalism work with Nick Bernabe and the *Anti-Media* community. True visionaries aren't just people with the courage to bring truth and justice into this world, but people who understand that defeating corruption must start with individual kindness, grace, friendship, and love.

Finally, there is no way to overstate my appreciation for my editor, Michaela Hamilton, who believed in and nurtured my vision for a gonzo true-crime book in which I could explore not only a tragic, mysterious case but the depths of my own mind. In my experience, truth blooms in the same soil as pain.

SOURCE NOTES

Chapter 1: Missing

4, **Press corps:** Elisa Lam, LAPD Press Conference, February 14, 2017, YouTube.com.

4, **Wallace Tennelle noted:** "No sign of missing Vancouver woman in LA," CityNews, February 10, 2013, citynews1130.com.

4, **posted flyers:** "Detectives Looking for Missing Canadian Woman" / "Young Woman's Disappearance from Downtown Hotel Is Suspicious," LAPD, February 6, 2013, lapdonline.org.

4, **son was murdered:** Bryant Tennelle, 18, The Homicide Report, May 11, 2007, Latimes.com.

5, **Extensive and exhaustive search:** "Separate Statement of Undisputed Material Facts in Support of Motion for Summary Judgement," Superior Court of California, County of Los Angeles, December 14, 2015.

5, **Missing Persons Unit:** "LAPD Adult Missing Persons Unit," LAPD, lapdonline.org.

6, **72 hours:** "Why the first 72 hours in a missing persons investigation are the most critical, according to criminology experts," ABC News, October 8, 2018, abcnews.go.com.

6, **750,000 cases:** "By the Numbers, Missing Persons in the US," *USA Today*, September 23, 2014, usatoday.com.

6, **"The difficulty with a missing persons,"** Adult Missing Persons Unit, LAPD, lapdonline.org.

6, **Most of the time:** "Majority of Missing Persons Cases Are Resolved," NPR, May 7, 2013, npr.org.

6, **said Todd Matthews:** "When adults go missing, only questions remain," Aljazeera America, February 15, 2014, america.aljazeera.com.

7, **In California:** California Missing Persons, State of California Department of Justice, oag.ca.gov.

7, **Rebekah Martinez:** "Woman Reported Missing in California Found on 'The Bachelor,'" NPR, February 3, 2018, npr.org.

7, **Blaze Bernstein:** "Suspect Now Charged With Hate Crime In Blaze Bernstein Slaying," CBS, August 2, 2018, losangeles.cbslocal .com.

7, **Sherrin Matthews:** "Sherin Mathews: Father of adopted girl charged with murder," BBC, January 13, 2018, bbc.com.

8, **"triangulate":** "What Your Cell Phone Can't Tell the Police," *The New Yorker,* June 26, 2014.

8, **Stalkers:** "Stalkers Exploit Cellphone GPS," *The Wall Street Journal,* August 3, 2010 blogs.law.nyu.edu.

13, **CIA declassified:** The Stargate Collection, The Black Vault, March 1, 2015, theblackvault.com.

13, **one report:** "CIA Posts More Than 12 Million Pages of CREST Records Online," January 17, 2017, cia.gov.

15, **2002 story:** "Vance students turn in lost church money," *Enid News & Eagle,* February 7, 2013.

15, **accused a fellow officer:** "The Manhunt for Christopher Dorner," December 8, 2013, latimes.com.

15, **Monica Quan:** "Dorner's 1st Victims Remembered a Year Later," ABC 7, February 3, 2014, abc7.com.

15, **Facebook manifesto:** "Christopher Dorner's Manifesto, In Full," Laist, February 7, 2013, laist.com.

17, **missing persons:** "Thousands of missing persons cases," July 7, 1993, nytimes.com.

Chapter 2: Found

18, **"funny, sweet, disgusting taste":** "How did woman's body come to be in L.A. hotel water tank?" February 23, 2013, cnn.com.

22, **Kolston Alderete:** "'Ghost' photo captured outside Cecil Hotel in downtown Los Angeles," ABC 7, January 27, 2014, abc7.com.

23, **sworn testimony:** "Declaration of Santiago Lopez Support of Defendants Motion for Summary Judgement," Superior Court of California County of Los Angeles, December 14, 2014.

Chapter 3: The Investigation Begins

25, **Authorities received a call:** "Update: Body of woman in water tank of LA hotel where Canadian tourist Elisa Lam last seen," SCPR, February 19, 2013, scpr.org.

26, **Later that day:** Laboratory Analysis Summary Report (Autopsy), Department of Coroner, County of Los Angeles, Forensic Science Laboratories.

27, **Tenants:** "Guests at L.A. Hotel Spent Weeks Drinking Water Contaminated by a Dead Body," February 20, 2013, gawker.com.

28, **Terrence Powell:** "Woman's body found in LA hotel cistern providing drinking water to guests," February 21, 2013, theguardian.com.

28, **In the days following:** "Agency checks water after body found in hotel tank," CBS News,February 20, 2013, cbsnews.com.

28, **Diaz:** "Update: Body of woman in water tank of LA hotel where Canadian tourist Elisa Lam last seen," February 19, 2013, scpr.org.

28, **preliminary autopsy:** "Elisa Lam Autopsy Yet to Determine Cause of Death," February 21, 2013, huffingtonpost.ca.

29, **age-old tactic:** Carlo, Philip. *The Night Stalker: The Life and Crimes of Richard Ramirez*. New York: Citadel, 2016, p. 113.

30, **every nook and cranny:** "Separate Statement of Undisputed Material Facts In Support of Motion for Summary Judgement," Superior Court of California County of Los Angeles, December 14, 2015.

31, **canines:** "Human Scent and Its Detection," cia.gov.

31, **skin particles:** "Bloodhounds Track Invisible Trail of Skin Cells," August 4, 1996, spokesman.com.

32, **cadaver dogs:** "Experts: Cadaver dogs 95 percent accurate, can smell remains 15 feet underground," July 29, 2014, syracuse.com.

33, **Jack the Ripper:** "The Hounds of Empire: Forensic Dog Tracking in Britain and its Colonies," UC Hastings, repository.uchastings .edu.

33, **Compound chemicals:** "The Nose Knows," April 19, 2012, slate .com.

35, **Stearns and Marcia:** "A Severed Head, Two Cops, and the Radical Future of Interrogation," May 24, 2016, wired.com.

36, **Teague:** "How a Los Angeles triple murderer skipped out on American justice only to face Chinese courts," May 6, 2018, scmp.com.

37, **Wallace "Wally" Tennelle:** Jill Leovy, *Ghettoside: A True Story of Murder in America*. New York: Penguin, 2015.

37, **Diaz:** "Residents disgusted after woman's body found in hotel water tank," February 19, 2013 latimesblogs.latimes.com.

Chapter 4: Rise of the Websleuths

39, **one third of murders** and **200,000 homicides:** "Open Cases: Why One-Third of Murders in America Go Unresolved," March 30, 2015, npr.org.

40, **40,000 unidentified individuals:** Halber, Deborah. *The Skele-*

ton Crew: How Amateur Sleuths Are Solving America's Coldest Cases. New York: Simon & Schuster, 2014, pp. 96–97.

41, **law enforcement officials and cops called them:** "The Searchers: Amateur Web Sleuths Are Teaming Up to Solve Cold Cases Online," *Pacific Standard,* July 15, 2014.

44, **transforming law enforcement's relationship with the public:** Halber, *Skeleton Crew,* 258.

45, **major urban police forces:** Halber, *Skeleton Crew,* 21.

Chapter 5: The West Coast Tour

63, **major changes to the biochemistry of the brain** Solomon, Andrew. *The Noonday Demon: An Atlas of Depression.* New York: Scribner, 2001, p. 56.

66, **ancient eras:** "'Spirit Possession' and Mental Health," December 31, 2014, psychologytoday.com.

Chapter 6: City of Demons

69, **75 percent of Americans:** "Three in Four Americans Believe in Paranormal," Gallup, June 16, 2005, gallup.com.

77, **schism:** "The Famous Break Up of Sigmund Freud & Carl Jung Explained in a New Animated Video." June 28, 2018, openculture.com.

77, **acausal parallelism:** *Jung on Synchronicity and the Paranormal,* Psychology Press, 1997.

78, **outbreak of tuberculosis:** "Tuberculosis outbreak in downtown L.A. sparks federal effort," February 21, 2013, latimesblogs.latimes .com.

78, **medical article:** "Clinical Utility of a Commercial LAM-ELISA Assay for TB Diagnosis in HIV-Infected Patients Using Urine and Sputum," March 24, 2010 ncbi.nlm.nih.gov.

Chapter 7: Further Down the Rabbit Hole

80, **Dr. Jack Brown:** "Nonverbal Communication Analysis # 2313: Elisa Lam Video in Elevator at Cecil Hotel—What Her Body Language Tells Us . . ." February 23, 2013, bodylanguagesuccess.com.

84, **Cody Fry:** "Elisa Lam Time Stamp Conspiracy, MUST SEE!" March 12, 2013 youtube.com.

86, **Elizabeth Short:** Gilmore, John. *Severed: The True Story of the Black Dahlia.* Los Angeles: Amok, 2006.

87, **eerie similarities:** "The Strange Similarities Between Elisa Lam and Beth Short, aka The Black Dahlia," February 22, 2013, esotouric .com.

88, **Black Dahlia case:** Gilmore, *Severed,* 139.

Chapter 8: The "Suicide Hotel"

89, **Cecil Hotel history:** "Hotel Cecil: Beyond the Lobby Doors," Kathy Tran, January 4, 2017, tranofthought.com.

89, **Birth of a Curse:** (hotel history): "The Hotel Cecil and the Mean Streets of L.A.'s Notorious Skid Row," September 29, 2015, kcet.org.

90, **Spanish leather** (and other details): *Los Angeles Times,* December 20, 1924.

92, **Grace E. Maguro:** "Woman Takes Death Plunge," *Los Angeles Times,* March 15, 1937.

92, **15 million people:** "Great Depression History," History.com.

92, **Great Recession:** "Comparing Great Depression and Great Recession," September 19, 2013, politifact.com.

93, **Dorothy Jean Purcell:** *Los Angeles Times,* September 8, 1944.

93, **Pauline Otton:** *Desert Sun,* Volume 36, Number 60, October 13, 1962.

94, **dozens of suicides:** Bartlett, James T. *Gourmet Ghosts 2: More Ghosts, Murders, Suicides and L.A. Weirdness.* N.p.: City Ghost Guides, 2016.

94, **"you can feel your victim dying through the knife":** Carlo, *Night Stalker,* 67.

95, **origin of Richie's violence:** "Was a Bad Childhood to Blame for 'Night Stalker' Richard Ramirez Becoming a Serial Killer?" November 1, 2017, aetv.com.

100, **underlying systemic economic injustices:** Torrey, E. Fuller. *American Psychosis: How the Federal Government Destroyed the Mental Illness Treatment System,* New York: Oxford University Press, 2013, pp. 115–20.

100, **"broken windows" campaign:** "Dismantling the Myth of Bill Bratton's LAPD," December 6, 2013, thenation.com.

Chapter 9: The 14th Floor

105, **"ALL LIVES END":** Nouvelle/Nouveau Tumblr, October, 2012, tumblr.com.

Chapter 10: The Autopsy

114, **autopsy:** Laboratory Analysis Summary Report (Autopsy), Department of Coroner, County of Los Angeles, Forensic Science Laboratories; Preliminary Examination Report; Forensics Consultant's Report; Microscopic Report; Medical Report; County of Los Angeles, Coroners Department Investigator's Narrative; Toxicology Medication Evidence.

Chapter 11: The Art of the Meltdown

124, **zaps:** "What Causes Brain Zaps?" October 2, 2017, psychologytoday.com.

128, **young woman, Jamie Minor:** "Body of missing hostess found trapped in ventilation system she had been stuck in for a month," August 24, 2018, dailymail.com.

128, **80 percent of bipolar patients:** "Bipolar Disorder and the Risk of Suicide," everydayhealth.com.

128, **data suggests:** "Suicide attempts in bipolar I and bipolar II disorder: a review and meta-analysis of the evidence," January 4, 2010, ncbi.nlm.nih.gov.

128, **suicide by drowning:** "US methods of suicide," lostallhope .com.

130, **combining an amphetamine:** "Stimulants for adult bipolar disorder?" November 7, 2008, mdedge.com.

130, **"secret weapon" against bipolar:** "Benefits of Wellbutrin—A Quick Reference Guide," bipolar-lives.com.

130, **patient experiencing severe hypomanic episodes:** "Antidepressants Risky for Bipolar II?" March 15, 2007, webmd.com.

131, **misdiagnosed as schizophrenic:** Hinshaw, Stephen. *Another Kind of Madness: A Journey Through the Stigma and Hope of Mental Illness.* New York: St. Martin's Press, 2017, p. 18.

133, **"Adventures in Hypomania":** "For your viewing pleasure," Nouvelle/Nouveau Tumblr, June 1, 2012, tumblr.com.

134, **"I'm sleeping a lot":** Nouvelle/Nouveau Tumblr, June 13, 2012, tumblr.com.

135, **"I want to kill myself":** Nouvelle/Nouveau Tumblr, September 17, 2012, tumblr.com.

136, **80 percent of teenage girls:** "80 percent of teenage girls suffer serious mental illness after sexual assault," July 22, 2018, theguardian. com.

136, **rape victims will often deny:** "Why most rape victims never acknowledge what happened," November 6, 2018, bbc.com.

139, **800,000 people die from suicide:** World Health Organization.

Chapter 13: Friends and Enemies of Occam's Razor

155, **New research on Psilocybin (mushrooms) and ketamine:** "Psychedelic drugs appear to fundamentally reorganize the brain— and they're starting to turn into approved treatments." https://www .businessinsider.com/new-drugs-from-mdma-mushrooms-ketamine -marijuana-2018-5/?op=1

157, **response from the LAPD:** "American Horror Story: The Cecil Hotel," October 27, 2015, medium.com.

160, **"one of the most mysterious disappearances":** Paulides, David. *Missing 411: A Sobering Coincidence.* North Charleston, SC: BookSurge, 2012, p. 239.

161, **the collective mentality of an organization of killers:** Gannon, Kevin, and Gilbertson, Lee D. *Case Studies in Drowning Forensics.* Boca Raton: CRC Press, 2014, p. 218.

161, **Can anything positive come from not telling the public:** Paulides, *Missing 411*, 319.

Chapter 14: Inbound Train

169, **civil trial:** received from Superior Court of California, County of Los Angeles, including: Complaint for Damages and Negligence Causing Wrongful Death; Declaration of Brad P Avrit in Support of Oppositions Motion For Summary Judgement; Declaration of Pedro Tovar in Support of Motion for Summary Judgement; Declaration of Santiago Lopez in Support of Motion for Summary Judgement; Separate Statement of Undisputed Material Facts in Support of Defendants Motion For Summary Judgement; Defendant Main Street Management LLC and Cecil Management LLC's Answer to Complaint

169, **plaintiff's primary argument:** "BrainScratch: The Final Word on Elisa Lam?" LordanArts, December 18, 2015, youtube.com.

Chapter 15: A World with Evil

175, **disturbing new disclosure:** "Elisa Lam: Canadian tragedy turned American Horror Story," October 31, 2015, cbc.ca.

179, **with a pistol pointed at her:** "Elisa," Wilhelm Werner Winther YouTube account, June 13, 2015, youtube.com.

Chapter 16: Dark Synchronicity

188, **Orchestrated Objective Reduction:** Steve Volk, "Down the Quantum Rabbit Hole," Discover Magazine, discovermagazine.com.

188, **The Global Consciousness Project:** "Meaningful Correlations in Random Data," The Global Consciousness Project, noosphere.princeton .edu.

188, *Margins of Reality*: Jahn, Robert and Dunne, Brenda. *Margins of Reality: The Role of Consciousness in the Physical World.* ICRL Press, 2009.

188, **Retroactive precognition:** Daryl J. Bem, "Feeling the Future: Experimental Evidence for Anomalous Retroactive Influences on Cognition and Affect," American Psychological Association, apa.org.

191, **two major forms of talk therapy:** Andrew Solomon, *The Noonday Demon: An Atlas of Depression*. New York: Scribner, 2015, p. 107.

192, **conversations with English professors:** Solomon, *Noonday Demon*, 111.

Chapter 17: The Last Bookstore

195, **story of the allegedly disturbing postcard:** Penny-Frances Edwards, *Elisa Lam—The Mystery*. Morrisville, NC: Lulu, 2015, p. 7.

198, **very outgoing, very lively, very friendly:** "Questions Remain 3 Years After Woman's Body Was Found Inside LA Hotel's Rooftop Water Tank," October 31, 2016, cbsloca.com.

Chapter 18: Return to the Cecil

207, **Paranormal Syndicate:** "Haunted Encounters: Face to Face S01E03 Ghosts of Skid Row, Kreischer Mansion," www.dailymotion.com/video/x3xnmr3.

211, **We should be glad there is a red-light district:** John Leake. *Entering Hades: The Double Life of a Serial Killer*. New York: Berkeley, 2009, p. 33.

212, **tie the nooses at maximum tension:** Ibid., 12.

212, **the hotel embodied a motif:** Ibid., 65.

214, **his best murder:** Ibid., 367.

215, **"remote viewing" session:** Chelsea Damali. "The Murder of Elisa Lam . . . the unexpected." February 23, 2013, chelseadamali.wordpress.com.

217, **multiple sexual harassment complaints:** Paul Krueger, "SDSU Prof Accused of Sexual Harassment Allowed to Leave Previous Job Quietly, Colleague Says," NBC San Diego, November 30, 2015 nbcsandiego.com.

217, **Pass the harasser:** Colleen Flaherty, "New Job, Old Habits," Inside Higher Ed, December 3, 2015, insidehighered.com.

Chapter 19: Revisiting the Cause of Death

235, **two independent coroners implied:** Marelise Van Der Merwe, "The Elisa Lam mystery: Still no answers," December 12, 2014, dailymaverick.co.za.

236, **report fewer suicides:** Christopher Shea, "The Subtle Politics of Suicide Rates," September 8, 2011, blogs.wsj.com.

236, **"coroner's determination about cause of death":** "It's time to abolish the coroner," December 12, 2017, washingtonpost.com.

236, **two cases in San Joaquin County:** Sam Stanton, Anita Chabria, Ryan Lillis, and Ed Fletcher, "Stephon Clark official autopsy released. Family autopsy was 'erroneous,' coroner says," Sacbee, May 1, 2018, sacbee.com & Julie Small, "Autopsy Doctor Resigns, Says Sheriff Overrode Death Findings to Protect Officers," December 4, 2017, kqed.com.

237, **date rape drugs:** "Rohypnol," Drugs.com.

237, **disturbs forensic pathologist Dr. Judy Melinek:** Julie Small, "Keeping Death Investigations Free From Pressure," KQED, September 13, 2016, kqed.com.

241, **leaked Coroner's Department memo:** twitter.com/ericspillman/status/1064654157469036544.

245, **accused of** *falsifying an autopsy***:** Paul Roupe, "9th Circuit Revives Lawsuit Over Falsfied Autopsy," Courthouse News, September 8, 2017, courthousenews.com.

245, **backlog of untested rape kits**, "The unconscionable backlog of unprocessed rape kits in California," May 21, 2018, latimes.com.

246, **under 5 percent:** "The Vast Majority of Perpetrators Will Not Go to Jail or Prison," Rainn, rainn.org.

246, **cost of rape kits:** Katy Waldman, "There Are 400,000 Unprocessed Rape Kits in the U.S. How Can This Be?" March 12, 2014, slate .com.

Chapter 20: Whoever Chases Monsters

247, **Christopher Dorner:** Christopher Goffard, Joel Rubin and Kurt Streeter, "The Manhunt for Christopher Dorner," LA Times, December 8, 2013, latimes.com.

248, **150 murders:** "Rampart scandal," PBS Frontline, pbs.org.

248, **revelations of the Rampart scandal**, Matt Lait and Scott Glover, "3 Ex-Rampart Officers Charged in Beating and Cover-Up," March 27, 2001, latimes.com.

249, **Tupac and Biggie assassinations:** Randall Sullivan, "The Unsolved Mystery of the Notorious B.I.G.," *Rolling Stone*, January 7, 2011, rollingstone.com.

249, **Perez and his lawyer:** "Perez's confessions," PBS Frontline, pbs.org.

251, **"most active rock cocaine area on earth":** Gary Webb. *Dark Alliance: The CIA, the Contras, and the Crack Cocaine Explosion.* New York: Seven Stories Press, 1998, p. 285.

251, **The CIA:** Ryan Devereaux, "Managing a Nightmare: How the CIA Watched over the Destruction of Gary Webb," September 25, 2014, theintercept.com.

251, **Washington Post:** Jeff Leen, "Gary Webb was no journalism hero, despite what 'Kill the Messenger' says," October 17, 2014, washingtonpost.com.

251, **mainstream media outlets:** Greg Grandin, "'The New York Times' Wants Gary Webb to Stay Dead," October 10, 2014, thenation .com.

252, **two gunshots:** Michael C. Ruppert, "Dispelling the Rumors: Gary Webb's Death Confirmed As Suicide," December 20, 2004, indybay.org.

252, **100 million:** "Millions in Cash Found in L.A. Fashion District Takedown of Alleged Drug-Money Laundering Operations," December 10, 2014, ktla.com.

252, **Business Insider:** Christopher Woody, "How the Sinaloa cartel reportedly laundered drug money with clothing and footwear," August 2, 2016, businessinsider.com.

252, **deputy Kenneth Collins:** Joel Rubin and Maya Lau, "LA County Sheriff's Deputy Charged with selling and offering to hire other cops to protect dealers," January 16, 2018, latimes.com.

252, **2014 *Los Angeles Times* investigation:** "LAPD misclassified nearly 1200 violent crimes as minor offenses," *Los Angeles Times,* August 9, 2014.

Chapter 21: Inside Job

255, **relatively new theory:** "BrainScratch: Elisa Lam Lawsuit—Questions and Theory," YouTube, October 16, 2015, "BrainScratch: Elisa Lam's Wrongful Death & Other Cecil Legal Troubles," June 19, 2015.

256, **Letter to the City Council:** Cecil Hotel owner Cordova to City Council, April 18, 2008, http://clkrep.lacity.org/onlinedocs/2008/08 -0644_misc_4-18-08.pdf.

257, **negotiations with CBRE:** "Multi Housing Capital Advisors Team Joins CBRE," *Commercial Real Estate News,* February 20, 2013, crenews.com.

Chapter 22: A Missing Element and a Bombshell

264, **bipolar spectrum:** "Do You Understand the Bipolar Spectrum?" psychcentral.com.

265, **"socio-emotional pollution":** Solomon, *Noonday Demon,* 32.

266, **"syndrome and symptom blur together":** Ibid., 63.

266, **"Impossible to see the line between":** Ibid., 78.

266, **"My body is uninhabitable":** *Kay Jamison. An Unquiet Mind: A Memoir of Moods and Madness.* New York: Vintage, 1996, p. 103.

266, **"between madness and sanity, and life and death":** Ibid., 102–03.

267, **Terror management theory:** Stephen Hinshaw. *The Mark of Shame: Stigma of Mental Illness and an Agenda for Change.* New York: Oxford University Press, 145.

269, **Anthony Weiner "sexting":** "Friend: Sydney Leathers in sexting scandal loves politics, 'idealized' Weiner," July 25, 2013, cnn.com.

270, **Universe is missing:** Evan Gough, "The universe has a lithium problem," February 20, 2017, phys.org.

270, **"Perhaps better than any other drug,"** Lauren Slater. *Blue Dreams: The Science and the Story of the Drugs That Changed Our Minds.* New York: Little, Brown, 2018, pp. 111–12

271, **recent resurgence of lithium:** Anna Fels, "Should We All Take a Bit of Lithium?" September 14, 2014, nytimes.com.

277, **"The drawings that are seen hanging":** IMDB: *The Night Stalker* (2016). www.imdb.com/title/tt1821657/trivia?ref_=tt_ql_2.

282, **team of scientists:** Thor Jenson, "New Study Links Conspiracy Theorists with a Mental Disorder," October 24, 2017 geek.com.

282, **"illusory pattern perception":** Jennifer A. Whitson and Adam D. Galinsky, "Lacking Control Increases Illusory Pattern Perception," Science Mag, October 3, 2008, sciencemag.org.

282, **Another study:** Matthew Hudson, "Conspiracy Theorists May Really Just Be Lonely," May 1, 2017, scientificamerican.com.

282, **A series of 2015 studies:** "Does Self-Love or Self-Hate Predict Conspiracy Beliefs? Narcissism, Self-Esteem, and the Endorsement of Conspiracy Theories," *Sage Journals,* November 13, 2015, sagepub .com.

286, **Of the estimated 48,000 homeless:** E. Fuller Torrey, *American Psychosis: How the Federal Government Destroyed the Mental Illness Treatment System.* Oxford: Oxford University Press, 2013, p. 124.

Chapter 23: What Happened to Elisa Lam?

294, **counterargument to Occam's:** Nathan Borden, MD, and Derek Linklater, "Hickam's Dictum," March 14, 2013, ncbi.nlm.nih.gov.

304, **high risk of overdose:** "Learn About GHB, Ketamine and Rohypnol," Here to Help, heretohelp.bc.ca.

305, **A one of a kind 2013:** Rock Nauert, "Do You Know the Differences Between These Two Types of Killers?" June 28, 2013, psychcentral.com.

309, **well-documented research:** Amanda Rosenberg, "Hiding my mental illness from my Asian family almost killed me," June 18, 2018, vox.com.

309, **"Many East Asians avoid the subject":** Solomon, *Noonday Demon*, 200.

311, **"adapt to culture and morph with history":** Rob Brotherton, *Suspicious Minds: Why We Believe Conspiracy Theories*. New York: Bloomsbury, 2017, p. 66.

311, **MKULTRA is an established historical reality:** Scotty Hendricks, "What was Project MKUltra? Inside the CIA's mind-control program," Big Think, April 17, 2018, bigthink.com.

314, **Stuck taking SSRIs:** Associated press, "Stuck on meds: Some can't quit antidepressants," NBC News, August 31, 2006, nbcnews.com.

318, **war going on in the websleuth community:** Halber. *Skeleton Crew*, 219.

319, **algorithmically suppress information:** Alex Hern, "When algorithms rule our news, should we be worried or relieved?" *The Guardian*, August 28, 2014, theguardian.com.

320, **early 20th Century lodging industry:** Bianca Barragan, "Downtown LA's creepy Hotel Cecil is now a city landmark," Curbed Los Angeles, March 2, 2017, la.curbed.com.

321, **Cecil Hotel has massive renovations planned:** Juliet Bennett Rylah, "New York Developer Reveals His Plans to Give the Cecil Hotel a Hip Makeover," Laist, May 31, 2016, laist.com.

321, **100 million:** Bianca Barragan, "Inside the $100M Overhaul at Downtown's Cecil Hotel," Curbed LA, June 1, 2016, lacurbed.com.

321, **Tongva peoples:** Annie Lloyd, "A Brief History of L.A.'s Indigenous Tongva People," Laist, October 9, 2017, laist.com.

INDEX

ABOUT THE AUTHOR

JAKE ANDERSON hails from Little Rock, Arkansas, and earned his undergraduate degree in film and digital media from the University of California at Santa Cruz. He currently lives in Portland, Oregon, where he is a writer, filmmaker, investigative journalist, activist, and web publisher. He also moonlights as a search engine optimizer. Jake runs the popular website The Ghost Diaries and is a contributing journalist for *The Anti-Media* and multiple alternative media outlets. He has been a featured guest on *Ground Zero with Clyde Lewis*, *Spaced Out*, *Nocturnal Frequency*, *West of the Rockies*, and *Common Ground*. Find more of his work at www.theghostdiaries.com (www.facebook.com/TheGhostDiaries), where he analyzes cold cases and unexplained mysteries. Follow him at twitter.com/OverTheMoonSF.